BASIC Programming for the IBM PC

Robin D. Raygor
Anoka-Ramsey Community College

Robert N. Bateson
Anoka-Ramsey Community College

Gregory W. Bitz
Illustrator

West Publishing Company

St. Paul New York Los Angeles San Francisco

Printed in the United States of America

Library of Congress Cataloging-in-Publication Data

Raygor, Robin D.
BASIC Programming for the IBM PC.

Includes index.
1. IBM Personal Computer—Programming. 2. BASIC (Computer program language) I. Bateson, Robert. II. Title.
QA76.8.I2594R39 1986 005.265 85-31484
ISBN 0–314–93407–3 (softcover)
ISBN 0–314–99077–1 (hardcover)

Cover Art: Delor Erickson
Copy editing: Northwind Editorial Service
Text design: Lucy Lesiak Design
Composition: Carlisle Graphics
Technical artwork: Century Design

PHOTO CREDITS

xvi Smithsonian Institution Photo No. 77-9543
xix Courtesy of Control Data Corporation
15 Courtesy of International Business Machines Corporations
20 Courtesy of International Business Machines Corporations

For our parents

CONTENTS

CHAPTER 1

Counting Eggs Using the LET Statement 27

CHAPTER 2

Doing It Right Programming Standards 35

CHAPTER 3

Getting Data In Two More Methods of Input 45

CHAPTER 4

Let's Do That Again Looping with GOTO and IF Statements 55

PREFACE

SOME WORDS ABOUT THIS TEXT

This book is intended as an introduction to programming in BASIC for people with little or no background in computers. It may be used in a class in programming or as a self-instruction manual. The information in the book is oriented to IBM or IBM-compatible microcomputers, although much of it applies to the many other microcomputers that are programmable in BASIC.

No knowledge of computer science or advanced mathematics is assumed of the student using this book. Even if you have never seen a computer before, you should be able to write moderately sophisticated programs (or modify existing programs) by the time you finish this text. We have tried to make this process as painless as possible and sincerely hope you enjoy your first encounter with small computers.

THE APPENDICES

APPENDIX A: The Mini-Manual

The Mini-Manual is a compact reference manual for the BASIC language. Some people prefer to work their way through the text, referring to the Mini-Manual only when necessary. Others like to read the Mini-Manual before going on to chapter 0. Whichever method you choose, it is certainly a good idea to familiarize yourself with the Mini-Manual now so that you will be able to make efficient use of it when you need it.

APPENDIX B: Error Messages

This is a list of the error messages you might see on the screen, with explanations of what they mean and how they usually occur. If you are ever confused about an error message, by all means consult this appendix. Note whether the error message you see on the screen has a question mark at the beginning; this will help you find it in the appendix.

APPENDIX C: BASIC Reserved Words

This is a list of words that may not be used as variable names. For example, CINT would not be a legal variable name because CINT is a reserved word.

APPENDIX D: Formatting a Diskette

This appendix describes how to format a new, blank diskette.

APPENDIX E: Flowcharts and Programming Techniques

This appendix contains information about flowchart symbols and program design.

APPENDIX F: Table of ASCII Character Codes

Appendix F gives the ASCII codes of each character available on the IBMpc.

APPENDIX G: Answers to the Self-testing Questions

Appendix G contains the answers to the self-testing questions that appear in each chapter of the book.

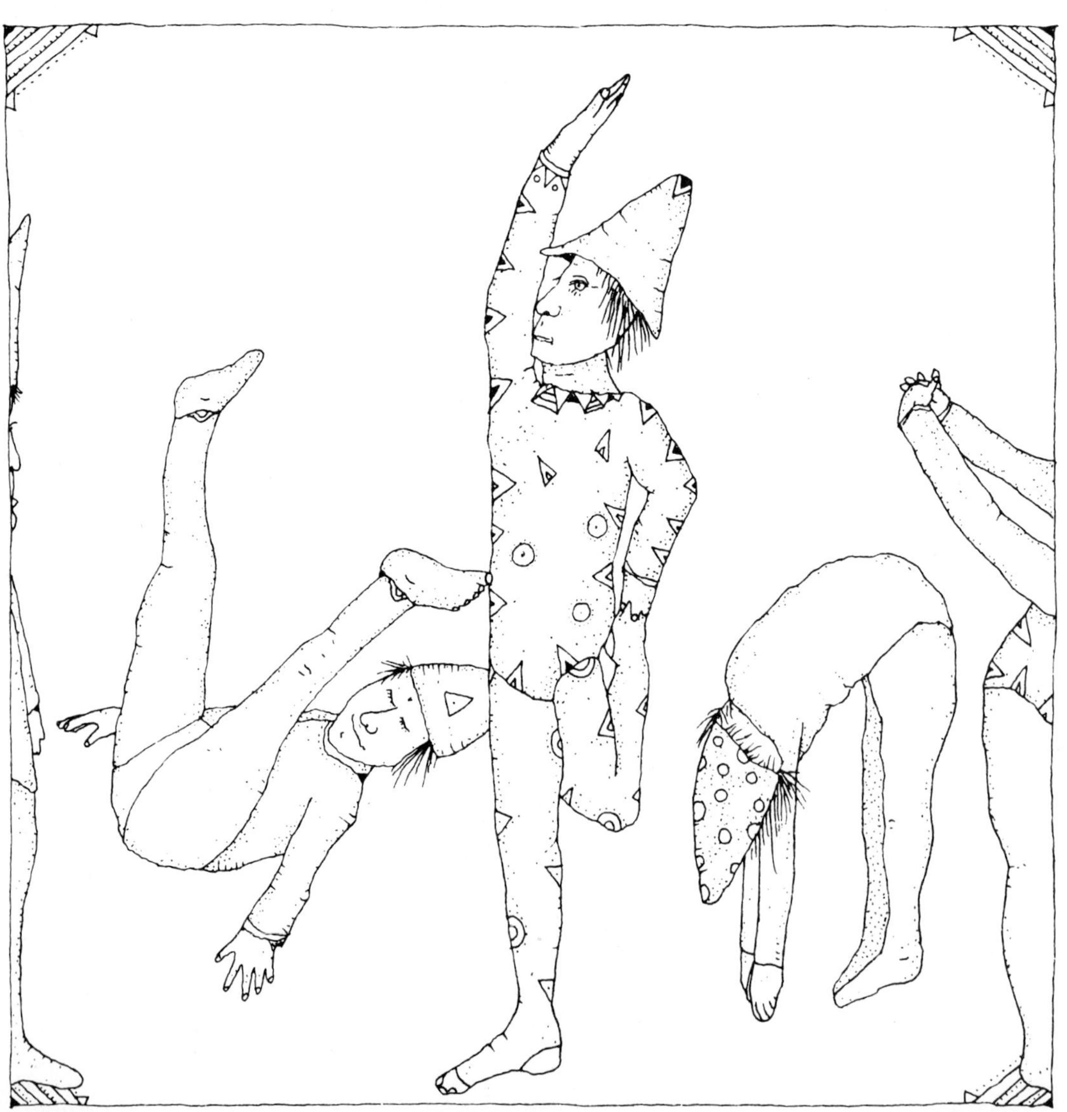

THE EXERCISES

At the end of each chapter, there is a series of exercises designed to test your knowledge of the concepts taught in that chapter. In the early chapters, you are advised to do all of the exercises, since each tests a different concept. In the later chapters, where you are asked to do just one of the exercises provided, we have tried to order the exercises according to their difficulty so that you can choose one that will challenge you without being frustrating. The easier exercises are presented first; the later ones are more difficult, with the last one or two being very difficult.

ACKNOWLEDGMENTS

Many people have been involved in the production of this book. Curt Austin, Tom Loftus, Jeff Cole, Sharon Raygor, Amelia Gast, John J. Rooney, Hartwick College; James W. Cox, Lane Community College; Pam Ogaard, Bismarck Junior College; Kathryn O. McCubbin, Christopher Newport College reviewed and tested early versions of the text and made many valuable suggestions. Peter Marshall, Tamborah Moore, John Carlisle, Jane Nieland, Lucy Lesiak, and numerous others at West Publishing and Carlisle Graphics worked tirelessly to support the authors and contribute to the design and production of the book.

The authors would especially like to thank the friends and family members who put up with us during the difficult phases of manuscript preparation.

Robin D. Raygor   Robert N. Bateson   Gregory W. Bitz

INTRODUCTION
Computers in Society

COMPUTERS OF THE FUTURE

Computers and computer components are becoming more powerful and at the same time less expensive every day. Economic and social forces are causing all of us to consider computers a part of our daily lives. Many of us have small computers on our wrists that tell the time, day, and date (many also play a different tune for each day and remember holidays and important events; some are also calculators or games). Not so long ago, these wrist "computers" would have cost hundreds of thousands of dollars. A little before that, they could not have been built at all.

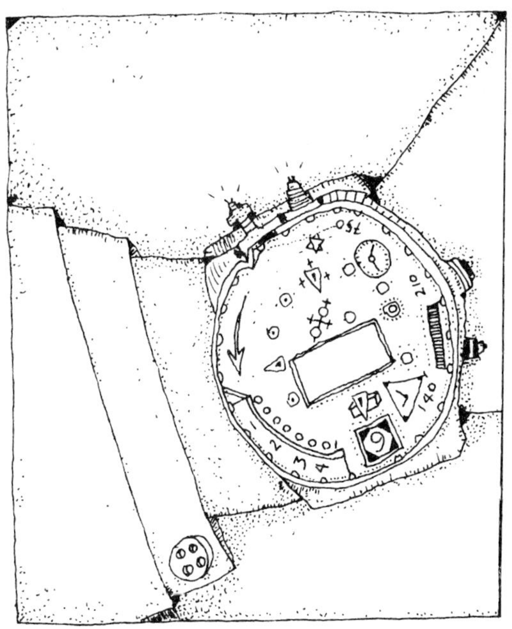

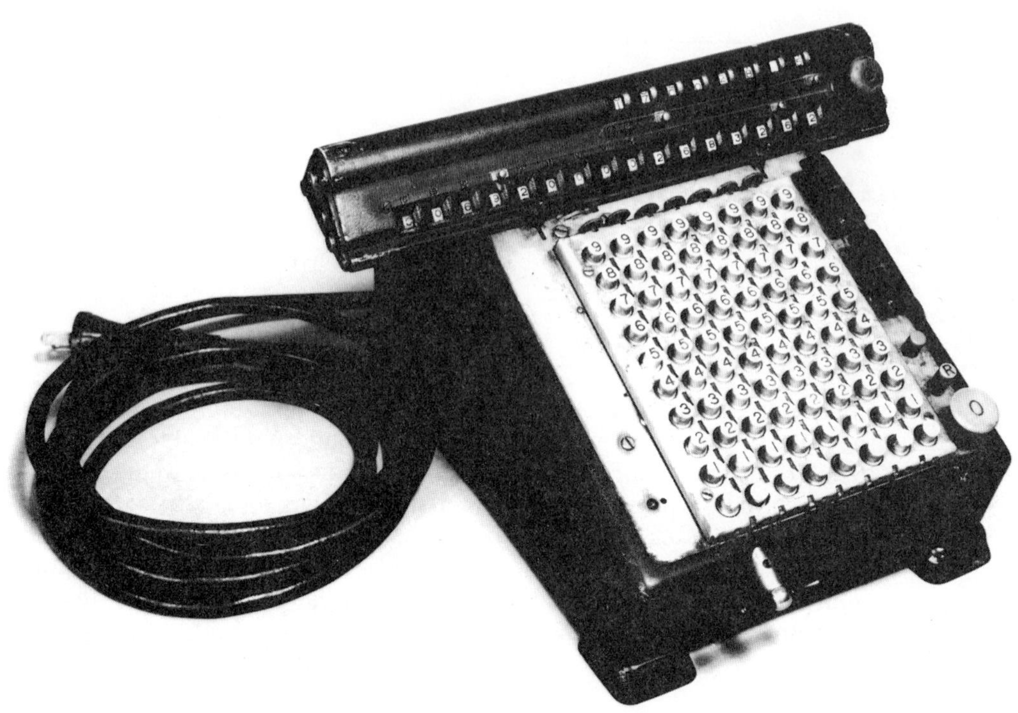

Not so long ago, this was considered to be a very modern calculator.

Not that long ago, a large business-machine company produced a desk calculator that was considered to represent the state of the art at that time. It was about the size of a very large typewriter and had a huge carriage that moved from left to right.

The numbers were on little drums that rotated to display each number in a small window. If you divided a fraction that was a repeating decimal, the machine would run until you unplugged it. The machine was extremely expensive and could only add, subtract, multiply, and divide. It couldn't even do square roots. One of the authors' fathers had such a machine, and quite often friends and neighbors would come by to admire it. It was considered to be a scientific wonder.

You don't have to be an expert in computer science to see how far the computer industry has come since then. This trend is clearly continuing, and soon the computers of today will seem like that dinosaur that was so admired in the past. Before long, computers will be designing, building, programming, and repairing other computers (it's already happening), and it's hard to imagine where this will all lead.

WHY LEARN PROGRAMMING?

Some have suggested that if the computers of the future will be so powerful, they'll probably speak English and be able to figure out what we want, thus making the learning of programming a waste of time.

There are several good replies to this argument. First, the kind of computers and programming necessary to fulfill this fantasy are some way off. Second, someone is going to have to program those computers to be so smart. And third and probably most important, we have found that people cannot learn to use computers and computer programs comfortably and efficiently unless they truly understand the structure and function of computers in general. There is no better way to come to understand how computers work than by learning to program.

THE BASIC LANGUAGE

A computer language is a set of rules that specify how to tell a computer what to do. Every computer language was designed with a specific function in mind. Some languages are designed primarily for accounting; others, like COBOL, for general business applications; and still others, like FORTRAN (and its cousin RATFOR), for scientific and mathematical applications.

BASIC (Beginner's All-purpose Symbolic Instruction Code) was originally designed as a teaching language. The "words" of the language were cho-

The computer room of a large company.

sen because they were easy to understand. Terms like PRINT, LOAD, SAVE, READ, and WRITE are easy for beginners to understand and use. Because of the tremendously widespread use of BASIC, however, it has expanded into a more sophisticated language that is used widely in personal computers and increasingly in business applications.

Because of the original purpose and limitations of early versions of BASIC, some programmers consider BASIC to be a "toy" language and don't take it seriously. They accuse BASIC of being an "unstructured" language, meaning that BASIC programs are poorly organized and hard to understand. The authors would like to argue that although BASIC does not *force* programmers to use structured techniques, it certainly does not prevent them. We believe that well-structured or poorly stuctured programs can be written in any language. We also believe that the techniques of structured, modular programming are best taught using a language that is easy to understand and that uses a "nonthreatening" vocabulary and syntax. Faster and more powerful versions of BASIC are becoming available all the time, some with all the structured programming capabilities of any other language. In this text we have tried to introduce the BASIC language in a way that is easy and painless without sacrificing the learning of programming standards and structured programming techniques.

CHAPTER 0

GETTING STARTED

Basic Computer Skills

NEW CONCEPTS TAUGHT

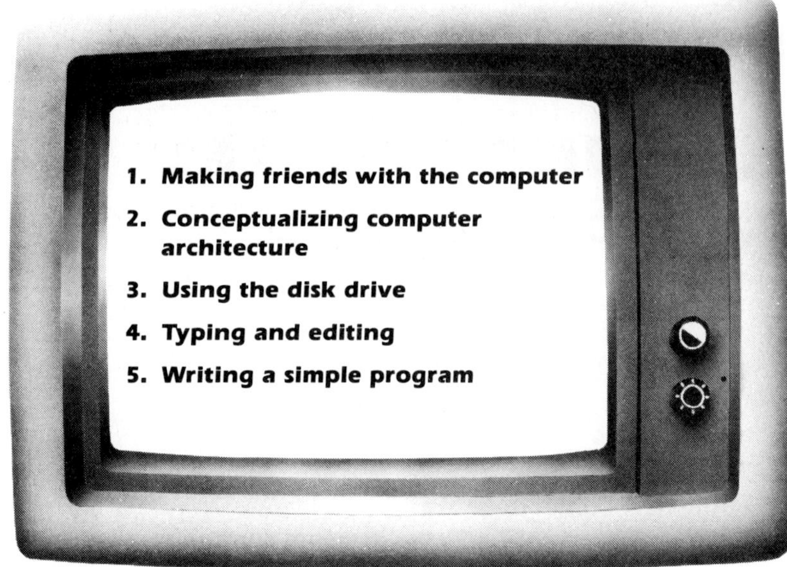

1. Making friends with the computer
2. Conceptualizing computer architecture
3. Using the disk drive
4. Typing and editing
5. Writing a simple program

OVERVIEW

We know that it's not common for books to have a chapter 0. We've done it here for two reasons. First, many computer operations do start their numbering at *zero*; it saves memory and sometimes makes things easier to understand. Second, this chapter is a little different than the other chapters of the book (though just as important). The purpose of this chapter is to make sure that you have the skills and knowledge necessary to carry you smoothly through the rest of the book. You may find that you can skip parts of this chapter. If you already know how to type, for example, the section on typing won't be much help to you. We warn you, however, not to neglect this chapter. Some of the material can save hours of your time; other parts of the chapter can save you from disaster.

We advise you to read this chapter while sitting at the computer. In this way, you can interact with the computer as you read. This will give you a much richer understanding of the concepts being taught. (It will also be more fun.)

MAKING FRIENDS

Many people have an initial fear of the computer that makes it harder for them to learn how to program it. Some of this fear is due to unfamiliarity. Much of it is really a fear that they might break the computer or damage it accidentally. Unlike the computers in TV comedy shows, which go up in smoke at the drop of a hat, the modern microcomputer is actually a pretty tough little machine. Unless you are using a hammer or blowtorch in your programming efforts, it is very unlikely that you will damage the computer. Like a pocket calculator, the computer is designed so that there is no way you can cause damage by pressing the wrong button. If you really knew what you were doing, you could enter commands that would alter the computer's memory in such a way that it wouldn't work properly, but (1) the chances of doing this by accident are very slim, and (2) the memory could be restored to normal simply by turning the machine off and turning it on again (don't try this while writing a program, though, since it erases the program from memory). So you can rest assured that no matter how serious an error might seem to you, it won't hurt the computer. What we mean by "memory" is explained in detail later in this chapter.

PLAYING AROUND

For your first experience with the computer, we recommend the following. First, you should have a diskette that has been formatted and contains the file named BASICA. Diskettes, as they come from the manufacturer, are not formatted; they are like blank keys that do not yet fit any lock. If you are using this book as part of a course in programming, the instructor will help you format your diskette. If not, see appendix D.

Diskettes should be treated very delicately. If you need to write on the label of a diskette, use a felt pen or, better yet, write on the label before putting it on the diskette. The gray or brown magnetic surface of the diskette is exposed at the read/write opening and hub-ring (see figure 0.1). Be careful not to touch

FIGURE 0.1

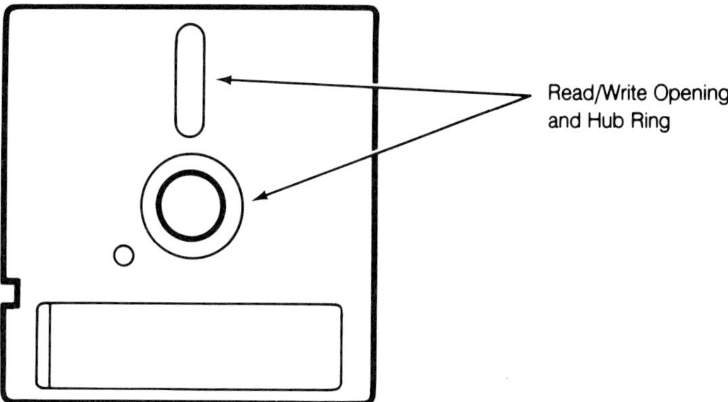

Be careful not to touch the magnetic surface of the diskette where it is exposed at the Read/Write opening and the Hub Ring.

FIGURE 0.2

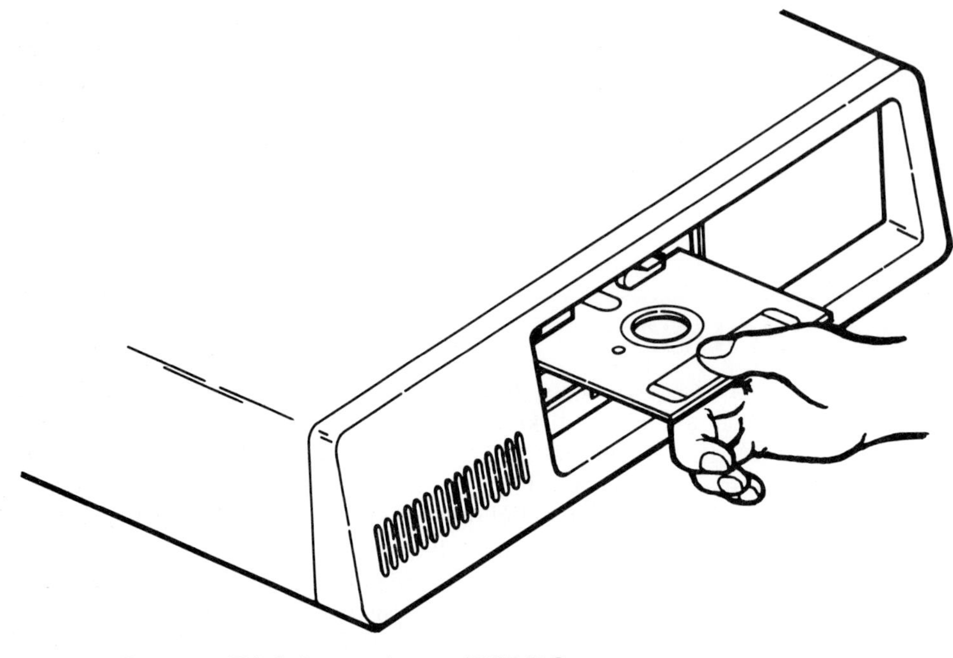

Correct Disk Insertion—IBM PC

these areas and try to protect them from dirt and dust. In addition, keep diskettes away from magnets and magnetic fields. The magnetic code on the diskette is very weak and can be easily damaged. A paper clip from a magnetic clip holder can make a diskette unusable.

With the computer turned off, gently slide the formatted diskette into the disk drive in the manner shown in figure 0.2. If your computer has more than one drive, put the diskette in the left-hand drive or, if the drives are stacked vertically, in the upper drive. Put your right thumb on the label as you insert it. This will make sure it is going in correctly. Next, close the disk drive door and turn the computer on. **Always** put the disk in before turning on the computer. This is done because the computer needs to read information off the diskette in order to get ready to work. This process is called *booting* or *boot-up*, and if it is not done, you may be able to write a program, but you won't be able to save it. Needless to say, this is somewhat unpleasant, as it means you must type the entire program over again.

When you turn on the computer's power switch, you will see the light on the disk drive go on and hear some noises from the drive. If the diskette is formatted properly and the disk drive door is closed, these noises will stop in a few moments and the light will go out. You should be able to see something now on the monitor (TV screen). If not, turn it on. You may be asked for the date and time; if so, enter them and press ⟨Enter⟩. The Enter key is marked differently on various keyboards. On some it may be marked Enter or Return, on others it is marked with a bent arrow.

Enter key The Enter key is on the right side of the keyboard and is marked differently on various keyboards. On some it may be marked Enter or Return, on others it is marked with a bent arrow like this: ↵

You must press the Enter key after each entry you type, such as the date, time, a command, or a program line. The Enter key initiates the computer's response to the line you just finished typing. The computer is very patient: it will wait all day for you to press the Enter key before it takes action.

Cursor The cursor is a blinking underline character that marks the current location on the screen. When a key is pressed, the character appears on the screen where the cursor was and the cursor is moved one position to the right.

Once you have gotten past the time and date questions, you will see what is called the DOS prompt, a letter followed by a symbol (usually A>). DOS stands for Disk Operating System, and this system controls the movement of information between the computer and the disk drive or drives. We will talk more about this later. The letter you see at the DOS prompt tells you which drive is active (called the *default* drive). The computer will use this drive until you tell it to use another. If you have only one drive, it will be drive A: (drive names are always followed by a colon) and you should see an A⟩. Many things can be done from the DOS prompt, but they are beyond the scope of this book. For more information about DOS, read your DOS manual. We also recommend Peter Norton's excellent book *MS-DOS and PC-DOS Users Guide.*

Since this book is about the BASIC language, you need to know how to get into the BASIC language system from the DOS prompt. This sounds complicated, but all you need to do is type BASICA. This will get you into advanced BASIC, where you will do all the work in the book. If you haven't done so, type:

```
BASICA  ⟨Enter⟩
```

If you are using the PCjr, you will need the BASIC cartridge; if it is not installed, you will see the message

```
"Cartridge Required"
```

If BASICA has loaded properly, you should see a message telling you that you are using IBM BASIC and, below this, the word OK followed by a blinking underline character. You will be seeing quite a lot of these two; the OK is the BASIC prompt, and the underline is called the *cursor*. The prompt is a signal that the computer is ready to accept information.

When you type characters from the keyboard, they will appear at the cursor location. Any information coming into the computer (from the keyboard, for example) is called *input*.

NOTE: We will show all programming commands and computer input and output in uppercase (capital letters). You may use lowercase if you like, but you may want to press the Caps Lock at the lower right of the keyboard so that your programs will match the ones in the book.

Try typing some characters on the keyboard. If things are going properly, they should appear on the screen. The computer will not respond to any input until you press the Enter key at the right side of the keyboard. This is your way of letting the computer know that you are done typing and want to be taken seriously. It is not really like the Return key on a typewriter, even though it often has the same effect (moving the cursor to the left side of the screen on the next line). As we mentioned earlier, this key is marked differently on various keyboards. Try typing some characters and then ⟨Enter⟩. Unless you are very lucky or know something about computers, the computer probably responded with "Syntax error." This is because what you typed was not a legitimate command. Don't let this bother you; just keep typing. If you like, you can try to guess words that the computer can understand (PRINT is one of them). Notice that you can use the right and left arrow keys at the right side of the keyboard or the backspace key at the upper right (it may be marked with a left arrow) to correct mistakes in typing. We will discuss editing and the correction of errors more fully later; for now, just play with the keys until you are comfortable with the keyboard.

Now let's try some legal commands. Try typing:

`BEEP` 〈Enter〉

You should hear something. To hear something else, type:

`SOUND 40,40` 〈Enter〉

Try the sound command with different numbers. The first is the pitch of the sound, the second is the duration.

> **Warning:** if you use a high value for the duration, you may have to listen to the sound for a while.

Audible pitch values range from 37 to about 10,000. When you get tired of the sound command, you might want to try the PLAY command. Type:

`PLAY "CDE"` 〈Enter〉 (enter the quotes as shown).

Try different letters inside the quotes. If you feel patriotic, type:

`PLAY "GGEEGGDDEFGABG"` 〈Enter〉.

Remember, all commands must be followed by 〈Enter〉.

Now try typing:

`PRINT "ABCDEF"` (enter quotation marks as shown).

Notice that when you press 〈Enter〉, the computer does exactly what it's told. This is what computers do best. Try putting some other things inside the quotes and see what happens.

By the way, the characters being printed on the screen in response to your print commands are called *output*. If the screen gets too full of output for your taste, you can clear it by typing:

`CLS` 〈Enter〉

> **CLS** CLS may be used when no program is running or in a program line. The result is to clear the screen and move the cursor to the upper left of the screen.
>
> Example:
>
> ```
> 10  CLS
> ```
>
> When no program is running, typing ⟨Ctrl-Home⟩ will have the same effect. On the PCjr, you must type ⟨Ctrl-Fn-Home⟩.

Let's try something fancier. Leave out the quotes and type:

```
PRINT A    ⟨Enter⟩
```

The computer probably responded by printing a "0." This is because you told it to print the value of the variable named A. Since A has no value yet, it prints 0. Now try typing:

```
LET A = 35    ⟨Enter⟩
PRINT A    ⟨Enter⟩
```

Now A has a value. If you give B a value by typing:

```
LET B = 12    ⟨Enter⟩
```

you can get even fancier by typing:

```
PRINT A + B    ⟨Enter⟩
```

or

```
PRINT A / B    ⟨Enter⟩
```

Something a little fancier yet would be to type:

```
IF A = 35 THEN PRINT "YES A DOES EQUAL 35"    ⟨Enter⟩
```

or

```
IF A > B THEN PRINT "A IS GREATER THAN B"    ⟨Enter⟩
```

If you don't completely understand what's going on here, don't worry; it will be explained in more detail later. Just continue to play with the keyboard until you feel comfortable with it.

A SIMPLE IMAGE

To many people, the computer is a strange territory. Their attitude is like that of a person waking up in the dark in a strange house. The sense of confusion this causes can interfere with learning. To help with this, we would like to offer the following simple image of a computer to give you a kind of mental map and, we hope, make you feel more at home in this strange territory.

A Simple Image of a Computer

The Image

Our image begins with a desk. On the desk are three things: a keyboard, an electronic calculator, and a printer. The keyboard is used to put messages into a box marked INPUT. The printer prints copies of messages from a box marked OUTPUT. The calculator and the printer are each operated by the brain of the computer (called the central processing unit, or CPU) under the direction of a set of internal instructions. Some of these instructions are etched in the circuits of the computer (hardware), and some are in the computer's memory only when it is turned on (software).

These instructions allow you to communicate with the computer and tell it what you want it to do. When you tell the computer to PRINT "HELLO," hundreds of operations take place inside the computer. In the old days, programmers had to program each of these operations individually. Now, because we have higher-level languages, like BASIC, we can give relatively simple commands and let the computer take care of the details. The set of commands we give the computer is called a program, and making up the set of commands that will do what we want is called programming.

Beginning students often don't realize that the computer understands only a relatively small set of commands, and takes them literally. The operations inside the computer take place at high speed, but the computer can't think for itself. It has to be told exactly what to do and it follows its orders blindly. If you tell it to wipe out a program that you spent six years working on, it will do it in an instant.

Now, back to our image. Behind the desk is a very large number of boxes, similar to the mailboxes in a post office. Each box has a place for a name card. A box can hold only one number or one group of letters; when a new number or group of letters is placed in the box, the previous contents are destroyed. We will call these boxes memory cells. We call the name placed on the box a variable name. While you were playing with your computer, you placed the number 35 in the memory cell named "A." It may still be there. "A" is the variable name. It is called that because its value may vary. If you type LET A = 23 or LET A = 48, the value of A (or the number stored in the memory cell named "A") will change. Instead of a number, a memory cell might contain a group of letters such as "BOB," "ABCDEF," or "HOLD THE ONIONS." These letters have to be handled differently than numbers by the computer, but it can't always tell numbers from letters; to help out, we place a "$" at the end of the names on the boxes that contain groups of letters.

You can make use of this by typing:

```
LET C$ = "HOLD THE ONIONS"   <Enter>
PRINT C$   <Enter>
```

If you don't put a dollar sign after the name of a variable containing letters, the computer will complain. Try typing:

```
LET A = "BOB"   <Enter>
```

for a demonstration.

Variable Names Variable names are used to identify memory cells that each contain a single number or a group of characters called a string. A variable name must begin with a letter of the alphabet and may be followed by additional letters of the alphabet or digits from 0 through 9. In some BASIC systems, only the first two characters of a variable name are significant (i.e., used to distinguish one variable name from another). However, in IBM BASIC, the first 40 characters are significant. Variable names may not be reserved words (i.e., words that have special meaning to BASIC—see appendix C).

A variable name determines whether a number or a string is stored in the named memory cell. For numbers, the variable name also determines the type and precision of the number. Numbers may be stored as integers, single-precision values (seven digits or less), or double-precision values (up to 17 digits). Single- and double-precision numbers generally include a decimal point and may be printed in an exponential form. (For further information, see appendix A, section 2.1, Number Format.)

String variable names end with a $. Integer variable names end with a %. Single-precision variable names end with a !. Double-precision variable names end with a #. If no explicit identifier is used, the variable is single-precision (unless it is predefined as described below).

Variables with no explicit identifier may be predefined to have a given precision using the BASIC statements DEFINT, DEFSNG, DEFDBL, and DEFSTR — which define variables to be integer, single, double, and string, respectively. The statement

```
10  DEFINT I,J,K
```

tells the computer to treat variables beginning with the letters I, J, and K as integer variables. The following statement does the same thing:

```
10  DEFINT I-K
```

Examples of variable names:

```
A      C$      B%      C2!      BOX      SUM      PRODUCT
```

In creating a program, we put our directions for the computer in the INPUT box by typing the program on the keyboard. When we want the computer to carry out our instructions, we type the word RUN on the keyboard and press ⟨Enter⟩. The computer takes the program from the INPUT box and then rushes around carrying numbers and messages between the INPUT box, the memory cells, the calculator, and the OUTPUT box as directed by the program. The calculator and the printer also do their thing as directed.

integer means whole number = %
String variable = $
single-precision = !
Double " = #

If you have ever seen a BASIC program, you may have noticed that there is a series of numbers in order at the left side of the page. These are the line numbers, and they tell the computer in what order to perform the tasks specified in the program. These instructions can be typed in any order, and the computer will put them in order by line number. Usually we number the lines by tens in case we're not perfect and have to insert some more lines into the program later on.

A SIMPLE PROGRAM

Now that you have some idea what goes on inside the computer, let's look at how a program completes a simple task. In this program we'll put the ages of three students in memory cells, calculate the sum of the three ages, place the sum in a fourth memory cell, and print the sum of the ages of the three students.

Let's assume that the three ages are 18, 24, and 32. Our first instruction will direct the computer to put the first age in a memory cell. We must give the computer a name to put on this memory cell. We will use A1 as the name of the memory cell that contains the first age. Since this is our first instruction, we will give it the line number of 10 and give the other lines higher numbers. Here is the first line of our program:

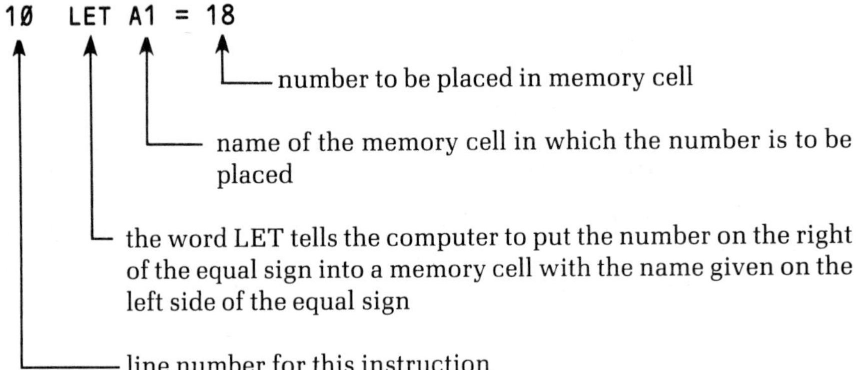
10 LET A1 = 18
number to be placed in memory cell
name of the memory cell in which the number is to be placed
the word LET tells the computer to put the number on the right of the equal sign into a memory cell with the name given on the left side of the equal sign
line number for this instruction

The next two instructions direct the computer to put the remaining two ages in the memory cells A2 and A3:

```
20  LET A2 = 24
30  LET A3 = 32
```

The fourth instruction directs the computer to send copies of the numbers in memory cells A1, A2, and A3 to the calculator with directions to add the three numbers and put the sum in memory cell S:

```
40  LET S = A1 + A2 + A3
```


The last instruction directs the computer to take a copy of the number in memory cell S and place it in the OUTPUT box:

```
50  PRINT S
```

Our completed program looks like this:

```
10  LET A1 = 18
20  LET A2 = 24
30  LET A3 = 32
40  LET S = A1 + A2 + A3
50  PRINT S
```

When the above program is carried out (if you would like to try it, just type NEW, and the program as it appears here, then type RUN), the number 74 should be printed.

> **NEW** If you type NEW and press ⟨Enter⟩, the program in your computer's memory will be removed. It cannot be recovered, so use this command carefully.

Although this image oversimplifies the interior of the computer, we hope it is useful and accurate enough to remove some of the mental blocks that have hindered students in the past.

THE DISK DRIVE

When you turn off the computer, your program and the value of all variables are wiped out of the computer's memory. It would be very tedious if we had to type in the whole program every time we wanted to run it. Luckily, programs can be stored on the diskette and loaded easily into the computer's memory. When you type a program on the keyboard, it is stored in a special part of the machine's memory. To store that program on a diskette, you simply type SAVE" followed by the name you have given the program. The name of the program must be contained in quotes and be in the proper form, with a filename of up to eight characters and an optional extension of up to three characters.

FILENAMES Legal names are made up of what might be called a first and last name. The first name is called the *filename* and can be up to eight letters long. The last name is called the *extension* and can be up to three letters long. The two names are separated by a period and **must contain no spaces**. Every program must have a name. If you type SAVE and just press 〈Enter〉, nothing will be saved. Usually the extension is used to help tell what category the file falls into. In BASIC, the language we will be using, the extension is not mandatory. If you leave it off, the computer will assume an extension of .BAS and will add it automatically. Filenames may be typed in either upper- or lowercase characters; the computer will convert them to upper case.

Examples of legal filenames:

```
FILENAME.BAS
NAMES
JUNE.83
```

SAVE If you type SAVE followed by a name for your program (in quotes) and press ⟨Enter⟩, the program in computer memory will be saved on your disk with the given name. If you give a name with no extension, the computer will add the extension "BAS". If the SAVE command is followed by ",A" as follows:

```
SAVE "PROGRAM1",A
```

the program will be saved to the disk in ASCII (American Standard Code for Information Interchange) format. Normally, BASIC programs are stored in an abbreviated code that is readable only by the BASIC language system. Using the ",A" option saves the program in a literal form, letter by letter. Saving a program in ASCII format is a little slower and is usually not necessary. An ASCII formatted file can be merged with another program using the MERGE command and can also be edited using most word processors.

IBM disk drive and keyboard.

If you type SAVE "PROGRAM.ONE" and there is already a PROGRAM.ONE on your diskette, the old version will be erased and replaced with the version currently in the computer's memory. If you type KILL "PROGRAM.ONE", PROGRAM.ONE will be erased and replaced with nothing. It is always a good idea to stop and think before typing SAVE" or KILL". WARNING! When you type SAVE" followed by the filename, the disk drive light will come on to indicate that your program is being written to the diskette. DO NOT press any keys while the file is being written. Typing a key while the computer is writing to the disk can cause the loss of the file being written and sometimes wrecks the entire diskette. If this happens and you have two drives, try putting your DOS diskette in drive A: and your bad diskette in drive B: and typing:

```
CHKDSK B:/F
```

KILL If you type KILL followed by the name of a program on the disk in the disk drive (in quotes) and press ⟨Enter⟩, the named program will be removed from the disk.

Example: `KILL "PROGRAM1.BAS"`

would remove PROGRAM1.BAS from the disk. Unlike the SAVE and LOAD commands, the KILL command will not work unless you include the file extension.

RUN" If you type RUN followed by the name of a program on the disk in the disk drive (in quotes) and then press ⟨Enter⟩, the named program will be copied from the disk into computer memory and a RUN will be executed.

Example: `RUN "PROGRAM1"`

will cause PROGRAM1 to be loaded and run. Any program in memory will be lost.

RUN If you type RUN and press ⟨Enter⟩, the computer will begin to carry out the program in memory (if any) at the lowest line number. ⟨F2⟩ may be used as a shortcut for this command.

Another possibility is: `RUN 60`

This will begin execution of the program at line 60.

Do not have to load program first. Just type run "program1" and it will automatically load and run it.

Programs on the diskette may be run by simply typing RUN" and the name, or they may be loaded into the machine's memory by typing LOAD" and the name. Then you may look at the program lines by typing LIST or run the program by simply typing RUN. The LLIST command will list the program on the printer.

LIST and LLIST If you type LIST and then press ⟨Enter⟩, your entire program will be listed on the screen. If you type LLIST and then press ⟨Enter⟩, your entire program will be listed on the printer. Other possibilities are illustrated below (any numbers may be substituted for 60 and 120 in the examples below as long as the second number is larger than the first).

Example 1:	`LIST 60`
	or
	`LLIST 60`
		will list only line 60 of your program.

Example 2:	`LIST 60-120`
	or
	`LLIST 60-120`
		will list all lines in your program from line 60 to line 120, inclusive.

Example 3:	`LIST 60-`
	or
	`LLIST 60-`
		will list all lines in your program from line 60 to the end of the program.

Example 4:	`LIST -60`
	or
	`LLIST -60`
		will list all lines in your program from the beginning to line 60, inclusive.

⟨F1⟩ can be used as a shortcut for the LIST command.

To make changes in a program called "BOB," you would type:

```
LOAD "BOB"
```

then make the changes; type RUN to see if the changed version works right; and type:

```
SAVE "BOB"
```

to replace the old version with the new one. Alternately, you might type:

```
SAVE "BOB2"
```

Then you would have both the old and new versions on the disk.

LOAD and MERGE If you type LOAD followed by the name of a program on the disk in the disk drive (in quotes) then press ⟨Enter⟩, the named program will be copied from the disk into the computer memory.

Example:

```
LOAD"PROGRAM1.BAS"
```

or

```
LOAD"PROGRAM1"
```

The extension need not be specified if it is "BAS."
⟨F3⟩ may be used as a shortcut instead of typing `LOAD"`

The MERGE command works like the LOAD command except that it merges the program on the disk with the one in memory. If there is any overlap in the line numbers, the ones in the merged program replace those in the program in memory. For this command to work, the file to be merged must have been saved in ASCII format with the ",A" option of the SAVE command (see SAVE).

After you run or save a program to the diskette, it is still in the memory of the computer and may be run or listed as many times as you like. The program will stay in memory until the machine is turned off, until you type NEW, or until you load or run another program, which replaces the first program.

The NEW command erases all programs and variables in memory, as does turning off the machine. Be sure you have saved your program before typing NEW or turning off the machine.

When you type LOAD" or RUN" followed by the name of a program on your diskette, any program in memory is wiped out and replaced with the named program, so be sure as well that the current program is saved before loading or running another program. Even experienced programmers sometimes lose programs that took them hours to type because of this oversight.

RUN", LOAD", NEW, and turning the computer's power off affect only the computer's memory. They have no effect on programs stored on the diskette.

Another important thing to remember is that if you or someone else has had a program in memory, it is still there unless the computer has been turned off or NEW has been typed. So if you finish working on one program and begin typing in a new program without clearing memory, you will end up with some combination of the two in memory—a condition that can lead to some very interesting effects when you try to run it.

FILES If there is a disk in the disk drive and you type FILES and press ⟨Enter⟩, a list of the programs stored on the disk will be displayed on the screen. FILES" *.BAS" will display only BASIC programs. If you have two disk drives,

```
FILES"B:*.BAS"
```

will list all BASIC programs on drive B:.

Typing FILES will show you the *directory* of the diskette in the drive. The directory is just a list of the programs on the diskette. It has no effect on memory, so that if you want to save a program called "BOB4" you can check to make sure you don't already have a version 4 before saving it. When writing a program, especially a long program, it is often a good practice to save successive versions of it so that if the one you are working on gets accidentally erased or stops working, you can fall back on a previous version.

NAME Files may be renamed by using the NAME command as follows:

```
NAME "OLDNAME.BAS" AS "NEWNAME.BAS"
```

The file to be renamed must exist, and both files must have legal filenames and include the extension.

TYPING AND EDITING

Now it's time to try writing a real program and at the same time learn some editing and typing techniques that can save you many hours in the future.

Typing

First, a few words about typing (if you have some typing experience, you can skip this paragraph). In the course of using this book, you will have to do a great deal of typing. If you have never typed before, or have never been taught how to type properly, we have a few suggestions that will seem uncomfortable at first but will save you a lot of time in typing the programs necessary to complete this book. These may seem simpleminded, but a surprising number of people ignore them.

The IBM-PC Keyboard.

1. Use both hands.
2. Put your left index finger on the ⟨F⟩ key.
3. Put your right index finger on the ⟨J⟩ key.
4. Try to leave them there.
5. Use the little finger of your left hand for the Control and shift keys on the left side.
6. Use the little finger of your right hand for the ⟨Enter⟩ and shift keys on the right side.
7. Rest your thumbs on the ⟨Space Bar⟩ and use them to press it.
8. Try to use all ten of your fingers.

NOTE: Remember that the computer has repeating keys. Don't hold them down too long.

These techniques may seem awkward at first, but we assure you that this will not last long and that your typing speed will rapidly increase to a point where you can easily type circles around a one- or two-finger typist.

Editing

Another thing you will have to do a lot of in the course of this book is changing the lines of programs to try to make them run properly. To eliminate an unwanted program line, carefully type the line number followed by ⟨Enter⟩. The line will be removed from memory. There is no way to get it back without retyping it. To get rid of a number of lines, you may type:

DELETE *line# − line#*

where the two line numbers specify the beginning and ending line of the block of lines you want to eliminate. Once deleted, the lines cannot be recovered. If there are no lines of your program in the specified range you will see the Illegal function call error message. One way of changing a program line is to simply retype it from the beginning, starting with the line number. The new line will replace the old line in memory, with the old line being lost forever. If the line is very long, however, this can be tedious and inefficient (also unnecessary). The computer has an excellent built-in editing system that is well worth the time and trouble it takes to learn to use it.

You have probably already noticed that the right and left arrows can be used to move the cursor back and forth over a line. Try typing the following line exactly as it appears (including the mistake) and press ⟨Enter⟩.

```
10  PRILT "THIS LINE NEEDS HELP"
```

Now think about how to correct this line without retyping it. What we need is a way to get the cursor back to the line and change the L in PRILT to an N. The cursor can be moved by using the four arrow keys at the right side of the keyboard. On some computers these keys are part of the numeric keypad. If this is the case, whether they work as numbers or as cursor keys depends on the Num Lock key at the upper right of the keyboard. If numbers are typed when you press the cursor keys, press the Num Lock key once and the keys will work as cursor keys.

Once you have the keys working correctly, move the cursor over the L in PRILT. The route you take is not important as long as the cursor ends up on the L. Now type an "N" and press the Enter key. Now type:

LIST ⟨Enter⟩

and check to see if the line is correct. If not, keep trying until you get it right.

Now let's try some more fancy editing. Type the following line just as it appears:

```
10  PRINT "THE QUICK FOX JUMPS"
```

Now we need to add the word "BROWN" between QUICK and FOX. Use the cursor arrows to move the cursor over the space between QUICK and FOX. Now, because we want to insert something, we press the Insert key (the key marked Ins at the lower right of the keyboard). Notice that the cursor changes shape when you are in the insert mode. Now type one space and the word "BROWN" and press ⟨Enter⟩.

IMPORTANT: After making a correction, you must press ⟨Enter⟩ while the cursor is STILL ON THE CORRECTED LINE, otherwise the correction will have no effect on the program in memory. Many beginning students make the mistake of correcting a line and then moving the cursor off the line with the up or down arrow without pressing ⟨Enter⟩. The changes in the line are not entered into the computer's memory unless you press ⟨Enter⟩ before leaving the corrected line.

If everything went well, the line should look like this:

```
10 PRINT "THE QUICK BROWN FOX JUMPS"
```

Don't feel bad if this doesn't work for you right away; it sometimes takes a little while to get good at it.

Now that you know how to insert extra material in the middle of a line, let's try deleting extra characters in a line. Type the following equation:

```
10  LET X = 23 * 253 / 100 + 6
```

Now suppose you discover that the first part should be divided by 10 instead of 100. Rather than retype the whole line, let's use our editing skill to fix it. We will also see a new way to get the cursor on the beginning of the line. Type:

```
EDIT 10  ⟨Enter⟩
```

As you can see, this command lists line 10 and puts the cursor at the beginning of the line. Now use the right arrow to move the cursor over to one of the zeros in 100; it doesn't matter which one. As you have probably guessed, the Delete key (the key marked Del, next to the Insert key) will delete unwanted material from a line. Use it to delete the unwanted zero, then press ⟨Enter⟩. The Insert and Delete keys can be used to add or remove any amount of material, as long as the resulting line doesn't get longer than 254 characters.

Here are some other editing techniques that can save you time and trouble. The cursor can be moved a word at a time instead of a character at a time by holding down the Control key (the key at the left of the keyboard marked Ctrl) while pressing the left or right arrow key. On some keyboards, the cursor can be moved to the beginning or the end of the line by pressing the Home and End keys at the right side of the keyboard. On the PCjr, you must press the Fn key at the upper right of the keyboard to use the Home or End keys.

If you are using an IBM PCjr, notice that a number of the keys have green labels on them. These are keys that have a special function when used with the Fn key. If you press the Fn key once and then one of these keys, the operation specified by the green label will be performed. The number keys at the top of the keyboard can be used as a shortcut for a number of standard BASIC commands. We will refer to these as the "function keys." On other IBM models, these keys are a separate set of function keys, usually located to the left of the keyboard. For PCjr users, when we refer to the F1 key, for example, we mean you to press the Fn key followed by the 1 key. See appendix A, the Mini-Manual, for more details about the use of the function keys and other special keys.

A REAL PROGRAM

Now that you have developed some typing and editing skills, it's time for you to do some actual programming. The following program won't exactly calculate the gross national product of Bolivia, but at least it's a real program. For the first step, type NEW and then type the program exactly as it appears in figure 0.3. Be sure to include all the line numbers, dollar signs, and quotation marks. When you are finished entering the program, type RUN and compare your run with the one in figure 0.3. If it does not run properly, type LIST and carefully compare your listing with the one in figure 0.3. Correct any differences and make sure the program runs correctly. Remember that you can type CLS at any time to clear the screen. This will have no effect on the program in memory.

FIGURE 0.3

```
LIST
10  REM MY FIRST PROGRAM
20  LET NA$ = "YOUR NAME"
30  LET AD$ = "YOUR STREET ADDRESS"
40  LET ST$ = "YOUR CITY, STATE, ZIP"
50  CLS
60  PRINT NA$
70  PRINT AD$
80  PRINT ST$
90  END
Ok
```

When your program produces the run pictured in figure 0.3, use the editing functions to replace the values for NA$, AD$, and ST$ with your actual name and address. Remember that to change the program, you must edit the actual program lines. To do this you must type LIST to get the lines on the screen. Editing the output of the program (changing the messages the program prints on the screen when it runs) will change what's on the screen, but will have no permanent effect on the program in memory.

When you get the new version to run properly, save the program to the diskette by typing:

```
SAVE "PROGRAM1"
```

Now type FILES to make sure it is there. After you have made sure the file is on the diskette, work up your nerve and type NEW. This wipes your program out of memory (but has no effect on the disk). Now type LIST and RUN to assure yourself that the program is really gone. Then type:

```
LOAD "PROGRAM1"
```

The F3 key may be used as a shortcut for the LOAD" command. If you get a "File not found" message, it means that you are typing the name incorrectly. It must be exactly the same as when you saved it. If you continue to have trouble, type FILES again and find your file, then type LOAD" followed by the complete filename including the extension. If you don't get an error message following your LOAD" command, the program has loaded properly and you may run or list it to your heart's content. If you like, you can now print the variables in immediate mode by running the program and then typing PRINT NA$ (or any of the other variables). This is extremely useful when trying to find and fix mistakes in a program (called "debugging" the program).

At this time you may also save the program under another name, in which case you will have two identical versions of it on the diskette. You may also erase one or both programs by typing KILL" and the program name. Keep at least one copy of the program; when you become a famous programmer, it will be a valuable collector's item.

CHAPTER 1

COUNTING EGGS
Using the LET Statement

NEW CONCEPTS TAUGHT

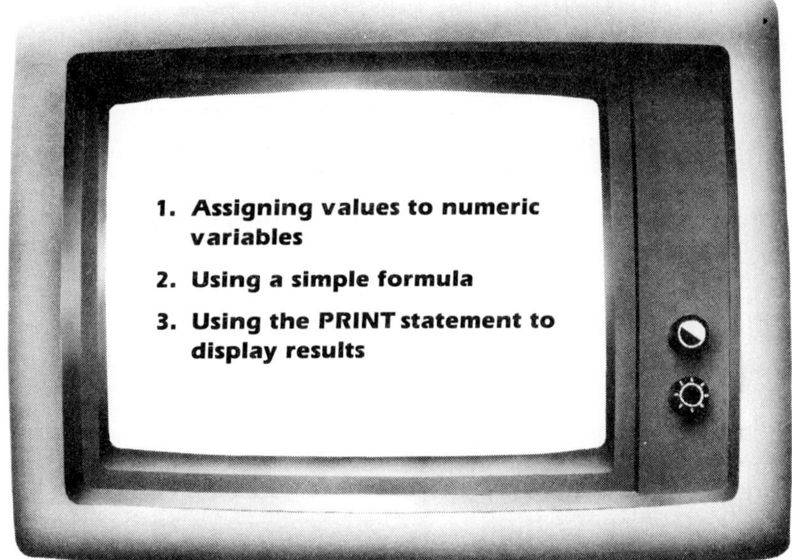

1. Assigning values to numeric variables
2. Using a simple formula
3. Using the PRINT statement to display results

HOW MANY EGGS?

Program 1A (see figure 1.1) is not very fancy or impressive, but it gets the job done and is easy to understand. It has only two variables, G for guests and E for eggs. Both variables are numeric variables; that is, the value they represent is a number.

In line 10 we set the value of G to 12. This places the number 12 in the memory cell called G. In line 20 we set the value of E to 2 times the value of G. The computer, when it gets to line 20, looks to see what value is currently stored in the memory cell labeled G; it then multiplies that value (which happens to be 12) times 2 and puts the result in the memory cell labeled E.

In line 30 we instruct the computer to print the number currently stored in the memory cell labeled E, and then in line 40 we tell the computer to relax.

Although this program is very simple, it can be useful; imagine that you are having a major banquet and serving many different kinds of food. With a little extension, this program could calculate the necessary amounts of the various foods. Best of all, when it was finished you could get results for various-sized parties simply by changing the value of G in line 10.

EXAMPLE 1A How Many Eggs?

Problem You are having a breakfast party where you will serve scrambled eggs. You estimate that you will need 2 eggs per guest and are expecting 12 guests. Write a program that will calculate the total number of eggs needed and print that value on the screen.

Solution

FIGURE 1.1

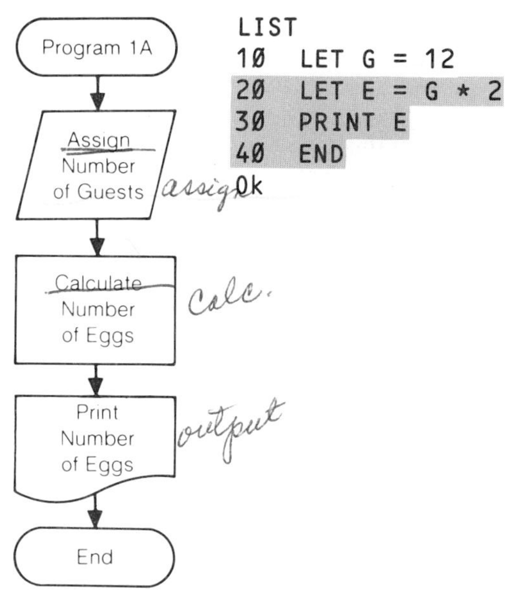

PRINT The PRINT statement is used to display the contents of memory cells or the value of an expression. The general form of the PRINT statement is:

line number PRINT *any combination of variable names, string variable names, and arithmetic expressions separated by commas or semicolons*

A *delimiter*, a punctuation mark used to separate one piece of information from another, may be used to separate the parts of a PRINT statement.

When the comma is used as the delimiter separating the items in the PRINT statement, the monitor screen is divided into print zones of 14 spaces each. The commas cause each succeeding variable to be printed in the next zone.

Semicolons may be used as the delimiter separating the items in a PRINT statement. When a semicolon is used at the end of a PRINT statement, the usual carriage return is suppressed. The PRINT statement prints a blank space in front of positive numbers, so that if X = 1, the statement

```
10  PRINT "THE NUMBER IS";X
```

will result in the printed output:

```
THE NUMBER IS 1
```

If X = −1, the result will be

```
THE NUMBER IS-1
```

While you are programming, the question mark (?) may be used as a shorthand for the word PRINT at any time.

Examples of PRINT statements:

Statement	Result
`70 PRINT`	Leaves a blank line on the screen or paper.
`80 PRINT X`	Displays the value of X in zone 1, beginning in position 1 (left adjusted)
`90 PRINT A,B,C`	Displays the value of A in zone 1, B in zone 2, and C in zone 3.
`100 PRINT "X = "; X`	Displays the message followed immediately by the value of X.

`200 PRINT A,`
`201 PRINT B,`
`202 PRINT C`
	Result is identical to 90 PRINT A,B,C as shown above.

`300 PRINT A`
`301 PRINT B`
`302 PRINT C`
	Displays the value of A in zone 1 of the first line, the value of B in zone 1 of the next line, and the value of C in zone 1 of the third line.

Flowcharts

The flowchart, or flow diagram, is one of the methods used by programmers to assist in writing a program. Flowcharts are most useful in keeping track of details in complex programs with decision points and multiple branches. The flowchart introduced in figure 1.1 (program 1A) presents some of the flowchart symbols used in this book. (Refer to appendix E for a complete list of flowchart symbols.) However, you should understand that the usefulness of a flowchart may not become apparent until you have to deal with more complex programming problems.

In the flowchart for program 1A, the oval-shaped symbol is used to designate the beginning and the end of a program. The name Program 1A is written in the beginning symbol, and the word End is written in the ending symbol. The parallelogram-shaped symbol is used for input operations, and the message ASSIGN NUMBER OF GUESTS identifies the input variable. The rectangle-shaped symbol is used for processing of data or anytime none of the other symbols apply. The processing step CALCULATE NUMBER OF EGGS is written inside the processing box. The torn-page symbol is used for output operations. The message PRINT NUMBER OF EGGS describes the output operation. The arrows in a flow diagram indicate the direction of flow and, hence, the order in which operations are performed. The order of operations is of paramount importance, and the flowchart is one method the programmer uses to keep the operations in the proper order. Obviously, we would not calculate the number of eggs before the input of the number of guests or print the number of eggs before calculating that value. However, a common error in beginning programs is incorrect order in the sequence of operations. Careful attention to a flow diagram would eliminate most, if not all, errors in the sequence of operations.

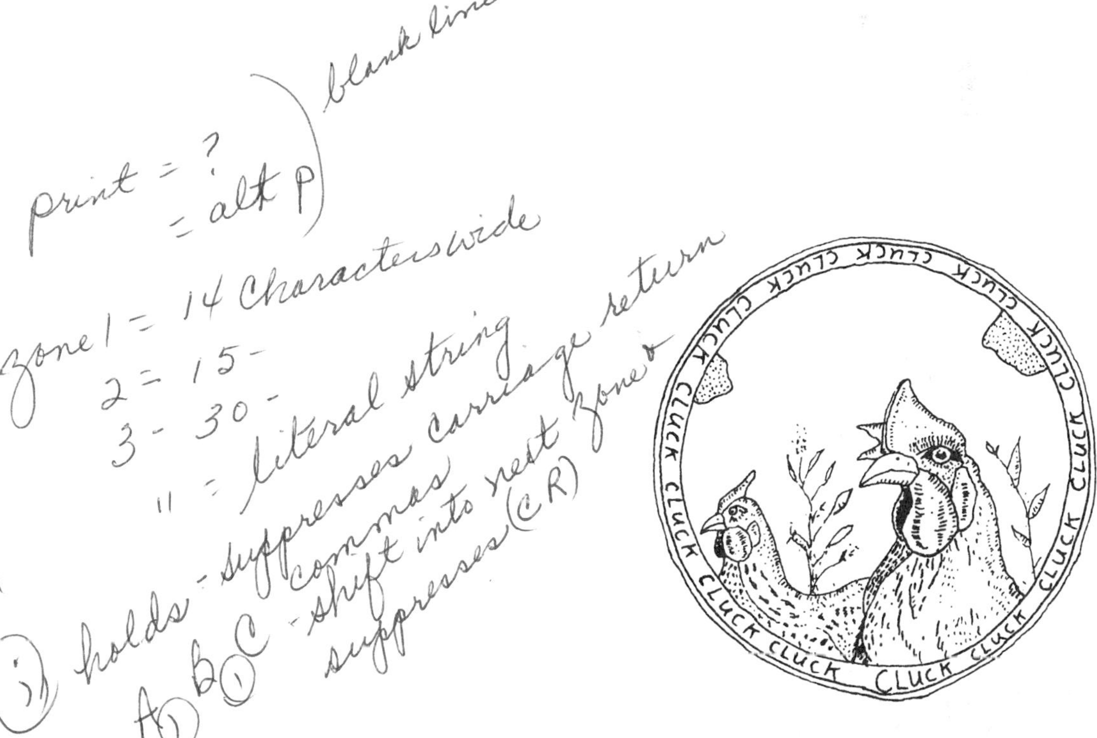

LET The LET statement is used to assign a name to a memory cell and put a number or message into the named memory cell. The general form of the LET statement is:

> *line number* LET *variable name* = *number or arithmetic expression whose value will be placed in memory*
>
> or
>
> *line number* LET *string variable* = "*message*"

The equal sign in the LET statement has a different meaning than it does in a mathematical equation. The LET statement instructs the computer to replace the contents of the memory cell named on the left side of the equal sign with the value of the expression on the right side. For this reason the equal sign in the LET statement is sometimes referred to as the "replaced by" symbol. Computer scientists would have preferred to use a left arrow rather than an equal sign to express this operation, but it wasn't available on the keyboard.

The statement LET X = X + 1 means replace the contents of the memory cell named X with the old contents of X plus 1. If the memory cell named X contains the number 3, the statement LET X = X + 1 will replace that 3 with a 4.

Examples of LET statements:

```
10  LET A = 2
20  LET X = 2 * A + 4.324
30  LET B$ = "JOHN JOHNSON"
```

The use of the word LET is optional; the statements

`10  LET A = 2` and `10  A = 2`

are equivalent.

SELF-TESTING QUESTIONS

Select the word from the list below that best matches each question.

A. Cursor keys	B. FILES	C. DELETE	D. KILL"
E. LLIST	F. CLS	G. LET	H. LIST
I. LOAD"	J. NEW	K. PRINT	L. Enter key
M. RUN	N. RUN "name"	O. SAVE"	P. SYNTAX ERROR

1.1 Used to remove the program from the computer's memory and leave a clear work space.

1.2 Used to clear the screen.

1.3 Used to enter (or conclude) a line or command.

1.4 Used to see the program in the computer's memory.

1.5 Used in a program to calculate the value of a variable.

1.6 Used in a program to show the results produced by the program.

1.7 Used to execute the program in the computer's memory.

1.8 A message the computer prints when something is wrong.

1.9 Used to move the cursor left, right, up, or down.

1.10 Used to list the program on the printer.

1.11 Used to remove lines from a program.

1.12 Used to store a program on a disk.

1.13 Used to list the names of the programs on a disk.

1.14 Used to copy a program from a disk into the computer's memory.

1.15 A single command used to copy a program from a disk into the computer's memory and execute the program.

1.16 Used to remove a program from a disk.

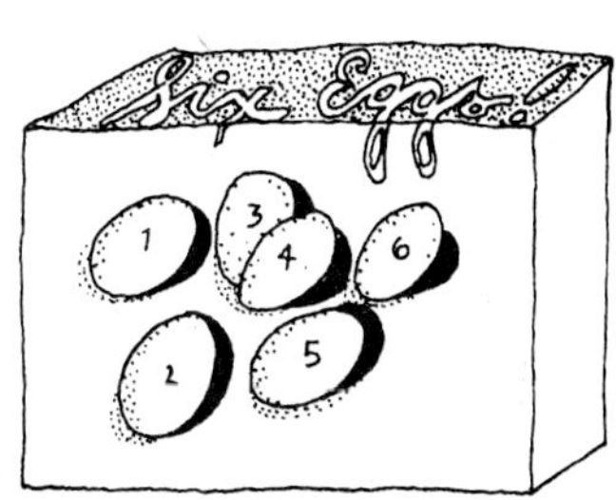

EXERCISES

1.1 Follow the nine steps listed below.

1. Type the program exactly as it appears in example 1A.
2. Run the program to make sure it gives you the run you see in figure 1.1.
3. When the program runs properly, save it by typing:

```
SAVE "P1A"
```

4. Using the BASIC editor, change line 10 and try various values of G (guests).
5. When you are satisfied with this, add shrimp to the menu and label this P1B.
6. Assume that you will need 3 shrimp per guest.
7. When this new version runs properly, save it by typing:

```
SAVE "P1B"
```

8. Type ⟨Ctrl-PrtSc⟩ to turn on the output to the printer (use ⟨Fn-Echo⟩ on the PCjr), then type RUN and LIST.
9. Type ⟨Ctrl-PrtSc⟩ again to turn off the output to the printer (use ⟨Fn-Echo⟩ on the PCjr).

TIPS

1. **Remember to type NEW before starting.**
2. **Note that you will need two new lines, one to calculate the number of shrimp and one to print this value.**
3. **Be sure to have the program calculate the number of shrimp before you have it print this value.**

CHAPTER 2

DOING IT RIGHT
Programming Standards

NEW CONCEPTS TAUGHT

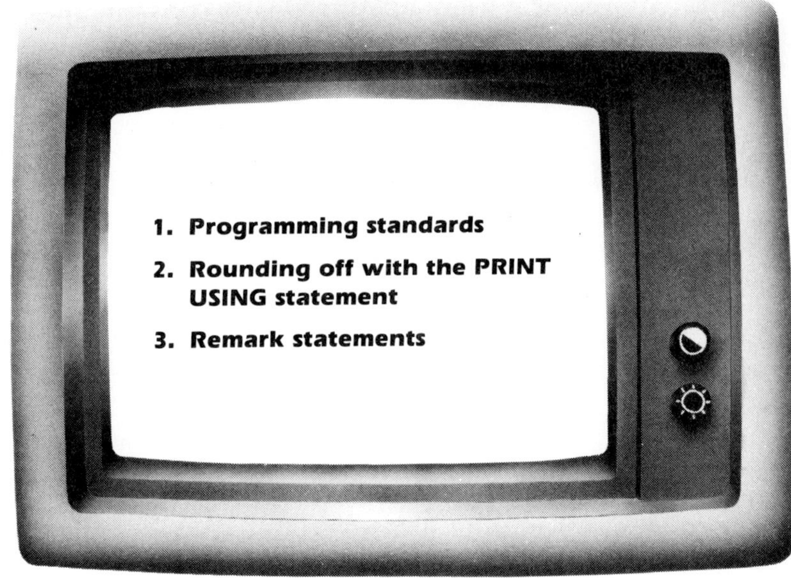

1. Programming standards
2. Rounding off with the PRINT USING statement
3. Remark statements

PROGRAMMING STANDARDS

In this chapter we are introducing several new concepts. One of them is the idea of programming standards. Most programmers have certain rules they follow in writing programs. Although these rules may seem restrictive to you at first, they are almost always to the advantage of the programmer. They make programs more reliable, easier to read, easier to modify, and in the long run, easier to write.

One of our rules is that every program should contain the program name, the name of the programmer, and the date. To make this information easy to find, we put it at the beginning, in lines 1, 2, and 3.

```
1     PN$ = "PROGRAM NAME"
2     NA$ = "YOUR NAME"
3     DA$ = "ØØ/ØØ/ØØ"
```

Another rule is that there should be standard sections of the program reserved for various purposes. In the program shown in figure 2.1,we have set aside lines 10 to 39 for the description of variables used in the program. The main program (the part of the program that does the real work) always starts at line 100.

EXAMPLE 2A The Starter Program

Problem Write a program that will serve as a starting point for future programs. Reserve space at the beginning for the name of the program, the programmer, and the date. Include a line that will print the name of the program (centered on the screen) when it is run. Have designated sections for variable descriptions and the main program. (Figure 2.1 shows the list for example 2A.)

Solution

FIGURE 2.1

```
LIST
1     PN$ = "STARTER"
2     NA$ = "YOUR NAME"
3     DA$ = "00/00/00"
10    '  ===== VARIABLES =====
100   '  ===== MAIN PROGRAM =====
101   CLS : PRINT TAB(40 - (LEN (PN$) / 2)) PN$
Ok
```

The colon symbol ":" between statements allows us to make multiple program statements in a single line. In line 101, for example, we have two program statements separated by a colon. It is legal to have many more as long as the entire line (including the line number) does not contain more than 256 characters.

```
101   CLS : PRINT TAB(40 - (LEN (PN$) / 2)) PN$
```

In line 101 the first statement uses the CLS command to clear the screen. Then we use the TAB statement and the PRINT PN$ statement to position and print the name of the program on the screen (PN$ is assigned in line 1). The TAB command moves the cursor to the column specified by the number following the word TAB. In this case we have used a formula so that this line will center the program name regardless of its length. The formula uses LEN(PN$), which is the length of the program name, divides it by 2, and tabs to 40 minus that number. Since 40 would be the center of the screen (the screen is 80 characters wide), this automatically centers the name on the screen. If you are working with a 40-column screen, use 20 rather than 40 in line 101.

If you don't understand this completely, don't worry; just copy the line exactly and everything will be fine.

The standards and rules we have talked about here will apply to all the programs in this book. All programs in this book will have the form of example program 2A. They will have the program name, the programmer's name, and the date assigned to the variables PN$, NA$, and DA$ in lines 1, 2, and 3 of the program. They will also maintain separate sections for variable descriptions, and the main programs as follows:

Variables—lines 10 through 39
Main Program—lines 100 through 199

Because you will be using this same form for all the programs you will write for this book, it will be convenient to write and save a kind of skeleton program like the one in figure 2.1. Call this program STARTER and save it under that name. That way you can start all future programs by typing NEW and then typing LOAD "STARTER". This will save you some typing and will make it easy to stick to the programming rules discussed above.

REMARK STATEMENTS

We usually use remark statements to designate parts of a program (as in lines 10 and 100 of figure 2.1). Remark statements are completely ignored by the computer; they have no effect on the execution of the program. We use them to make the program easier to understand and to make comments about the program to remind us how it works. Remark statements may begin with the word REM or the single quote mark '. In the section beginning at line 10 we will put a series of remark statements listing the variables in a program and explaining how they are used.

ROUNDING OFF

Often when the computer divides one number by another or does a square root, the answer is some awkward number with many decimal places. Many times we don't need such accuracy and would like to have the number rounded off before printing it. IBM BASIC provides the PRINT USING statement, which is used when we want to print the rounded value of a number. We use

```
140  PRINT USING "## MILES PER GALLON";MPG
```

in line 140 of program 2B to print the value of MPG rounded to a whole number. The PRINT USING statement allows us to format information so that the computer will print it the way we want it to. It provides a kind of picture for the computer to use. The # signs are used to represent numbers. If we had wanted the number rounded to one decimal place, we would have used ##.# instead of ##. The best way to understand the PRINT USING statement is to experiment with it. Type in the example program and try several variations of the PRINT USING statement until you feel you understand how it formats decimal numbers. We will explore some more sophisticated uses of the PRINT USING statement in later chapters.

PRINT USING The PRINT USING statement allows the programmer a great deal of control over the format of printed output. A complete explanation of the PRINT USING statement is beyond the scope of this book. The following are some common forms and their effects. The # sign is used to represent numbers in the PRINT USING statement. The symbols in the PRINT USING statement give the computer a kind of "picture" of what you want the output to look like. A decimal point may be placed in the format string to tell the computer where the decimal point goes in the printed output. If the number to be printed does not fill the whole field, a zero will be added in front of the decimal point. If the number to be printed extends beyond the right of the format string, it will be rounded off. If the number to be printed is larger than the specified format string, a percent sign (%) is printed in front of the number. A dollar sign ($) in front of the format string causes the number to be printed with a leading dollar sign. Two dollar signs ($$) in front of the format string cause the dollar sign to be placed right next to the first digit of the number. Several numbers or variables may be placed at the end of the PRINT USING statement separated by commas. They will be formatted according to the PRINT USING format string.

Examples:

```
STATEMENT                           RESULT

PRINT USING "##.##";.99             Ø.99
PRINT USING "###.##";123.456        123.46
PRINT USING "##.##";999.11          %999.11
PRINT USING "$####.##";25           $  25.ØØ
PRINT USING "$$####.##";25             $25.ØØ
PRINT USING "    ##";1,2,3              1    2    3
```

COMPUTING MILEAGE

One of the things a microcomputer is best at is arithmetic. Our example of this is a simple program for computing mileage. If you go a certain distance in your car and use a certain number of gallons of fuel getting there, you can easily figure out your miles per gallon by dividing the number of miles by the number of gallons. This procedure is the basis for example 2B.

One problem we must solve here is how to tell the computer how many miles we traveled and how many gallons of fuel we used. There are several ways to do this. In lines 110 and 120 of this program, we enter the values right into the program.

```
110  LET DIST = 200
120  LET GAL = 30
```

In chapter 3 we will see two other ways to do this. In line 110 of figure 2.2, the variable DIST, which stands for distance traveled, is set equal to 200 (miles); in line 120 the variable GAL, which stands for gallons of fuel used, is set equal to 33; and then in line 130, MPG (miles per gallon) is computed.

```
130  LET MPG = DIST / GAL
140  PRINT USING "## MILES PER GALLON"; MPG
150  END
```

In line 140 we print the value of MPG (rounded to a whole number with the PRINT USING statement) followed by the phrase "MILES PER GALLON" to make it clear what the number being printed represents.

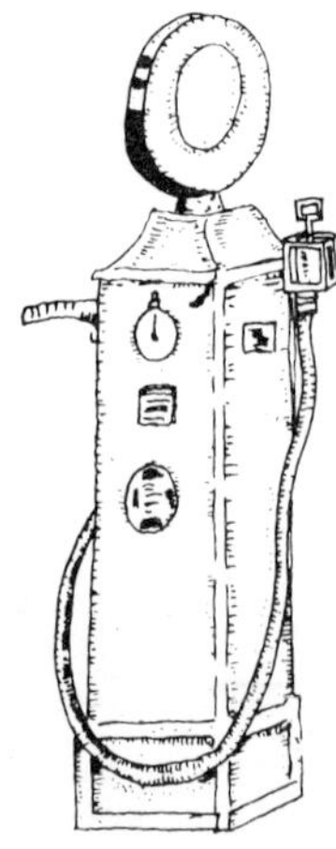

EXAMPLE 2B Miles per Gallon (LET)

Problem Using the program from example 2A as a starting point, write a program that will calculate the miles per gallon for your car on a single trip. Use LET statements to assign values to the variables for distance traveled and gallons used. In the variable section, describe the variables used with remark statements. Round your result to a whole number using the PRINT USING statement.

Solution

FIGURE 2.2

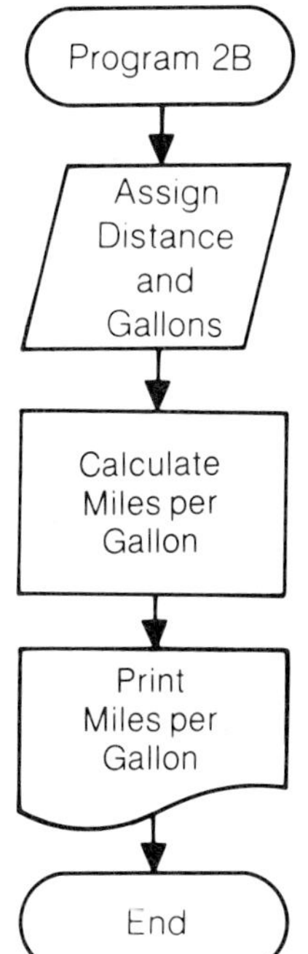


```
LIST
1     PN$ = "P2B-MPG"
2     NA$ = "YOUR NAME"
3     DA$ = "00/00/00"
10    ' ===== VARIABLES =====
11    ' DIST = DISTANCE TRAVELED
12    ' GAL = GALLONS USED
13    ' MPG = MILES PER GALLON
100   ' ===== MAIN PROGRAM =====
101   CLS : PRINT TAB(40 - (LEN (PN$) / 2)) PN$
110   LET DIST = 200
120   LET GAL = 30
130   LET MPG = DIST / GAL
140   PRINT USING "## MILES PER GALLON"; MPG
150   END
Ok
```

RUN

SELF-TESTING QUESTIONS

Step through the program in each question and write the output produced when the program runs.

2.1

```
110  LET DIST = 500
120  LET GAL = 20
130  LET MPG = DIST / GAL
140  PRINT USING "## MILES PER GALLON"; MPG
```

2.2

```
110  LET DIST = 60
120  LET GAL = 9
130  LET MPG = DIST / GAL
140  PRINT USING "## MILES PER GALLON"; MPG
```

2.3 Same as question 2.2, except change line 140 to the following:

```
140  PRINT USING "##.# MILES PER GALLON"; MPG
```

2.4 Same as question 2.2, except change line 140 to the following:

```
140  PRINT USING "##.## MILES PER GALLON"; MPG
```

2.5 Same as question 2.2, except change line 140 to the following:

```
140  PRINT USING "##.### MILES PER GALLON"; MPG
```

EXERCISES

Do Both Exercises

2.1 Type the starter program exactly as it appears in figure 2.1, then run the program. If you get the "SYNTAX ERROR" message, you probably have made one or more typing errors. If you have typed the program correctly, nothing should happen when you type RUN, except that the word STARTER should be printed in the center of the line at the top of the screen.

When you are satisfied that the program has been typed correctly, save it by typing:

```
SAVE "STARTER".
```

You can then use this program as a beginning for all future programs.

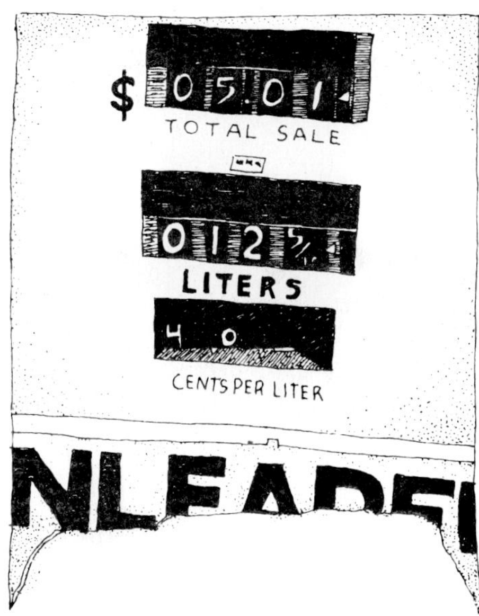

TIPS

1. **Remember to type NEW before starting.**
2. **Type carefully.**
3. **Be especially careful to have the parentheses in line 101 in the right places.**

2.2 Write a program that will calculate the miles per gallon for your car on a single trip. Use LET statements to put into the program the values for miles traveled and gallons of fuel used. Start by typing LOAD "STARTER". Then use the BASIC editor to change the program name in line 1 to "P2-MPG" (we use the hyphen to separate P2 from MPG in the name—remember, spaces are not allowed in a program name). Change line 3 to indicate the date. Use the program from figure 2.2 as a model for your program. Use 60 as the number of miles traveled and 9 as the number of gallons of fuel used.

Do four versions of the program: one to round MPG to a whole number, then to one decimal place, to two decimal places, and finally to three decimal places. Change the PRINT USING statement in line 140 to accomplish this. For each of the four versions, get a printout of the LIST and RUN by typing:

⟨Ctrl-PrtSc⟩ (use ⟨Fn-Echo⟩ on the PCjr)
`LIST`
`RUN`
⟨Ctrl-PrtSc⟩ (use ⟨Fn-Echo⟩ on the PCjr)

Do this four times, once for each version. When the program runs properly, save it by typing:

```
SAVE "P2-MPG"
```

NOTE: If you save the program immediately after a run of the program, you can make use of the variable PN$ stored in the computer memory and save the program as follows:

`SAVE PN$` ⟨Enter⟩

Saving the program this way guarantees that the program is saved under the exact name as on line 1 of the program. Remember, to use this method, the program must have been run at least once and the name in line 1 of the program must be correct. Before saving the program using this method, type PRINT PN$ or ?PN$ to make sure that PN$ has the correct value.

TIPS

1. **Follow these directions very carefully.**
2. **If you find out there was an error in your starter program, be sure to go back and correct it after you finish this assignment.**

CHAPTER 3

GETTING DATA IN

Two More Methods of Input

NEW CONCEPTS TAUGHT

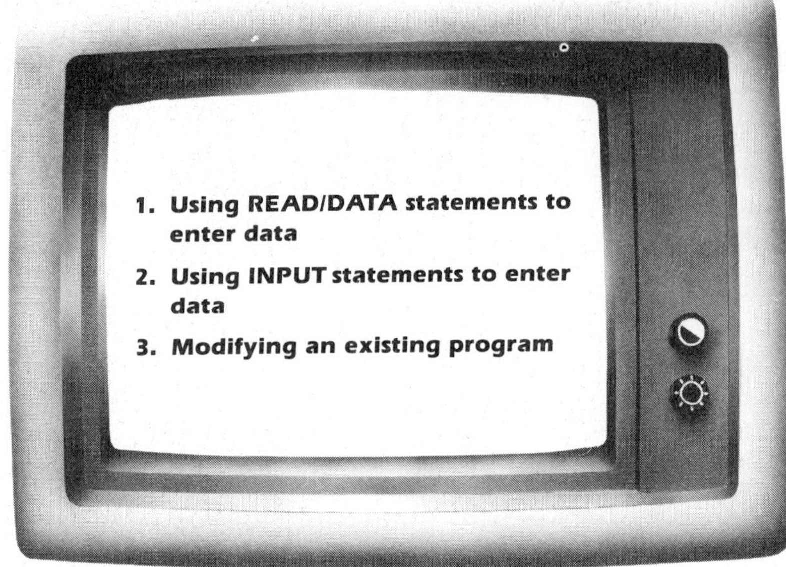

1. Using READ/DATA statements to enter data
2. Using INPUT statements to enter data
3. Modifying an existing program

METHODS OF INPUT

In chapter 2 we used the computer to calculate our miles per gallon on a trip. We used LET statements to tell the computer how far we traveled and how much fuel we used on our trip. In this chapter we will see two other methods of giving a computer the information it needs to do its work.

READ/DATA Statements

READ statements and DATA statements are really two different things, but since each is useless without the other, they always go together; thus, we usually refer to them as READ/DATA statements. You have probably seen the word data used in other contexts to refer to information; that's exactly what it means here. The DATA statement contains information the computer needs to do its job. The READ statement tells the computer that there is a DATA statement around somewhere that it should be aware of. Confused?

The concept of READ/DATA statements will be much clearer if we look at program 3A in figure 3.1. In line 150 there are two data values separated by a comma. This line could actually be placed anywhere in the program, even after the END statement, and it would still work. In any program that has a DATA statement, there is a kind of imaginary pointer, pointing to the first DATA value in the program, wherever it is. In this case it points to the 400 in line 150.

When the computer encounters the READ statement in line 110, it knows this means it should put the value that the DATA pointer is pointing at (400) in the memory cell labeled DIST and move the DATA pointer ahead one notch (which leaves it pointing at the 19 in line 150). When the computer gets to the second READ statement (in line 120), it puts the second data value (19) in the memory cell labeled GAL. It then calculates MPG, rounds it off, and prints the result as before. The DATA statement in line 150 is ignored. In fact, DATA statements are always ignored except when being referred to specifically by a READ statement. While the DATA statements could be placed anywhere, the placement and order of the READ statements is extremely important.

EXAMPLE 3A Miles per Gallon (READ/DATA)

Problem Write a program that will calculate and print your miles per gallon for a single trip. Use READ/DATA statements to enter the values of distance traveled and gallons of gas used.

Solution

FIGURE 3.1

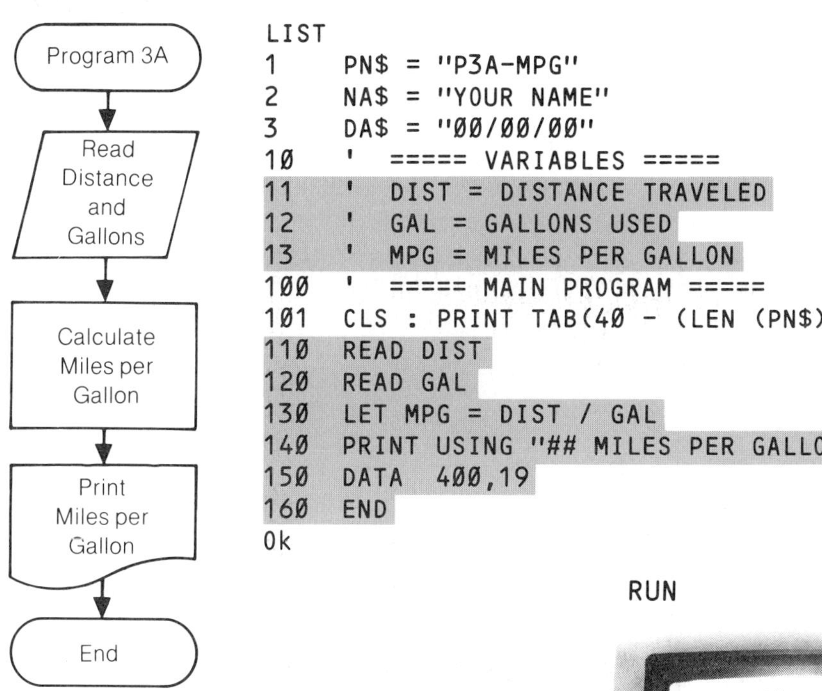


```
LIST
1      PN$ = "P3A-MPG"
2      NA$ = "YOUR NAME"
3      DA$ = "ØØ/ØØ/ØØ"
1Ø     '  ===== VARIABLES =====
11     '  DIST = DISTANCE TRAVELED
12     '  GAL = GALLONS USED
13     '  MPG = MILES PER GALLON
1ØØ    '  ===== MAIN PROGRAM =====
1Ø1    CLS : PRINT TAB(4Ø - (LEN (PN$) / 2)) PN$
11Ø    READ DIST
12Ø    READ GAL
13Ø    LET MPG = DIST / GAL
14Ø    PRINT USING "## MILES PER GALLON"; MPG
15Ø    DATA  4ØØ,19
16Ø    END
Ok
```

RUN

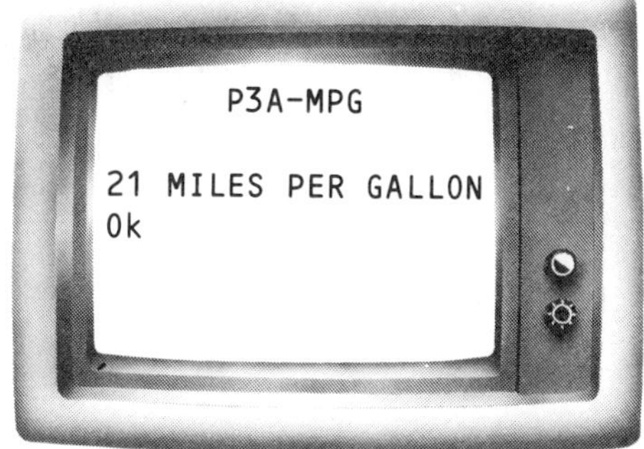

Some programs have many data values taking up many lines of the program. Here we needed only two, so we put them on a single line. We could have put them on two lines if we had wanted to, like so:

```
150  DATA 400
155  DATA 19
```

INPUT STATEMENTS

The INPUT statement is a way of getting the computer to pay attention to the person sitting at the keyboard *during* the execution of the program. When an INPUT statement is encountered, the program stops and waits for something to be entered at the keyboard (followed by 〈Enter〉, of course). So that the person at the keyboard knows what they are supposed to be entering, we usually have the program print a message on the screen. This message is called a "prompt" and is often in the form of a question.

In program 3B (see figure 3.2), we use INPUT statements to set the values of DIST and GAL. In line 110 the message "HOW MANY MILES" is printed on the screen. The semicolon (;) following the prompt is not necessary, but it lets the user enter the number of miles on the same line just to the right of the prompt. Without the semicolon, the number of miles would be entered at the left side of the screen on the line below the prompt. (You might say that the semicolon suppresses the carriage return that would normally follow this kind of statement.) Notice that we use no question mark in lines 110 and 130. This is because the INPUT statements on the following lines (120 and 140) will print a question mark before accepting any input. In line 120 the computer puts whatever value the user types at the keyboard into the memory cell labeled DIST.

In line 130 the program prints another prompt on the screen, and in line 140 puts the value typed at the keyboard into the memory cell labeled GAL. In lines 150 and 160, the miles per gallon for the trip are calculated, and printed as before.

In chapter 4 we will use an alternate form of the INPUT statement that allows the prompt to be included in the INPUT statement itself.

EXAMPLE 3B Miles per Gallon (INPUT)

Problem Write a program that calculates and prints your miles per gallon for a single trip. Use INPUT statements to enter the number of miles traveled and gallons of gas used.

Solution

FIGURE 3.2

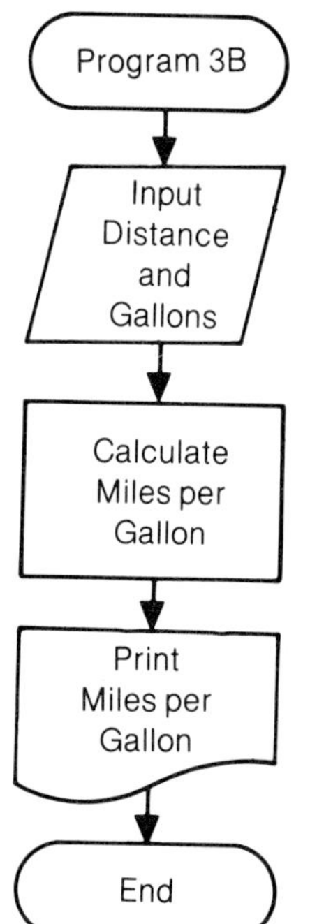


```
LIST
1     PN$ = "P3B-MPG"
2     NA$ = "YOUR NAME"
3     DA$ = "ØØ/ØØ/ØØ"
1Ø    '  ===== VARIABLES =====
11    '  DIST = DISTANCE TRAVELED
12    '  GAL = GALLONS USED
13    '  MPG = MILEAGE
1ØØ   '  ===== MAIN PROGRAM =====
1Ø1   CLS : PRINT TAB(4Ø - (LEN (PN$) / 2)) PN$
11Ø   PRINT "HOW MANY MILES";
12Ø   INPUT DIST
13Ø   PRINT "HOW MANY GALLONS";
14Ø   INPUT GAL
15Ø   LET MPG = DIST / GAL
16Ø   PRINT USING "##.# MILES PER GALLON" ; MPG
17Ø   END
Ok
```

RUN

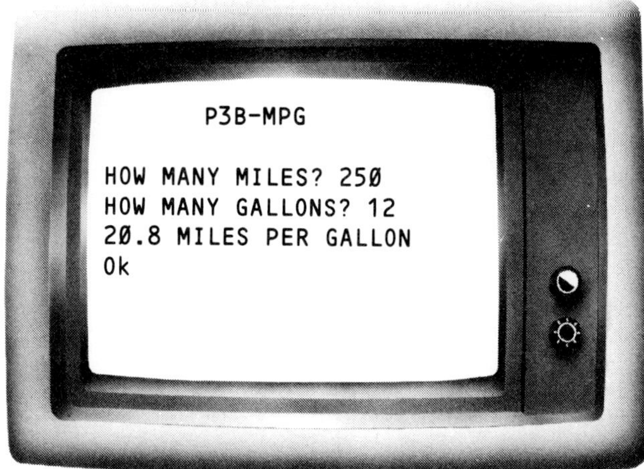

P3B-MPG
HOW MANY MILES? 25Ø
HOW MANY GALLONS? 12
2Ø.8 MILES PER GALLON
Ok

READ, DATA, and RESTORE The READ and DATA statements are used together to assign names and put numbers or messages in memory cells. The READ statement gives the names for the memory cells. The DATA statement gives the numbers or messages that go into the named memory cells. The names and numbers or messages must be in exactly the same order in the READ and the DATA statements. All the DATA statements in a program are considered to be part of one overall DATA statement with the same order of occurrence of the numbers and messages. When the program run begins, the computer sets a DATA pointer above the first quantity in the overall DATA list. Each time the computer encounters a variable name in a READ statement, it puts that name on a memory cell, copies the quantity under the DATA pointer into the named memory cell, and moves the DATA pointer over the next quantity in the overall DATA list.

The computer prints the message OUT OF DATA when it encounters a name in a READ statement and the DATA pointer has moved past the last quantity in the overall DATA list.

The RESTORE statement moves the DATA pointer back to the first quantity in the overall DATA list. If the RESTORE statement is followed by a line number (e.g., RESTORE 100), the DATA pointer will be moved to point at the first data value on the specified line.

The general form of the READ and DATA statements are:

> *line number* `READ` *any combination of variable names and string variable names separated by commas*
>
> and
>
> *line number* `DATA` *a corresponding combination of numbers and messages*

Note: A message that includes a comma or colon must be enclosed in quotation marks.

Examples:

```
10 READ X
20 DATA 7.642

50 READ X,Y,Z
60 DATA 7.642,3.25,-1.43

120 READ A$
200 DATA PETER

220 READ N$,M$
230 DATA "JONES, PETER", "MACKEY, ORVILLE"

500 READ N$,S1,S2,S3
510 DATA "JONES,PETER"
511 DATA 364,34,7652
```

INPUT The INPUT statement is used to assign names to memory cells. When the program runs and the INPUT statement is executed, the computer waits for the user to type the data to be put in the memory cell named in the INPUT statement. The most common form of the INPUT statement is:

line number **INPUT** *prompt; variable name*
or
line number **INPUT** *prompt, variable name*

The prompt is optional. If a semicolon (;) is used before the variable name, a question mark will be printed. If a comma is used, no question mark will appear.

Examples of INPUT statements:

```
1Ø INPUT X
2Ø INPUT A$
3Ø INPUT "HOW MANY TRIPS? ",T1
4Ø INPUT "TYPE YOUR NAME"; NAME$
```

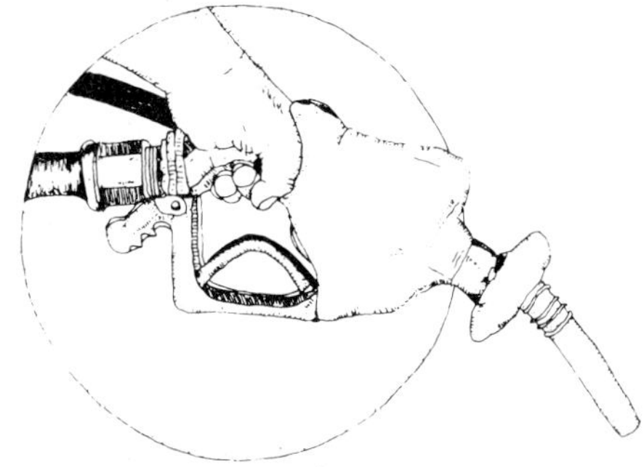

SELF-TESTING QUESTIONS

Step through the program in each problem and write the output produced when the program runs.

3.1

```
110  READ DIST
120  READ GAL
130  LET MPG = DIST / GAL
140  PRINT USING "## MILES PER GALLON"; MPG
150  DATA 425, 15.2
```

3.2 Same as question 3.1, except change lines 140 and 150 to the following:

```
140  PRINT USING "##.# MILES PER GALLON"; MPG
150  DATA 285, 9.3
```

3.3 The first two lines of two runs of PROGRAM 3B are shown below. Write the output produced when each run is completed.

a.
```
HOW MANY MILES? 315
HOW MANY GALLONS? 8.6
```

b.
```
HOW MANY MILES? 405
HOW MANY GALLONS? 11.2
```

3.4

```
110  READ A
120  READ B
130  READ C
140  READ D
150  PRINT "THE LAST NUMBER IS ";D
160  DATA 4, 1, 8, 7, 3
```

EXERCISES

Do Both Exercises

3.1 Load the STARTER program you wrote in chapter 2 and change the name of the program in line 1 to P31-READ. Revise the chapter 1 program you wrote to calculate the number of eggs and shrimp for the party. Start the program at line 110 and use a READ/DATA statement instead of a LET statement to set the number of guests. Also, add REM statements at lines 11, 12, and 13 to describe the variables G, E, and S. Assume that you will need 1.25 eggs and 1.33 shrimp per person. After calculating the necessary amounts of eggs and shrimp, round off to the nearest whole egg or shrimp. When the program runs properly, get a list and run on paper as described in chapter 1, and save program 3.1 by typing:

SAVE "P31-READ" ⟨Enter⟩

or immediately after a run by typing:

SAVE PN$ ⟨Enter⟩

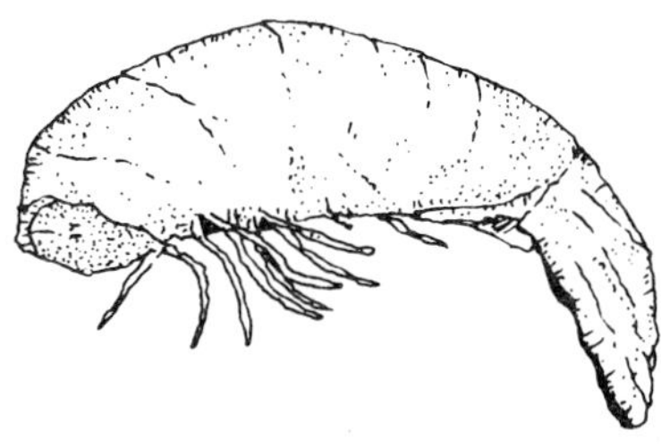

TIPS

1. **Be sure to change line 1 as soon as you load the program.**
2. **If things get too messed up, you can type NEW, reload STARTER, and start over; if you do this, be sure you change line 1 again.**
3. **Look at the changes we made in example 2B to make it into example 3A.**

3.2 After you have program 3A working and safely saved and you have a successful list and run, change the name of the program in line 1 to P32-INP. Then modify the program so that it uses an INPUT statement to enter the value of guests. Have the program ask you "HOW MANY GUESTS?" before inputting the number. When the program runs properly, get a list and run in the usual way and save this program by typing:

```
SAVE "P32-INP"
```

or immediately after a run by typing:

```
SAVE PN$
```

TIPS

1. **Follow these directions *very* carefully.**
2. **This is a minor change from P31, so don't expect to make a lot of changes.**
3. **Remember that when the program gets to the INPUT statement, it will stop and wait for you to type something.**
4. **Be sure to have the program print a prompt so that you will know things are working right.**

CHAPTER 4

LET'S DO THAT AGAIN

Looping with GOTO and IF Statements

NEW CONCEPTS TAUGHT

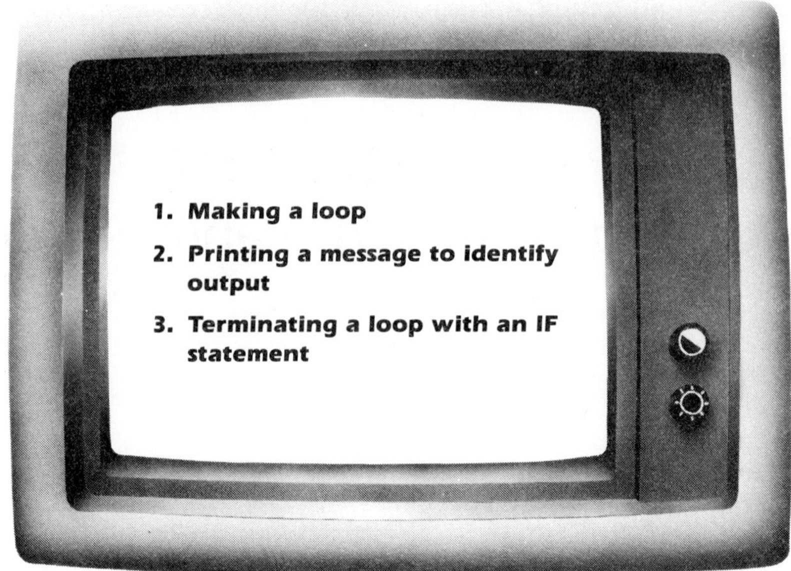

1. Making a loop
2. Printing a message to identify output
3. Terminating a loop with an IF statement

LOOPING

All of the programs we have seen so far have done a single task by proceeding directly from beginning to end. This method is simple and effective if you want to do a task only once. The real treat of having a computer, however, is in getting it to do boring, repetitive tasks while we are out reclining in the sun. Repetition in computer jargon is called "looping" and can be accomplished in several ways. One of these ways is to form a loop with a simple GOTO statement.

A Primitive Loop

In program 4A the loop includes lines 110 through 160. As soon as the program gets to line 160, it is sent back to line 110. The END statement in line 210 is about as effective as sunglasses on an owl; the program will never reach line 210.

EXAMPLE 4A Miles per gallon (READ/DATA and GOTO Loop)

Problem Write a program that uses a GOTO loop to print your miles per gallon for a series of trips. Use READ/DATA statements to enter the values of distance traveled and gallons of gas used.

Solution

FIGURE 4.1

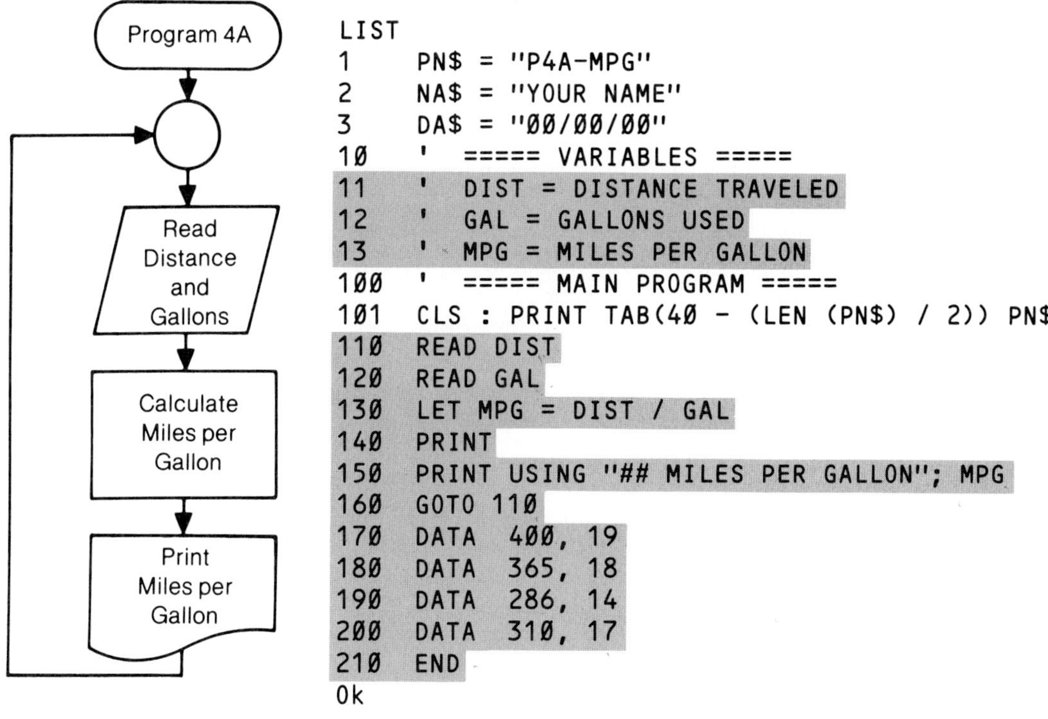


```
LIST
1     PN$ = "P4A-MPG"
2     NA$ = "YOUR NAME"
3     DA$ = "ØØ/ØØ/ØØ"
1Ø    '  ===== VARIABLES =====
11    '  DIST = DISTANCE TRAVELED
12    '  GAL = GALLONS USED
13    '  MPG = MILES PER GALLON
1ØØ   '  ===== MAIN PROGRAM =====
1Ø1   CLS : PRINT TAB(4Ø - (LEN (PN$) / 2)) PN$
11Ø   READ DIST
12Ø   READ GAL
13Ø   LET MPG = DIST / GAL
14Ø   PRINT
15Ø   PRINT USING "## MILES PER GALLON"; MPG
16Ø   GOTO 11Ø
17Ø   DATA  4ØØ, 19
18Ø   DATA  365, 18
19Ø   DATA  286, 14
2ØØ   DATA  31Ø, 17
21Ø   END
Ok
```

RUN

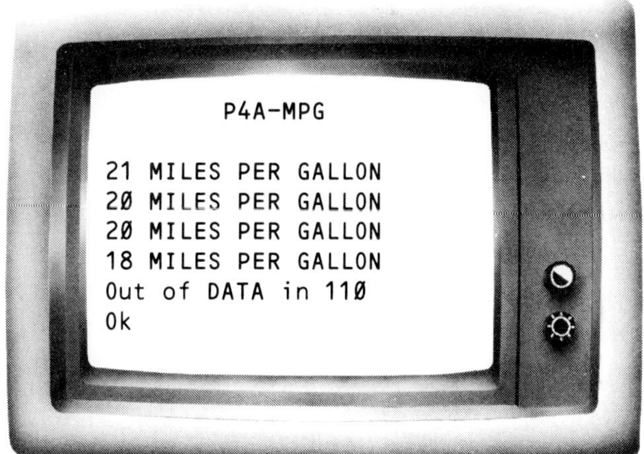

P4A-MPG
21 MILES PER GALLON
2Ø MILES PER GALLON
2Ø MILES PER GALLON
18 MILES PER GALLON
Out of DATA in 11Ø
Ok

The DATA statements in lines 170 through 200 are all right, however, since DATA statements can be anywhere in a program. When the program encounters the READ statement in line 110, it searches the whole program, disregarding all commands, looking faithfully for the first DATA statement and finding it in line 170. As we explained before, after the DATA value is read, the DATA pointer is pointed at the next DATA value in the program (also on line 170). Line 120 reads this DATA value and then leaves the pointer aimed at the first DATA value in line 180. The mileage is calculated and printed, and when the loop executes again, the DATA in line 180 are read.

We have put two DATA values on each line since two values are read each time through the loop. This makes the program easier to understand but is not strictly necessary. Actually we could have put all the DATA values on one line, provided they were in the right order.

After the loop has executed four times, the DATA pointer is left pointing past the end of the DATA. When the loop sends the program back to line 110 for the fifth time, the DATA pointer is not pointing to any DATA (you might think of it as pointing off into space), so the READ statement in line 110 causes the program to crash and produces the Out of DATA in 110 message you see at the end of the run. Needless to say, this is not what we would call elegant programming. One of your tasks for this chapter is to learn how to terminate a loop more gracefully than this.

The Small Circle

A new symbol, the small circle, is introduced in the flowchart for program 4A. The circle is used as a connector symbol to join two branches at the beginning of the loop. One branch comes from the beginning of the program, the other branch is the return from the end of the program to start another pass through the input-processing-output operations. The term *loop* comes from the closed path formed in the flow diagram by the return branch.

A Better Loop

A more graceful method of terminating a loop can be seen in program 4B (figure 4.2). The loop in this program includes lines 140 through 210. Notice how the IF statement in line 210 determines whether the program loops or ends. The variable C in lines 200 and 210 is called the loop counter. Every time the loop is completed, the variable C is increased by 1. That is, the first time through the loop, line 200 raises C from zero to 1; the second time through, it is raised from 1 to 2. Since in this example we entered 2 as the number of trips (N), when C reaches 2, line 210 does not send the program back to line 140; rather, it "falls through" to the END statement in line 220.

EXAMPLE 4B Miles per Gallon (INPUT and GOTO loop)

Problem Write a program that uses a GOTO loop to print a list of your miles per gallon on a series of trips. Use INPUT statements to enter the number of trips, miles traveled, and gallons of gas used. Use a loop counter to stop the looping after the specified number of trips.

Solution

FIGURE 4.2

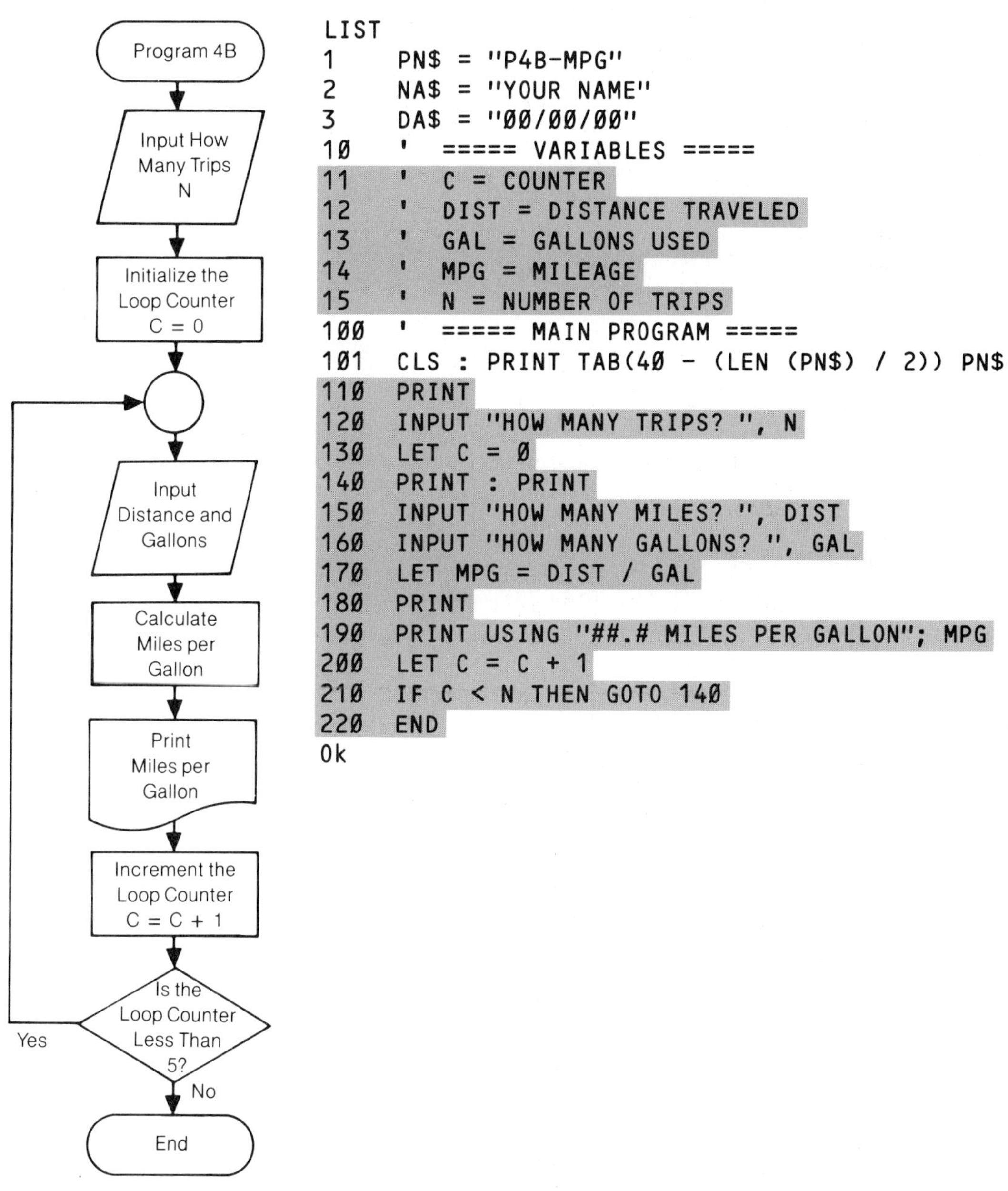


```
LIST
1     PN$ = "P4B-MPG"
2     NA$ = "YOUR NAME"
3     DA$ = "00/00/00"
10    '   ===== VARIABLES =====
11    '   C = COUNTER
12    '   DIST = DISTANCE TRAVELED
13    '   GAL = GALLONS USED
14    '   MPG = MILEAGE
15    '   N = NUMBER OF TRIPS
100   '   ===== MAIN PROGRAM =====
101   CLS : PRINT TAB(40 - (LEN (PN$) / 2)) PN$
110   PRINT
120   INPUT "HOW MANY TRIPS? ", N
130   LET C = 0
140   PRINT : PRINT
150   INPUT "HOW MANY MILES? ", DIST
160   INPUT "HOW MANY GALLONS? ", GAL
170   LET MPG = DIST / GAL
180   PRINT
190   PRINT USING "##.# MILES PER GALLON"; MPG
200   LET C = C + 1
210   IF C < N THEN GOTO 140
220   END
Ok
```

(Figure continued)

(Figure 4.2 continued)

RUN

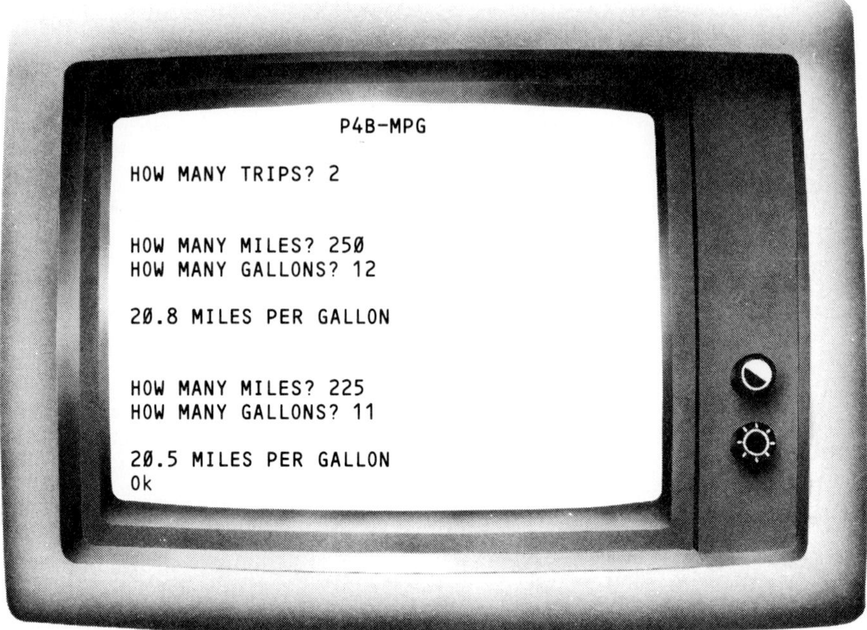

P4B-MPG
HOW MANY TRIPS? 2
HOW MANY MILES? 25Ø
HOW MANY GALLONS? 12
2Ø.8 MILES PER GALLON
HOW MANY MILES? 225
HOW MANY GALLONS? 11
2Ø.5 MILES PER GALLON
Ok

The first part of line 210, "IF C < N", we call a conditional. In any IF/THEN statement, if the conditional (the statement between the IF and the THEN) is false, everything else on the line is ignored and the program goes on to the next line. Terminating a loop is only one use of this concept, as we'll see later. In this example, when C is no longer less than N, the program goes on to line 220. Notice that this technique could be used to avoid the crash that occurred in program 4A.

In some programs, you might not want to have to enter N. (For example, you might not know exactly how many entries there will be.) Another way to handle this loop would be to delete lines 120, 130, and 200; change lines 150 and 210; and add a line 155 as follows:

```
15Ø  INPUT "HOW MANY MILES (ENTER 9999 TO QUIT): ";DIST
155  IF DIST = 9999 THEN GOTO 22Ø
21Ø  GOTO 14Ø
```

With the program changed like this, you can enter as many numbers as you wish and quit at any time by entering 9999 when prompted. This is one of many ways that programs can be made more convenient to use.

A New Form of the INPUT Statement

Notice the new version of the INPUT statement we have used in lines 120, 150, and 160 of program 4B. Compare this version with the combined PRINT and INPUT statements we have used previously. This new form of the INPUT statement provides a more concise way of printing a prompt and getting input from the user. It is also possible to avoid the question mark that is always printed with the other form of the INPUT statement; with this form you may use a comma just before the variable name to suppress the question mark. This way you can use a colon or other symbol at the end of your prompt. If you want to have the program print a question mark, use a semicolon (;) instead of a comma.

The Decision Symbol

The flowchart for program 4B introduces an important flowchart symbol, the diamond-shaped decision symbol. An expression called the conditional is written inside the decision symbol. In program 4B the conditional is the expression C < N. Two branches leave the decision symbol, one marked "yes," the other marked "no." If the conditional is true, the branch marked "yes" is taken; if the conditional is false, the branch marked "no" is taken. In program 4B the conditional is used to decide whether to loop back and calculate the miles per gallon for another trip, or to stop looping. In the BASIC program the decision symbol is implemented by the following statement:

```
240 IF C < N THEN GOTO 150.
```

> **GOTO** The GOTO statement tells the computer to jump to the line number that is written after the word GOTO and continue the run of the program.

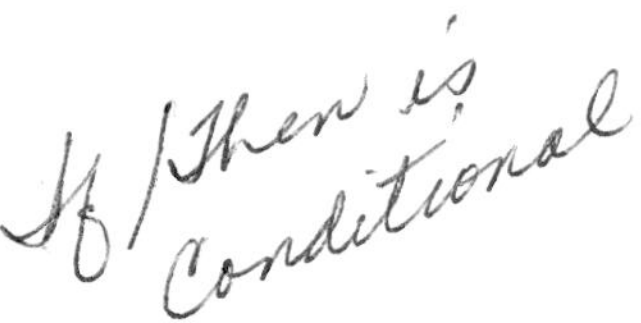

IF/THEN The IF/THEN statement tells the computer to either execute or ignore the instruction following the word THEN, depending on the conditional (the statement written between the word IF and the word THEN). If the conditional is true, the computer will execute the instruction that follows the word THEN. If the conditional is false, the computer will ignore the instruction after the word THEN and go on to the next line.

Example:

```
180  IF X < 5 THEN GOTO 120
```

The above instruction tells the computer to check the value of X to see if it is less than 5. If the value of X is less than 5, the computer goes to line 120 for the next instruction. If X is not less than 5, then the computer ignores the GOTO 120 instruction and goes on to the next line after line 180.

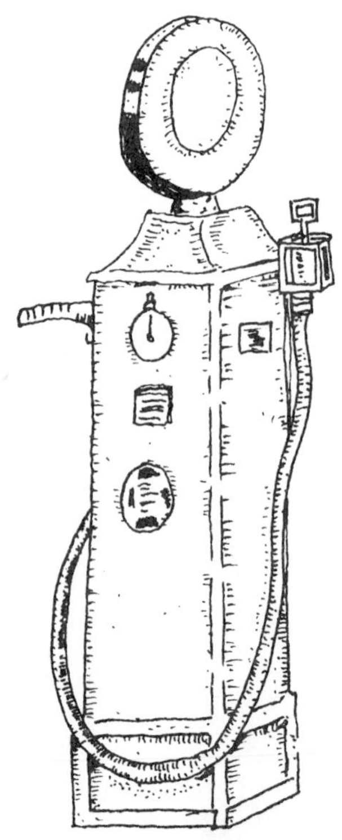

SELF-TESTING QUESTIONS

Step through the program in each problem and write the output produced when the program runs.

4.1
```
110  READ A
120  READ B
130  PRINT B
140  GOTO 110
150  DATA 4, 7, 3, 8, 9
```

4.2 Write everything that is printed when program 4B is run with the following three trips as input.

Trip 1: 412 miles and 11.8 gallons
Trip 2: 360 miles and 21.2 gallons
Trip 3: 385 miles and 14.5 gallons

4.3 An alternate version of program 4B is given below. Write everything that is printed when this program is run using the input from the following two trips:

Trip 1: 250 miles and 12 gallons
Trip 2: 225 miles and 11 gallons

```
110  PRINT "ENTER A DISTANCE OR 9999"
120  PRINT "TO TERMINATE THE PROGRAM."
130  PRINT
140  INPUT "HOW MANY MILES? ",DIST
150  IF DIST = 9999 GOTO 210
160  INPUT "HOW MANY GALLONS? ",GAL
170  LET MPG = DIST / GAL
180  PRINT
190  PRINT USING "##.# MILES PER GALLON"; MPG
200  GOTO 130
210  END
```

4.4 The termination of the program in question 4.3 is quite abrupt. The following version has a more graceful termination. Write everything that is printed when this program is run with the same input as question 4.3.

```
110  PRINT "ENTER A DISTANCE OR 9999"
120  PRINT "TO TERMINATE THE PROGRAM"
130  LET C = 0
140  PRINT
150  INPUT "HOW MANY MILES? ",DIST
160  IF DIST = 9999 GOTO 230
170  INPUT "HOW MANY GALLONS? ",GAL
180  LET MPG = DIST / GAL
190  PRINT
200  PRINT USING "##.# MILES PER GALLON"; MPG
210  LET C = C + 1
220  GOTO 140
230  PRINT
240  PRINT "PROGRAM TERMINATED AFTER"
250  PRINT C; " TRIPS.  GOODBYE."
260  END
```

EXERCISES

Do Both Exercises

4.1 Load the program you wrote for exercise 3.1 and change the name of the program in line 1 to P41–READ. Now change the program so that it prints out the number of eggs and shrimp needed for various values of G (guests). Use a GOTO loop and READ/DATA statements to enter the different values of guests (use at least four values). Put a PRINT statement inside the loop so that the printout looks like this:

```
2 GUESTS -  3 EGGS   3 SHRIMP
3 GUESTS -  4 EGGS   4 SHRIMP
5 GUESTS -  6 EGGS   7 SHRIMP
9 GUESTS - 11 EGGS  12 SHRIMP
```

As before, use 1.25 eggs and 1.33 shrimp per person and round off to the nearest whole egg or shrimp. When the program runs properly, save it and get the usual list and run on paper.

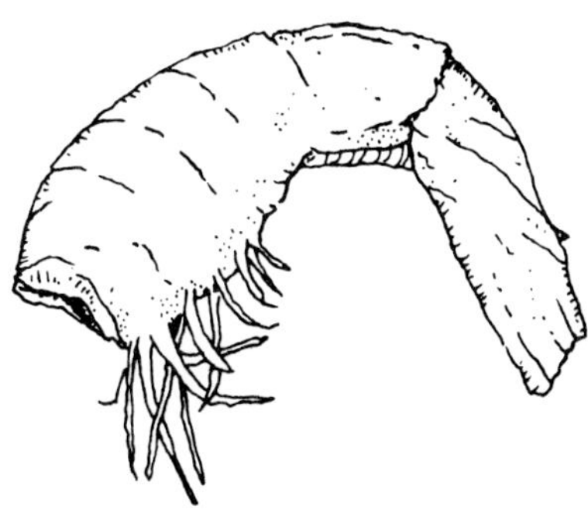

TIPS

1. **If the program runs endlessly and the cursor does not reappear, it means that your READ statement is outside your loop. Use ⟨Ctrl-Break⟩ to stop the program. Remember, the Ctrl key and the Break key must be held down at the same time. Use ⟨Fn-Break⟩ on the PCjr.**

4.2 Load program 4.1 and change the name of the program in line 1 to P42–INP. Then modify the program so that it has a loop and a loop counter and uses INPUT statements to let you enter various values of G (guests). The program should print a prompt before getting the input and print out the value of E (eggs) and S (shrimp) each time through the loop. As before, use 1.25 eggs and 1.33 shrimp per person and round to the nearest whole egg or shrimp. Your run should look like the following:

```
HOW MANY PARTIES? 4

HOW MANY GUESTS? 2

 3 EGGS   3 SHRIMP

HOW MANY GUESTS? 3

 4 EGGS   4 SHRIMP
 .
 .
 .
```

etc.

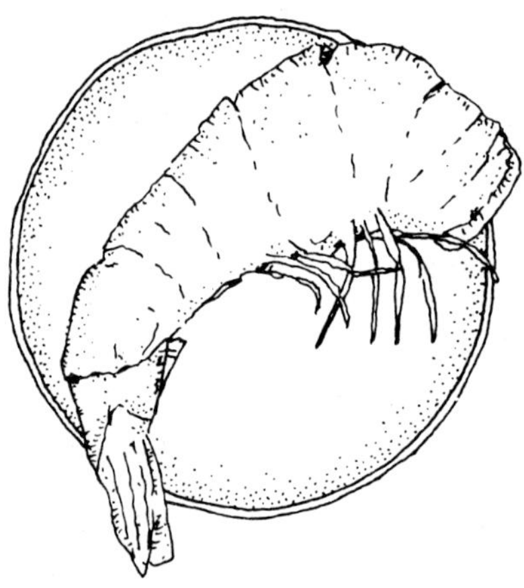

TIPS

1. **Remember that during the run, the program is expecting input from the keyboard. At this time commands such as LIST, RUN, LOAD, etc., will not be executed.**
2. **If the program loops endlessly, the loop counter is not working and you must use ⟨Ctrl-Break⟩ or ⟨Fn-Break⟩ to stop things.**
3. **Look at program 3.2 to help remind you of what changes are necessary.**

CHAPTER 5

GOING AROUND AGAIN

Looping with a FOR/NEXT Statement

NEW CONCEPTS TAUGHT

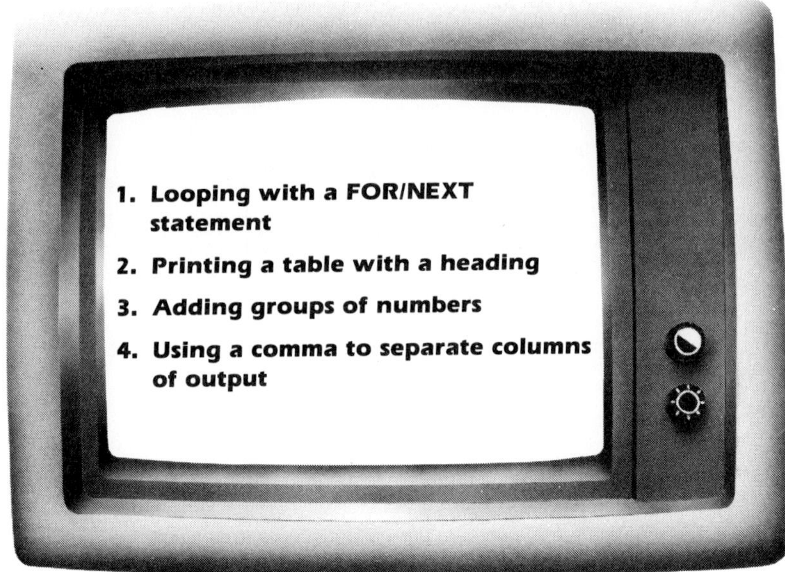

1. Looping with a FOR/NEXT statement
2. Printing a table with a heading
3. Adding groups of numbers
4. Using a comma to separate columns of output

FOR/NEXT LOOPS

A FOR/NEXT loop is more sophisticated than a GOTO loop; it runs faster and has a built-in loop counter. Whenever the computer sees a FOR statement, it knows that this marks the beginning of a FOR/NEXT loop. It does whatever it's directed to do, and when it reaches the NEXT statement, it goes back to the beginning of the loop (if the loop counter has not passed its limit) and starts again. If the loop counter is above the limit, the program skips the loop and goes to the line following the NEXT statement.

Celsius to Fahrenheit

In program 5A in figure 5.1, we see a simple FOR/NEXT loop with only two variables used in the whole program. F stands for degrees Fahrenheit and C does double duty since it stands for both degrees Celsius and the loop counter. The program begins in line 110 by printing the program name, two blank lines, and then, in line 120, the headings for each column. (Notice the comma between the two headings—we'll explain that later in this section.)

FOR and NEXT The FOR and NEXT statements are always used together to form a loop that counts the number of times the instructions inside the loop are repeated. The general form of a FOR/NEXT loop is:

line number `FOR` *variable name* `=` *a* `TO` *b* `STEP` *c*

. . . .
. . . . } instructions inside loop

line number `NEXT` *same variable name as in FOR statement*

1. STEP *c* is optional; if omitted, the step defaults to 1.
2. The variable name on the right of the FOR statement is called the loop counter (or control variable) of the FOR/NEXT loop.
3. The letters *a*, *b*, and *c* in the FOR statement represent numbers, variable names, or arithmetic expressions. During the first pass through the loop, the loop counter has the value of the number, variable, or expression represented by the letter *a*. At the end of each pass through the loop, the value of the number, variable, or expression represented by the letter *c* is added to the loop counter. If the number in the loop counter is not greater than the number represented by the letter *b*, then the computer goes on to the instruction after the NEXT statement.

Example:

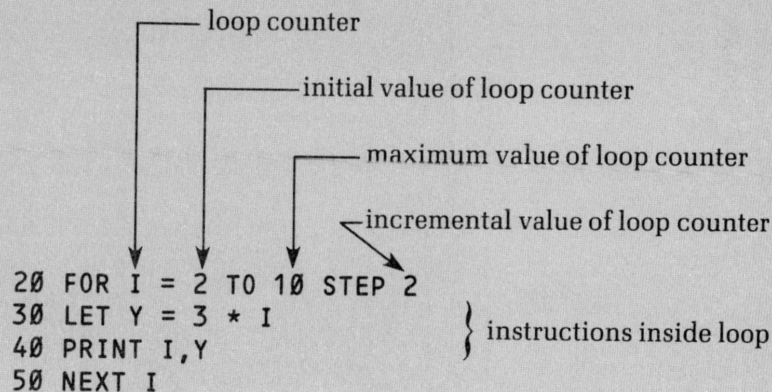

A Modified Decision Symbol

One type of conditional, the IF/THEN statement, was introduced in program 4B. Program 5A in figure 5.1 introduces a second type of conditional, the FOR/NEXT statement. FOR/NEXT statements are a convenient method for creating a loop when a definite number of passes through the loop are required. A modified decision symbol is used in this text to indicate the beginning of a FOR/NEXT loop, and the circle is used to indicate the end of the loop, as shown in the flowchart for program 5A.

The loop in program 5A begins at line 140 with the FOR/NEXT statement:

```
140  FOR C = Ø TO 1ØØ STEP 1Ø
```

Notice that lines 150 and 160 are indented to show that they are inside of the loop. The C in line 140 is the loop counter; the first part of the line tells the computer to set C to 0. The STEP 10 command tells the computer to increase C by 10 each time through the loop. (The STEP command is optional; if it is left out, the loop steps by 1.) Within the loop, F is calculated by using a formula to convert from Celsius to Fahrenheit (line 150), and then C and F are printed (line 160).

The comma in line 160, like the one in line 120, splits the output into two columns. In IBM BASIC, the screen is divided into vertical sections called columns. A comma in a PRINT statement tells the computer to print whatever follows the comma in the next screen column. This program uses only two columns.

When the computer sees the NEXT statement in line 170 for the first time, it changes C from 0 to 10 and then checks to see if C is greater than 100 (the limit set in line 140). Since C is not greater than 100, the program loops back to the FOR statement in line 140 and executes the loop again. The program repeats the loop until C is greater than 100. In this example, C will have the value of 110 when the looping stops.

When C is greater than 100, the program skips to the line after the NEXT statement (line 180 in this example) and the program ends.

EXAMPLE 5A Celsius to Fahrenheit (FOR/NEXT loop)

Problem Write a program that uses a FOR/NEXT loop to print a two-column table of degrees Celsius vs. degrees Fahrenheit. Print CELSIUS at the top of the Celsius column and FAHRENHEIT at the top of the Fahrenheit column for your column headings.

Solution

FIGURE 5.1

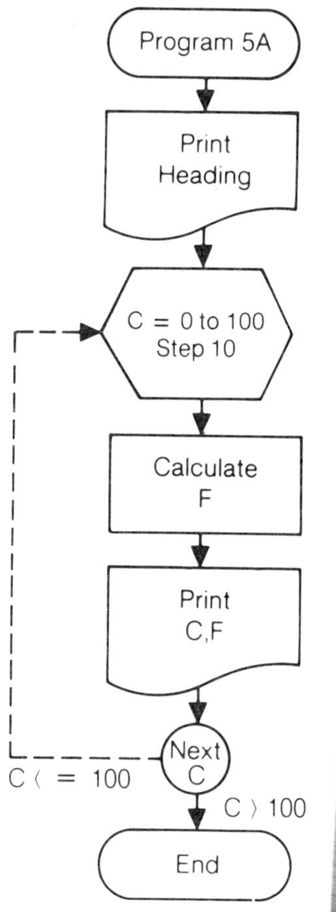


```
LIST
1     PN$ = "P5A-CTOF"
2     NA$ = "YOUR NAME"
3     DA$ = "00/00/00"
10    '  ===== VARIABLES =====
11    '  C = DEGREES CELSIUS
12    '  F = DEGREES FAHRENHEIT
100   '  ===== MAIN PROGRAM =====
101   CLS : PRINT TAB(40 - (LEN (PN$) / 2)) PN$
110   PRINT : PRINT
120   PRINT " CELSIUS"," FAHRENHEIT"
130   PRINT
140   FOR C = 0 TO 100 STEP 10
150      LET F = 9 / 5 * C + 32
160      PRINT C,F
170   NEXT C
180   END
Ok


RUN
```

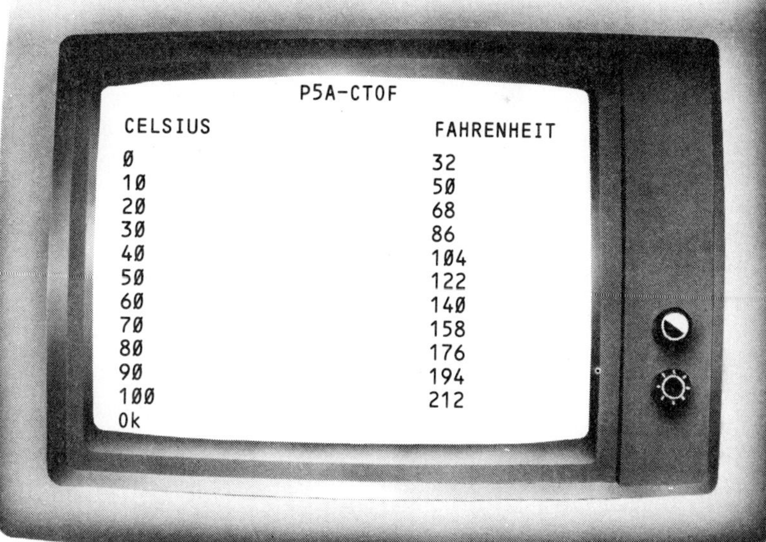

It All Adds Up

In program 5B we have a flexible program that allows us to tell the program how many numbers we want to add, enter them at the keyboard, and then have the sum printed for us on the screen. Unlike the loop counter in program 5A, the loop counter in this program (designated by I) is not used for anything else. The letters I, J, and K often are used by programmers as loop counters in situations like this.

The program begins by printing the program name, two blank lines, and then in line 120 setting SUM to 0. Line 130 asks us how many numbers we will be entering, line 140 gets the answer, and line 150 prints another blank line.

The FOR/NEXT loop in this program begins at line 160:

```
FOR I = 1 TO N
```

Notice that this line is somewhat different than the line at the beginning of the loop in program 5A. For one thing, we have left out the STEP command, which means that the loop counter will increase by only 1 each time through the loop. Another difference is that we have used a variable (N) as the upper limit of the loop rather than a number. This adds flexibility to the program because the loop will execute as many times as there are numbers we want to add. Just as the variables I, J, and K mentioned above are used as loop counters, N is often used as a limit variable for loops.

Notice that all three of the variables (I, X, and SUM) change their value every time through the loop. Each time through the loop, X is whatever number we enter from the keyboard, SUM is the previous SUM plus the number just entered, and the loop counter, I, is increased by 1. In this particular run of the program, after three times through the loop all three numbers have been added to SUM (which was set to zero in line 120), and, when we get to the NEXT statement in line 190, I is set to 4. Since 4 is greater than N (which in this run of the program is set to 3), the program skips to line 200. In line 210 the results are printed and in line 220 the program ends.

EXAMPLE 5B Sum of N Numbers (FOR/NEXT Loop)

Problem Write a program that asks: "HOW MANY NUMBERS DO YOU WANT TO ADD?", inputs the answer to the question, inputs each number to be added, and prints: SUM = followed by the sum of the numbers entered.

Solution

FIGURE 5.2

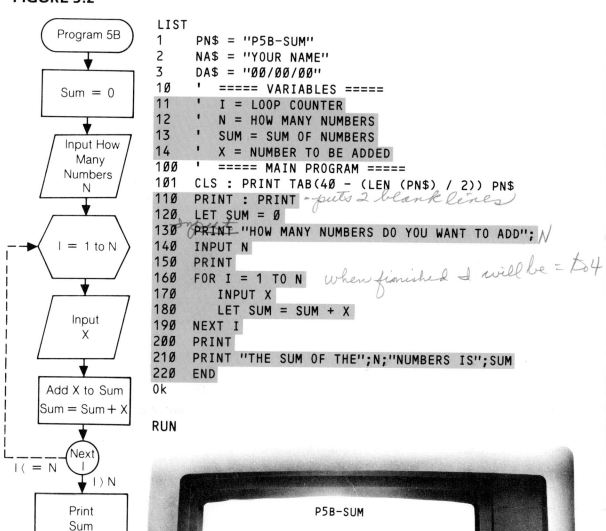

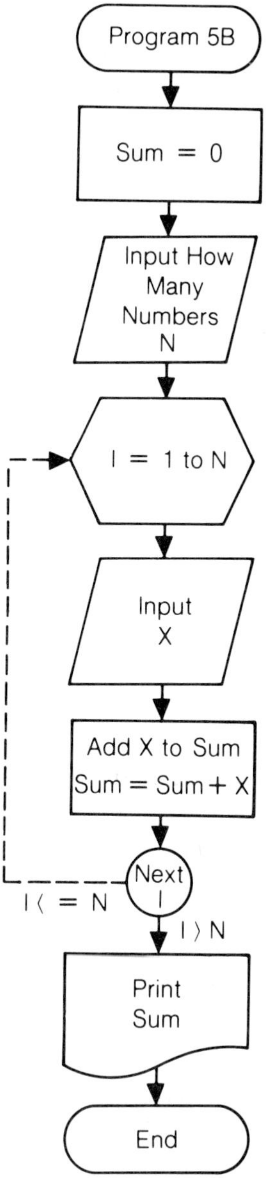

Program 5B

Sum = 0

Input How Many Numbers N

I = 1 to N

Input X

Add X to Sum
Sum = Sum + X

Next I

I < = N

I > N

Print Sum

End

```
LIST
1      PN$ = "P5B-SUM"
2      NA$ = "YOUR NAME"
3      DA$ = "00/00/00"
10     '  ===== VARIABLES =====
11     '  I = LOOP COUNTER
12     '  N = HOW MANY NUMBERS
13     '  SUM = SUM OF NUMBERS
14     '  X = NUMBER TO BE ADDED
100    '  ===== MAIN PROGRAM =====
101    CLS : PRINT TAB(40 - (LEN (PN$) / 2)) PN$
110    PRINT : PRINT
120    LET SUM = 0
130    PRINT "HOW MANY NUMBERS DO YOU WANT TO ADD";
140    INPUT N
150    PRINT
160    FOR I = 1 TO N
170       INPUT X
180       LET SUM = SUM + X
190    NEXT I
200    PRINT
210    PRINT "THE SUM OF THE";N;"NUMBERS IS";SUM
220    END
Ok
```

RUN

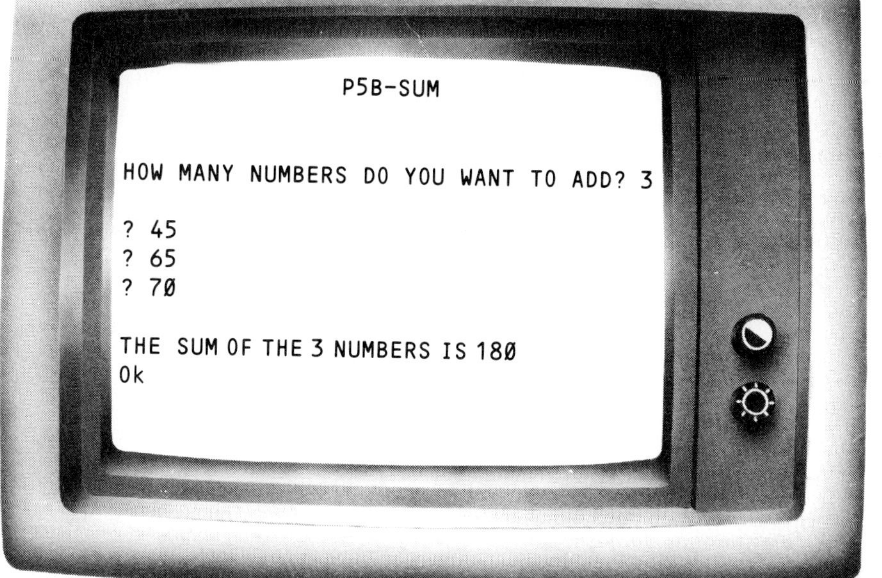

P5B-SUM
HOW MANY NUMBERS DO YOU WANT TO ADD? 3
? 45
? 65
? 70
THE SUM OF THE 3 NUMBERS IS 180
Ok

SELF-TESTING QUESTIONS

EXAMPLE: Step through the following program and write the output produced when the program runs.

```
110  LET S = 0
120  READ N
130  IF N = 9999 THEN PRINT "SUM = ";S : END
140  LET S = S + N
150  GOTO 120
160  DATA 4, 8, 9, 6, 9999
```

Construct a step-through table as shown below. Each row represents one pass through the loop. Values of variables are printed to show the changes that occur.

Line Number:	120		130	140
Variables:	S	N	N = 9999?	S
Pass 1:	0	4	no	4
Pass 2:	4	8	no	12
Pass 3:	12	9	no	21
Pass 4:	21	6	no	27
Pass 5:	27	9999	yes	

ANSWER: SUM = 27

Step through the program in each problem and write the output produced when the program runs.

5.1

```
110  PRINT "YARDS","FEET"
120  FOR Y = 1 TO 5
130      LET F = 3 * Y
140      PRINT Y,F
150  NEXT Y
```

5.2

```
110  FOR Y = 1 TO 5
120      PRINT "YARDS","FEET"
130      LET F = 3 * Y
140      PRINT Y,F
150  NEXT Y
```

5.3 Assume that the following sequence of numbers is entered during a run of the program below: 7, 18, 5, 9, 6, 9999. Write the output produced by the program.

```
110  LET S = 0
120  LET C = 0
130  PRINT "ENTER NUMBERS TO BE ADDED"
140  PRINT "OR ENTER 9999 TO QUIT"
150  INPUT N
160  IF N = 9999 GOTO 200
170  LET S = S + N
180  LET C = C + 1
190  GOTO 150
200  PRINT C;" NUMBERS WERE ADDED"
210  PRINT "THE TOTAL IS ";S
220  END
```

5.4
```
110  FOR I = 1 TO 5
120     PRINT I;
130  NEXT I
```

5.5
```
110  FOR I = 1 TO 8 STEP 2
120     PRINT I;
130  NEXT I
```

5.6
```
110  FOR I = 1 TO 15 STEP 3
120     PRINT I;
130  NEXT I
```

5.7
```
110  FOR I = 1 TO 4
120     READ X
130     PRINT X;
140  NEXT I
150  DATA 8, 7, 9, 4, 3
```

5.8
```
110  READ X
120  FOR I = 1 TO 8 STEP 3
130     PRINT X;
140  NEXT I
150  DATA 3, 8, 7
```

5.9
```
110  FOR I = 1 TO 5
120     READ X
130     PRINT X;
140  NEXT I
150  PRINT X
160  DATA 5, 9, 4, 7, 8, 2
```

5.10
```
110  FOR I = 1 TO 10 STEP 2
120     READ X
130     PRINT I;X;
140  NEXT I
150  DATA 5, 4, 3, 2, 1
```

EXERCISES

Choose One of the Following

5.1 Write a program that uses a FOR/NEXT loop to produce the table of areas of a rectangle shown below using the formula AREA = L * W. Use READ/DATA statements to enter ten sets of length and width values. Use hand calculations or a calculator to verify two of the AREA values in the table.

LENGTH	WIDTH	AREA
1Ø	2Ø	2ØØ
.	.	.
.	.	.
11	8	88

TIPS

1. **Use a separate loop counter like I.**
2. **Use commas to format the columns on the screen.**
3. **Don't put the line that prints the headings inside a loop.**
4. **You will need to use the command WIDTH 80 in your program to get more than two columns across if you are using a PCjr.**

5.2 Write a program that uses a FOR/NEXT loop to produce the table of price, quantity, and value shown below using the formula V = P * Q. Use READ/DATA statements to enter ten sets of price and quantity values. Use hand calculations or a calculator to verify two of the values in the table.

```
PRICE          QUANTITY          VALUE

12.97          13                168.61
.              .                 .
.              .                 .
11.25          7                 78.75
```

TIPS

1. Use a separate loop counter like I.
2. Use commas to format the columns on the screen.
3. Don't put the line that prints the headings inside a loop.
4. You will need to use the command WIDTH 80 in your program to get more than two columns across if you are using a PCjr.

5.3 An airline is preparing a booklet for passenger use on long-distance flights. They would like to include a table for converting altitude from miles to feet. Write a program that will use a FOR/NEXT loop to produce the altitude conversion table shown below. The conversion formula for feet-to-miles is:

```
FEET = MILES * 5280
```

Use hand calculations or a calculator to check at least two of your altitude-in-miles values.

```
ALTITUDE               ALTITUDE
IN MILES               IN FEET

0                      0
1                      5280
.                      .
.                      .
.                      .
5                      26400
```

TIPS

1. **Use a comma to print the two columns.**
2. **Print the headings before entering the loop.**
3. **Use one line to print ALTITUDE, ALTITUDE and another line to print IN MILES, IN FEET.**
4. **Use the variable MILES for both the altitude in feet and also the loop counter.**

5.4 Write a program that will use a FOR/NEXT loop to produce the following table of X, X squared, and the square root of X for values of X from 1 to 10. Use hand calculations or a calculator to check at least two of the values of X squared and square root of X.

```
                                   SQUARE
                    X              ROOT
X                   SQUARED        OF X

1                   1              1
2                   4              1.414213
3                   9              1.732051
.                   .              .
.                   .              .
.                   .              .
10                  100            3.162278
```

TIPS

1. Print the headings before entering the loop.
2. Use one line to print , , SQUARE. Use a second line to print , X, ROOT and a third line to print X, SQUARED, OF X.
3. Use commas to separate the three columns.
4. Use X * X for X squared.
5. Use X ^ 0.5 for the square root of X.
6. Use X as the loop counter.
7. Use the command WIDTH 80 if you are using a PCjr.

5.5 Two thousand dollars is invested at 14 percent interest, compounded yearly. Write a program using a FOR/NEXT loop that will produce the table shown below. The compound interest formula is :

```
A = P * (1 + I / 100) ^ N
```

where: A = amount after N years
P = original amount deposited
I = yearly interest rate
N = number of years

Use hand calculations or a calculator to check at least two of the values of AMOUNT in the table.

```
YEAR        AMOUNT

1           2280
2           2599.2
.           .
.           .
.           .
20          27486.98
```

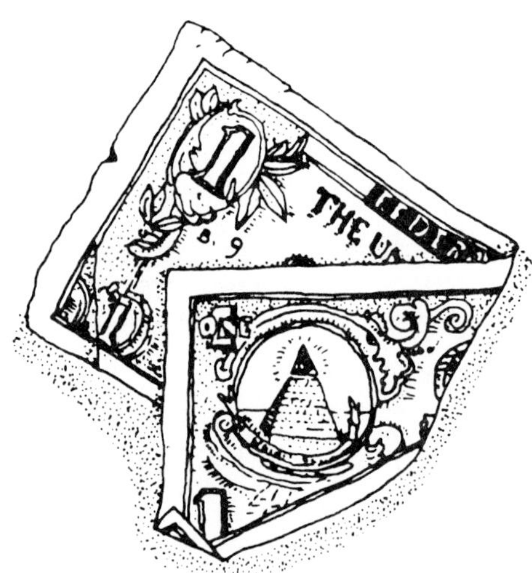

TIPS

1. **Use the variable N for years and the loop counter.**
2. **Print the headings before entering the loop.**
3. **Use the variable names listed above.**
4. **Use commas to separate the two columns.**

5.6 The Ark Manufacturing Company produces an item called Noah's Gizmo. In an effort to maximize profit, the accounting department made a cost analysis of each product. A fixed cost of $1,250 per day was charged to Noah's Gizmo. Direct production costs are $120 per Gizmo, and secondary costs such as breakdowns and overtime pay are closely approximated by 0.75 * N ^ 2 dollars per day. Profit is given by the following equation in which N is the number of Gizmos produced each day.

```
PROFIT = 212 * N - (125Ø + 12Ø * N + Ø.75 * N ^ 2)
         ↑ Revenue        ↑ Cost
```

Write a program that will use a FOR/NEXT loop to produce the profit table shown below. Circle the maximum value of profit. Use hand calculations or a calculator to check at least two of the values of PROFIT in the table.

```
# OF GIZMOS          PROFIT

5                    -8Ø8.75
1Ø                   -4Ø5
15                   -38.75
.                    .
.                    .
1ØØ                   45Ø
```

TIPS

1. **Use N as the number of Gizmos produced and also as the loop counter.**
2. **Print the headings outside the loop.**
3. **Use commas to separate the columns.**
4. **This is a difficult program; try it at your own risk.**

5.7 Write a program that will use a FOR/NEXT loop to read ten scores from a DATA statement and compute the sum and average of the ten scores. Then print a table with two columns as shown below. Round the average value to the nearest hundredth. Use hand calculations or a calculator to check at least two of the values of SCORE and SCORE MINUS AVERAGE.

```
THE AVERAGE VALUE IS 14.2


SCORE                  SCORE MINUS AVERAGE

18.47                   4.27
11.68                  -2.52
.                       .
.                       .
.                       .
17.84                   3.64
```

TIPS

1. **Write one FOR/NEXT loop that calculates the average value and another FOR/NEXT loop that prints the table.**
2. **You will have to use the RESTORE command between the two parts from tip 1.**
3. **Use the variable I as a loop counter; don't use I for anything else.**
4. **This program is difficult; don't try it unless you're prepared for some frustration.**

CHAPTER 6

WHERE DO WE GO FROM HERE?

Branching with IF Statements

NEW CONCEPTS TAUGHT

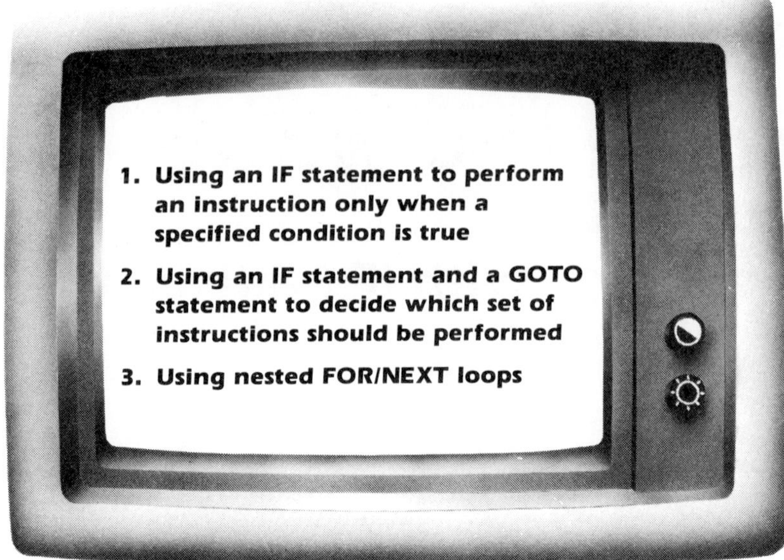

1. Using an IF statement to perform an instruction only when a specified condition is true
2. Using an IF statement and a GOTO statement to decide which set of instructions should be performed
3. Using nested FOR/NEXT loops

IF STATEMENTS

In previous programs, all lines of the program have been executed in each run. Many times, however, we need to write sections of a program that will be executed only under certain conditions. This is accomplished with an IF statement that tells the computer that the instructions that follow it should be performed only if the conditions are right.

IF/THEN The general form of the IF/THEN statement is:

> *line number* `IF` *conditional* `THEN` *one or more instructions separated by colons, :*

If the conditional is true, then the computer will execute all of the instructions that follow the word THEN. If the conditional is false, then the computer will ignore all of the instructions after the word THEN and go on to the next line.

Example:

```
180 IF X < 5 THEN X = X + 1 : Y = Y + 2
```

The above instruction tells the computer to check the value of X to see if it is less than 5. If the value of X is less than 5, then the computer adds 1 to the value of X and adds 2 to the value of Y. If X is not less than 5, then the computer ignores both of the instructions to the right of the word THEN and goes on to the next line after line 180.

Gross Pay

Program 6A in figure 6.1 shows how to use an IF statement. We need a way of calculating overtime pay and adding it to gross pay for employees who work over 40 hours per week, but we would soon go broke if we gave everyone overtime pay regardless of the number of hours they worked. One way of handling this is to have instructions, like the ones on lines 140 and 150, that are performed only if a specified condition is true (or false). In program 6A the variable H is used for hours worked and the variable W is the wage rate per hour. If the person works 40 hours or less, their pay is simply H times W with no overtime pay. This is accomplished entirely by line 140. If their hours (H) total more than 40, line 140 will not be executed and their pay (P) will be calculated by line 150.

```
140  IF H <  = 40 THEN P = H * W
150  IF H > 40 THEN P = 40 * W + (H - 40) * 1.5 * W
```

Let's take a closer look at line 150. Since the employee has worked more than 40 hours, we need to calculate the first 40 of their hours at the regular rate and then add the pay they should receive for their overtime hours at the overtime rate of time and a half. We could use separate lines to do this, but it is simpler and saves memory if we can do it all on one line. The equation in line 150 does all three of these at once. To the left of the + sign, we see the first 40 hours are multiplied by W to give the pay for the employee's first 40 hours. To the right of the + sign, we see their total hours minus the ones we have already accounted for (H − 40) are multiplied by the overtime wage rate (1.5 * W). When these two products are added together, they yield P, or gross pay. Line 180 demonstrates some new ways to use the PRINT USING command.

```
180  PRINT USING "GROSS PAY IS $$#,###.##";P
```

The double dollar sign ($$) is used to cause a single dollar sign to be printed right next to the beginning of the number regardless of the size of the number. A comma is also used in specifying the number format so that if the pay is over a thousand dollars, the amount printed will have a comma printed in the appropriate place.

Notice that in a single run of the program, lines 140 and 150 can't both be executed. We describe this by saying that they are mutually exclusive. If one is executed, it is impossible for the other one to be executed and *vice versa.* When using mutually exclusive conditionals like this, it is important to make sure that the conditionals, when taken together, take care of all possibilities. If line 140 stated the condition as H < 40 instead of H < = 40, the program would fail when H was exactly equal to 40 because neither line would be executed; then line 180 would print GROSS PAY IS 0 DOLLARS. A mistake like this can lead to some very unhappy employees.

EXAMPLE 6A Gross Pay (IF/THEN)

Problem Write a program that will input the number of hours worked in one week and the hourly wage rate. Calculate the gross pay using time and a half for all hours over 40. Print the message "GROSS PAY IS" followed by the amount of gross pay.

Solution

FIGURE 6.1

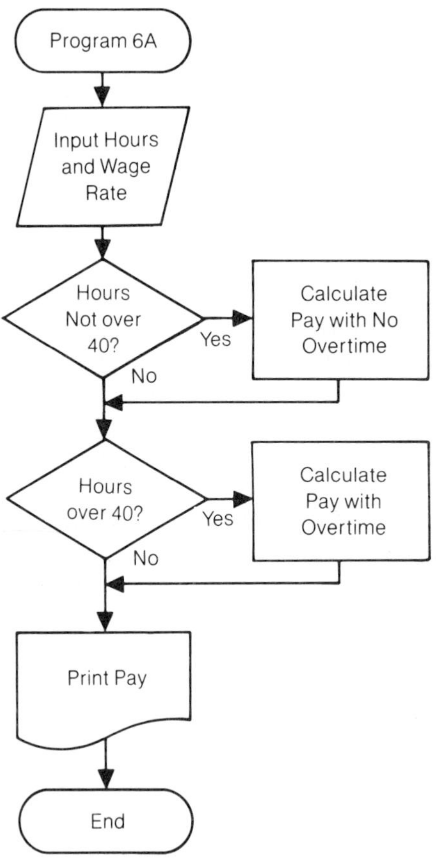

(Figure continued)

(Figure 6.1 continued)

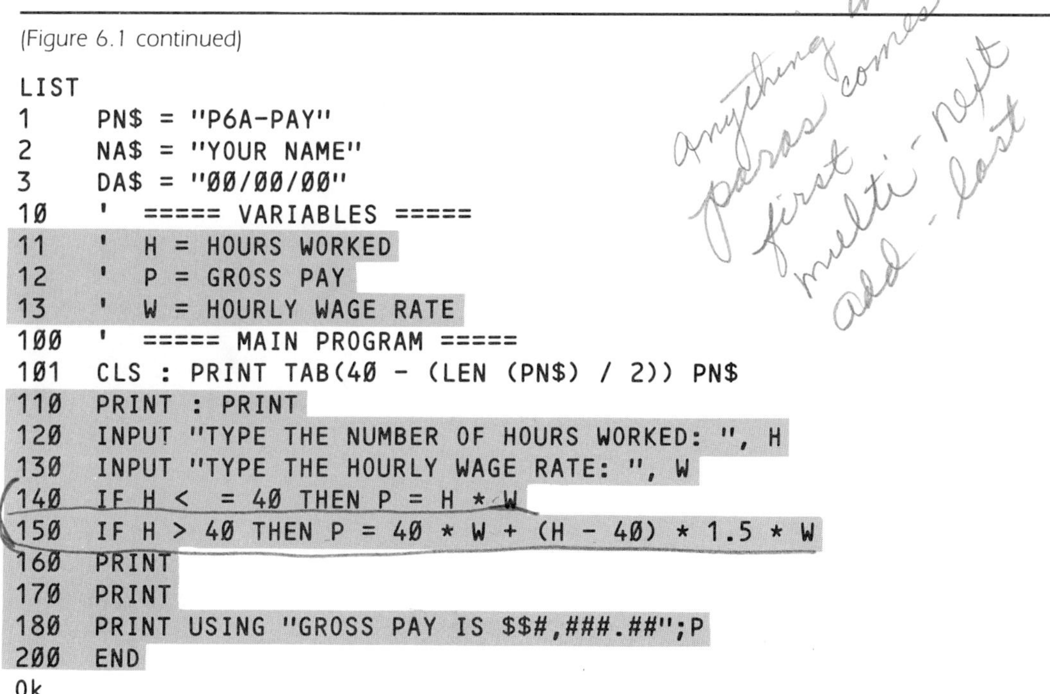

```
LIST
1     PN$ = "P6A-PAY"
2     NA$ = "YOUR NAME"
3     DA$ = "00/00/00"
10    '  ===== VARIABLES =====
11    '  H = HOURS WORKED
12    '  P = GROSS PAY
13    '  W = HOURLY WAGE RATE
100   '  ===== MAIN PROGRAM =====
101   CLS : PRINT TAB(40 - (LEN (PN$) / 2)) PN$
110   PRINT : PRINT
120   INPUT "TYPE THE NUMBER OF HOURS WORKED: ", H
130   INPUT "TYPE THE HOURLY WAGE RATE: ", W
140   IF H <  = 40 THEN P = H * W
150   IF H > 40 THEN P = 40 * W + (H - 40) * 1.5 * W
160   PRINT
170   PRINT
180   PRINT USING "GROSS PAY IS $$#,###.##";P
200   END
Ok
```

RUN 6A *(to check equation in line 140)*

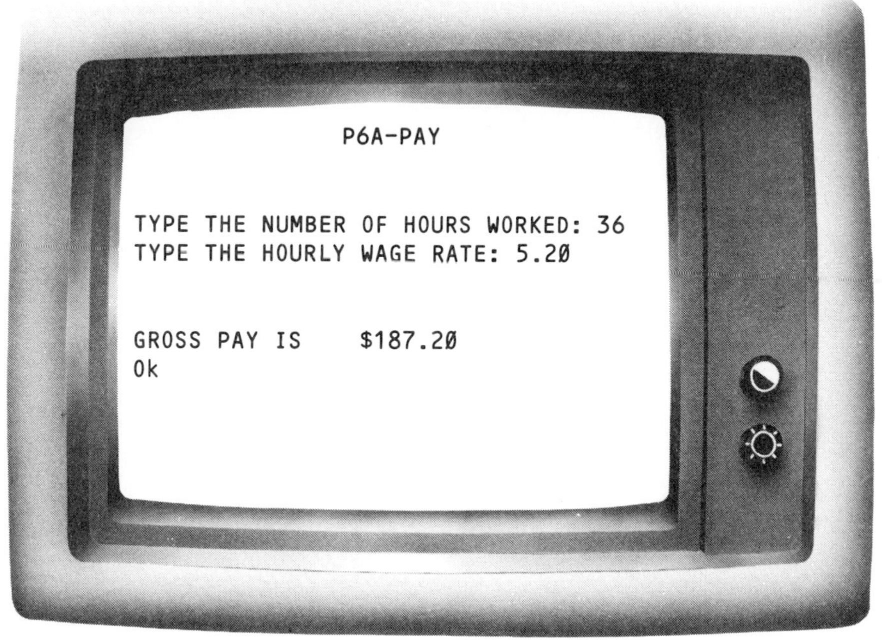
P6A-PAY
TYPE THE NUMBER OF HOURS WORKED: 36
TYPE THE HOURLY WAGE RATE: 5.20
GROSS PAY IS $187.20
Ok

(Figure continued)

(Figure 6.1 continued)

RUN 6A (to check equation in line 150)

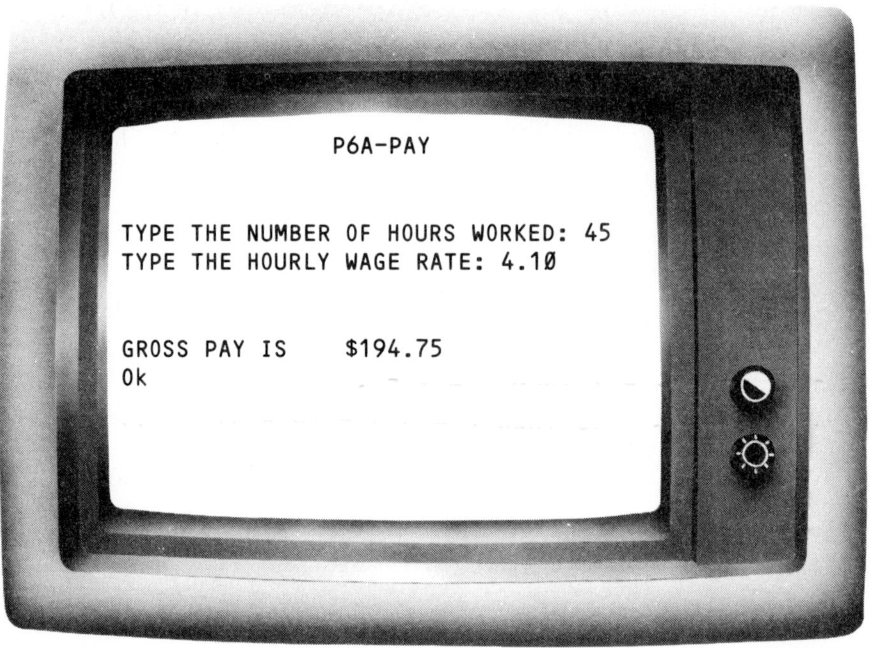

P6A-PAY
TYPE THE NUMBER OF HOURS WORKED: 45
TYPE THE HOURLY WAGE RATE: 4.10
GROSS PAY IS $194.75
Ok

Relational Symbols A conditional consists of two expressions separated by one of the following relational symbols:

Relational Symbol	Meaning
=	equal to
>	greater than
<	less than
< > or > <	not equal to
<=	less than or equal to
>=	greater than or equal to

Examples of relational expressions:

```
A = B + C
X - Y < = 27
2 * X - 2 > = 5 * Y +2
```

The Gas Bill

Program 6B in figure 6.2 is a little more complicated than program 6A, but it works much the same way. One difference is that it requires four mutually exclusive statements; these appear in lines 150, 160, 170, and 180. If a customer uses 3 CCF (hundred cubic feet) of gas or less in one month, they are charged a flat rate of $3.50 per month. This is calculated in line 150, and, if the CCF is 3 or less, the program jumps to line 190, where the output is printed. If the customer used more than 3 CCF of gas, but not more than 40, their bill is calculated in line 160 by adding the cost of the first 3 CCF to the cost of the other CCF used; again, the program jumps to line 190 to print the bill. If they used over 40 CCF but not more than 100, what they owe is calculated in line 170. If they used over 100 CCF, their bill is calculated in line 180. Notice that if the conditions stated in lines 150, 160 and 170 are all false, the customer *must* have used more than 100 CCF of gas. Therefore no IF statement is necessary in line 180.

```
150  IF G < = 3 THEN C = 3.5 : GOTO 190
160  IF G < = 40 THEN C = 3.5 + (G - 3) * .35 : GOTO 190
170  IF G <=100 THEN C = 3.5 + 37 * .35 + (G - 40) * .31 : GOTO 190
180  LET C = 3.5 + 37 * .35 + 60 * .31 + (G - 100) * .3
```

Since we want only one of these four statements to be executed, it is important to have the GOTO 190 at the end of each conditional; otherwise with a CCF amount of 3, for example, all of the statements would execute because 3 is less than 40, less than 100, and so forth. What this means is that the statements are not mutually exclusive in the strict sense of the phrase; however, we have made them mutually exclusive in the execution of the program by the addition of the GOTO statements. As this program is written, only one of these statements could be executed in a single run of the program.

EXAMPLE 6B Gas Bill (IF/THEN)

Problem The Sota Gas Company has the following rate structure for natural gas (note: CCF = hundred cubic feet).

First 3 CCF, $	3.50 flat fee
Next 37 CCF, $ per CCF	0.35
Next 60 CCF, $ per CCF	0.31
CCF over 100,$ per CCF	0.30

The present and previous meter readings are to be entered using an INPUT statement. Write a program that prints the CCF used and the monthly gas bill.

Solution

FIGURE 6.2

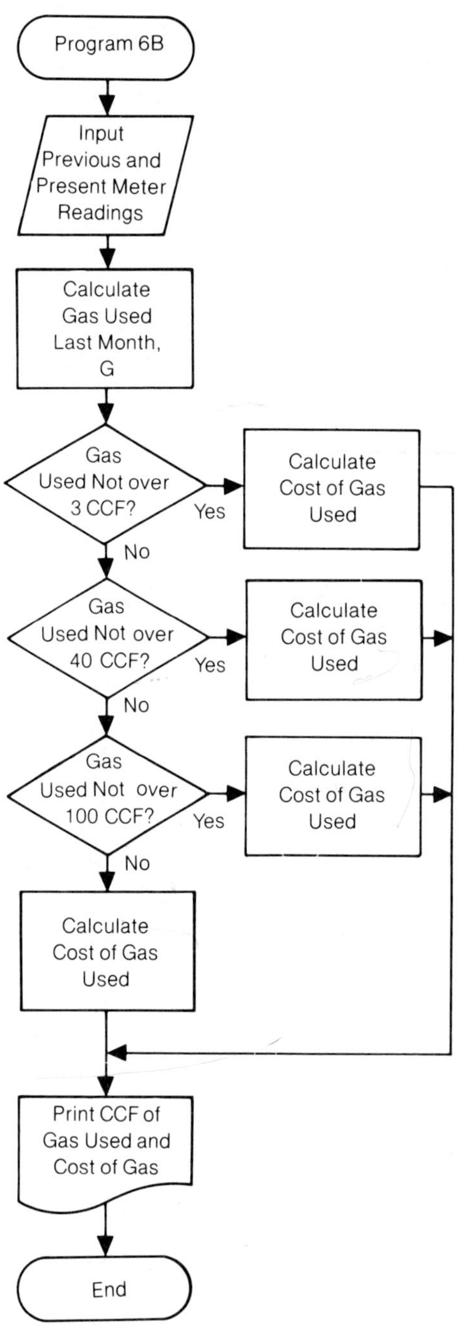

(Figure continued)

(Figure 6.2 continued)

```
LIST
1     PN$ = "P6B-GAS"
2     NA$ = "YOUR NAME"
3     DA$ = "ØØ/ØØ/ØØ"
1Ø    '  ===== VARIABLES =====
11    '  C = MONTHLY GAS BILL
12    '  G = CCF OF GAS USED
13    '  P1 = PREVIOUS METER READING
14    '  P2 = PRESENT METER READING
1ØØ   '  ===== MAIN PROGRAM =====
1Ø1   CLS : PRINT TAB(4Ø - (LEN (PN$) / 2)) PN$
11Ø   PRINT
12Ø   INPUT "THE PREVIOUS READING IN CCF IS"; P1
13Ø   INPUT "THE PRESENT READING IN CCF IS"; P2
14Ø   G = P2 - P1
15Ø   IF G < = 3 THEN C = 3.5 : GOTO 19Ø
16Ø   IF G < = 4Ø THEN C = 3.5 + (G - 3) * .35 : GOTO 19Ø
17Ø   IF G <=1ØØ THEN C = 3.5 + 37 * .35 + (G - 4Ø) * .31 : GOTO 19Ø
18Ø   LET C = 3.5 + 37 * .35 + 6Ø * .31 + (G - 1ØØ) * .3
19Ø   PRINT "YOU USED ";G;" CCF THIS MONTH"
2ØØ   PRINT USING "YOUR GAS BILL THIS MONTH IS $$###.##";C
21Ø   END
Ok
```

(Figure continued)

(Figure 6.2 continued)

RUN 6B (to check equation in line 150)

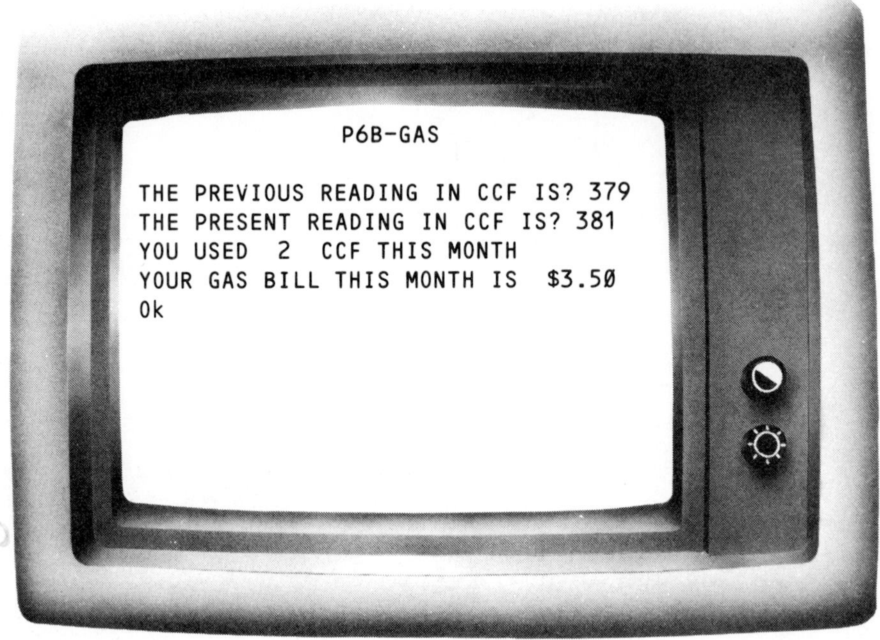

P6B-GAS
THE PREVIOUS READING IN CCF IS? 379
THE PRESENT READING IN CCF IS? 381
YOU USED 2 CCF THIS MONTH
YOUR GAS BILL THIS MONTH IS $3.5Ø
Ok

RUN 6B (to check equation in line 160)

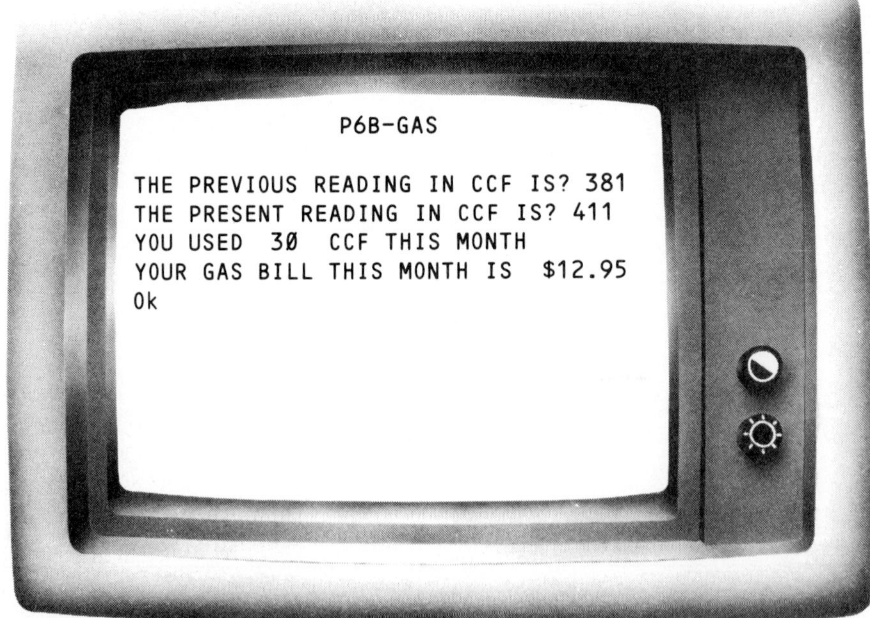

P6B-GAS
THE PREVIOUS READING IN CCF IS? 381
THE PRESENT READING IN CCF IS? 411
YOU USED 3Ø CCF THIS MONTH
YOUR GAS BILL THIS MONTH IS $12.95
Ok

(Figure continued)

(Figure 6.2 continued)

RUN 6B (to check equation in line 170)

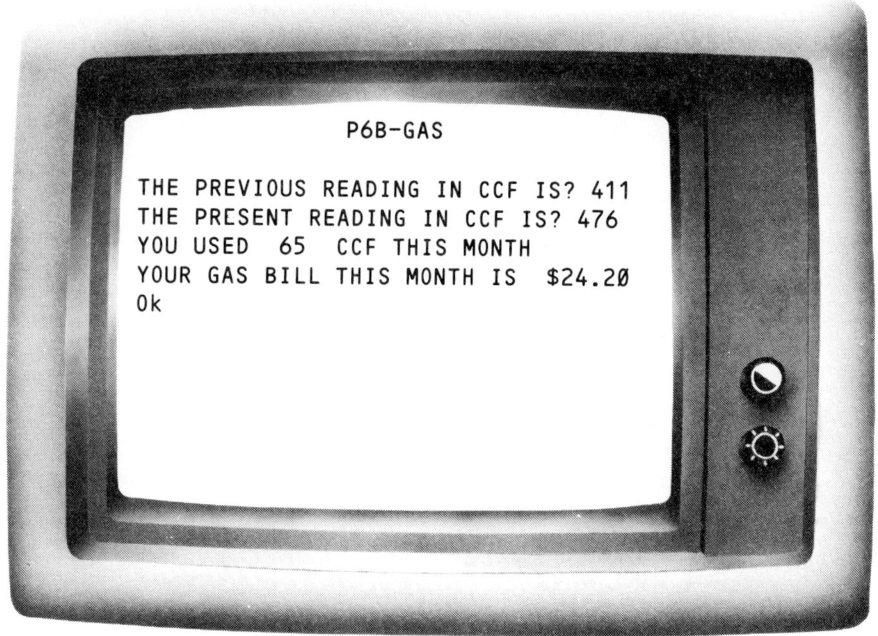
P6B-GAS
THE PREVIOUS READING IN CCF IS? 411
THE PRESENT READING IN CCF IS? 476
YOU USED 65 CCF THIS MONTH
YOUR GAS BILL THIS MONTH IS $24.20
Ok

RUN 6B (to check equation in line 180)

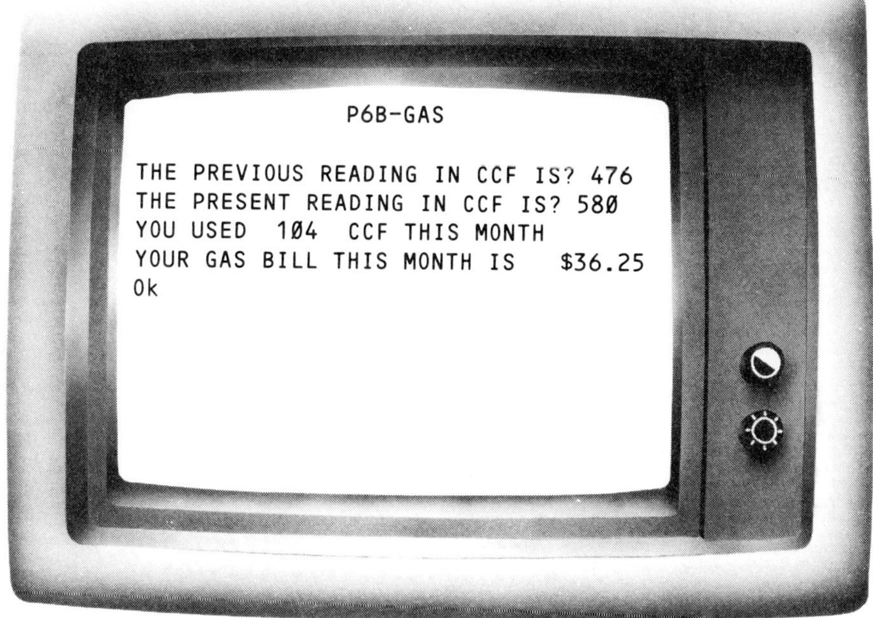
P6B-GAS
THE PREVIOUS READING IN CCF IS? 476
THE PRESENT READING IN CCF IS? 580
YOU USED 104 CCF THIS MONTH
YOUR GAS BILL THIS MONTH IS $36.25
Ok

Getting Rich

Program 6C is a more complicated program than the other two; it involves several steps and has one loop inside another loop. We call loops set up like this *nested* loops. In this program the inside loop includes lines 140 through 220 and the outside loop includes lines 150 through 200. The outer loop is performed three times because we want the results to include three quarters. The inner loop executes three times because there are three months in each quarter. It makes sense to call this inner loop the month loop and the outer loop the quarter loop.

In a complex program like this, it is best to try to copy the real-life process step-by-step. In this program, for example, we should try to follow the procedures of the bank, step-by-step.

In line 17 we have set the initial balance in the account and in line 18 we have set the yearly interest rate. In line 19 we set the value of the monthly deposit. These three values will not change during the program, and there is no sense in setting their value each time through the loop; this would only slow down the program. Therefore we set their value before we enter the loops.

With nested loops it is often best to think about the inside loop first. Lines 150 through 200 describe the events of each month as they happen. In line 160 you deposit your hard-earned $120 on the first of the month and the bank adds it to the amount already in the account. Notice that A, the amount in the account, is continually changing. In line 170 the bank figures out the interest for this month (I) by multiplying the amount in the account by the yearly interest rate (R) divided by 12 to get monthly interest and divided by 100 to convert it to a proper decimal. In line 180 the interest calculated in line 170 is added to the amount in the account to get a new value of A. In line 190, A is printed using a more sophisticated PRINT USING statement than we have seen before. There are three separate numbers (using #) in the PRINT USING statement. At the end are the three variables to be printed, separated by commas. The month loop executes three times, and then the program goes on to line 210, which prints the blank line between quarters. After the quarter loop has executed four times (each time meaning three executions of the month loop), the program ends and it's time to try to figure out what to do with all that money.

EXAMPLE 6C Savings Account (Nested FOR/NEXT Loop)

Problem You have a savings account in the Duckburg City Bank. The account earns 9.6 percent interest compounded monthly. At the end of each month, the bank computes the interest earned during the month, adds the interest to the account, and prints a statement showing the balance in the account. The December statement showed a balance of $3,500. Write a program that will print your account balance each month for the next three quarters if you make a deposit of $120 on the first of each month. The printed table should indicate the quarter and month and the balance at the end of each month.

Solution

FIGURE 6.3

```
LIST
1      PN$ = "P6C-SAVE"
2      NA$ = "YOUR NAME"
3      DA$ = "00/00/00"
10     '   ===== VARIABLES =====
11     '   A = AMOUNT IN ACCOUNT
12     '   D = MONTHLY DEPOSIT
13     '   I = MONTHLY INTEREST
14     '   M = NUMBER OF MONTHS
15     '   R = YEARLY INTEREST RATE
16     '   Q = NUMBER OF QUARTERS
17     LET A = 3500     <-- Assign initial amount in account
18     LET R = 9.6      <-- Assign interest rate
19     LET D = 120      <-- Assign amount of monthly deposit
100    '   ===== MAIN PROGRAM =====
101    CLS : PRINT TAB(40 - (LEN (PN$) / 2)) PN$
110    PRINT : PRINT "QUARTER - MONTH     BALANCE ON LAST DAY"
120    PRINT"---------------------------------------"
130    PRINT
140    FOR Q = 1 TO 4
150       FOR M = 1 TO 3
160          LET A = A + D                 <-- Make monthly deposit on first of month
170          LET I = A * R / 100 / 12      <-- Calculate interest on last day of month
180          LET A = A + I                 <-- Add interest to account on last day
190          PRINT USING "   #       ##         $$##,###.##";Q,M,A
200       NEXT M
210       PRINT
220    NEXT Q
230    END
Ok
```

(Figure continued)

(Figure 6.3 continued)

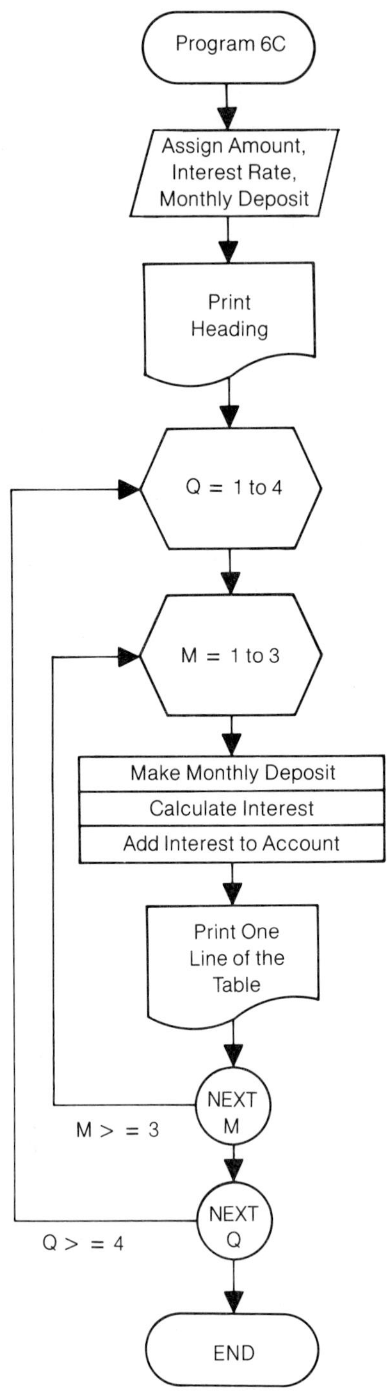

(Figure continued)

(Figure 6.3 continued)

RUN

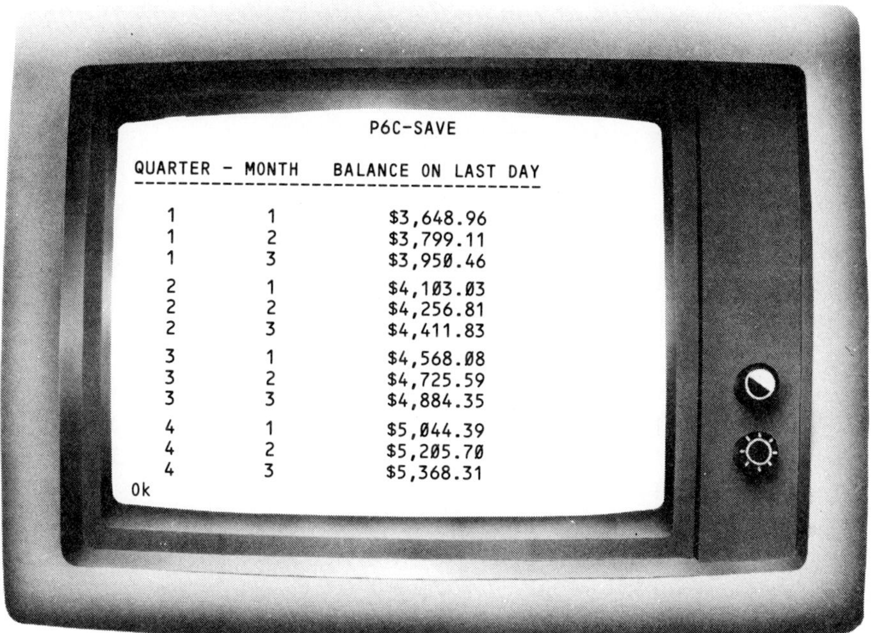

```
                P6C-SAVE

QUARTER - MONTH   BALANCE ON LAST DAY
--------------------------------------

   1        1        $3,648.96
   1        2        $3,799.11
   1        3        $3,950.46

   2        1        $4,103.03
   2        2        $4,256.81
   2        3        $4,411.83

   3        1        $4,568.08
   3        2        $4,725.59
   3        3        $4,884.35

   4        1        $5,044.39
   4        2        $5,205.70
   4        3        $5,368.31
Ok
```

SELF-TESTING QUESTIONS

Step through the program in each question and write the output produced when the program runs.

EXAMPLE:

```
110  LET S = 0
120  IF S > 4 GOTO 160
130  PRINT "D";
140  LET S = S + 1
150  GOTO 120
160  END
```

The step-through table is shown below:

Line Number:		120	130	140
Variables:	S	S > 4?	PRINT D	S = S + 1
Pass 1:	0	no	D	1
Pass 2:	1	no	D	2
Pass 3:	2	no	D	3
Pass 4:	3	no	D	4
Pass 5:	4	no	D	5
Pass 6:	5	yes		

The output is: DDDDD.

6.1

```
110  FOR I = 1 TO 4
120    READ A,B
130    IF A > B THEN PRINT "A IS GREATER"
140    IF A = B THEN PRINT "EQUAL"
150    IF A < B THEN PRINT "B IS GREATER"
160  NEXT I
170  DATA 4,5, 6,2, 5,5, 7,6
```

6.2

```
110  LET S = 0
120  IF S > = 5 GOTO 160
130  PRINT "E";
140  LET S = S + 1
150  GOTO 120
160  END
```

6.3

```
110  LET S = 1
120  PRINT "B";
130  LET S = S + 1
140  IF S < 3 GOTO 120
150  END
```

6.4
```
11Ø  LET S = 1
12Ø  PRINT "A";
13Ø  IF S > 3 GOTO 16Ø
14Ø  LET S = S + 1
15Ø  GOTO 12Ø
16Ø  END
```

6.5
```
11Ø  LET S = Ø
12Ø  LET S = S + 1
13Ø  IF S > 4 GOTO 16Ø
14Ø  PRINT "K";
15Ø  GOTO 12Ø
16Ø  END
```

6.6
```
11Ø  FOR I = 1 TO 3
12Ø    FOR J = 1 TO 3
13Ø      PRINT I;
14Ø    NEXT J
15Ø  NEXT I
```

6.7
```
11Ø  FOR I = 1 TO 3
12Ø    FOR J = 1 TO 3
13Ø      PRINT J;
14Ø    NEXT J
15Ø  NEXT I
```

6.8
```
11Ø  FOR I = 1 TO 3
12Ø    FOR J = 1 TO 2
13Ø      PRINT I;J;
14Ø    NEXT J
15Ø  NEXT I
```

6.9
```
11Ø  FOR I = 3 TO 1 STEP -1
12Ø    FOR J = 1 TO 3
13Ø      PRINT J;
14Ø    NEXT J
15Ø  NEXT I
```

6.10
```
11Ø  FOR I = 3 TO 1 STEP -1
12Ø    FOR J = 3 TO 1 STEP -1
13Ø      PRINT J;
14Ø    NEXT J
15Ø  NEXT I
```

6.11
```
11Ø  FOR I = 3 TO 1 STEP -1
12Ø    FOR J = 3 TO 1 STEP -1
13Ø      PRINT I;
14Ø    NEXT J
15Ø  NEXT I
```

6.12
```
110  FOR I = 1 TO 3
120    FOR J = 1 TO 3
130      PRINT J;
140    NEXT J
150    PRINT
160  NEXT I
```

6.13
```
110  FOR I = 1 TO 2
120    FOR J = 1 TO 2
130      FOR K = 1 TO 2
140        PRINT K;
150      NEXT K
160    NEXT J
170  NEXT I
```

6.14
```
110  FOR I = 1 TO 2
120    FOR J = 1 TO 2
130      FOR K = 1 TO 2
140        PRINT K;
150      NEXT K
160      PRINT
170    NEXT J
180  NEXT I
```

6.15
```
110  FOR I = 1 TO 2
120    FOR J = 1 TO 2
130      FOR K = 1 TO 2
140        PRINT K;
150      NEXT K
160      PRINT
170    NEXT J
180    PRINT
190  NEXT I
```

6.16
```
100  CLS
110  FOR Y = 1 TO 3
120    PRINT "YEAR = ";Y
130    FOR Q = 1 TO 4
140      PRINT "QUARTER = ";Q": ";
150      PRINT "MONTHS = ";
160      FOR M = 1 TO 3
170        PRINT M + 3 * (Q - 1);
180        IF M < 3 THEN PRINT ",";
190      NEXT M
200      PRINT
210    NEXT Q
220    PRINT
230  NEXT Y
```

EXERCISES

Choose One of the Following

6.1 The wholesale cost of an item is to be entered using an INPUT statement. If the wholesale cost is less than $100, the markup is 20 percent. Otherwise the markup is $20 (20 percent of the first $100), plus 30 percent of the amount over $100. Write a program that will enter the wholesale cost and print the retail price as shown below.

```
WHAT IS THE WHOLESALE COST? 450

THE RETAIL PRICE IS $575.00
```

Your printed output must include at least three runs of your program, one with a wholesale cost less than $100, one with a wholesale cost of $100, and one with a wholesale cost greater than $100. Your printed output should also include a written calculation verifying the selling price from each run.

Gosub needs Return with it!

turn in this program on 11/12

To Print: Control PrtSc make sure printer is ready on line

Return brings you back to next statement

must have END before Subroutine

If not return without Gosub error

TIPS

1. **Be sure one of your conditionals has an equal sign in it, otherwise the program will fail when the wholesale cost is exactly $100.**

6.2 A salesperson's total weekly sales are to be entered using an INPUT statement. The commission is 8.3 percent of the first $5,000 in sales and 3.5 percent of any amount over $5,000 in sales. Write a program that will enter the sales and print the commission as shown below.

```
WHAT IS THE WEEKLY SALES TOTAL? 8200

YOUR COMMISSION IS $527.00
```

Your printed output must include at least three runs of the program: one with weekly sales less than $5,000, one with weekly sales of $5,000, and one with weekly sales greater than $5,000. Your printed output should also include written calculations verifying the commission for each run.

TIPS

1. **One of your conditional statements must contain an equal sign, otherwise a sales amount of exactly $5,000 will cause an error.**

6.3 A student's three exam scores are to be entered using an INPUT statement. The average score is used to determine the letter grade as follows:

95 < = AVG	GRADE = A
85 < = AVG < 95	GRADE = B
70 < = AVG < 85	GRADE = C
60 < = AVG < 70	GRADE = D
AVG < 60	GRADE = F

Write a program that will enter a student's three exam scores, calculate the average grade, and print the student's letter grade as shown below:

```
ENTER YOUR THREE EXAM SCORES.
? 85,88,86
YOUR AVERAGE SCORE IS  86.3
YOUR LETTER GRADE IS B
```

Your printed output must include five runs with all five possible letter grades appearing. At least one of the average values should be on a grade borderline (e.g., 95, 85, 70, etc.). Also include a written calculation verifying two of the average values. Use INPUT S1,S2,S3 to input the three scores.

TIPS

1. **Write double conditionals as two conditions enclosed in parentheses, separated by the word AND. For example: IF (85 < = AVG) AND (AVG < 95).**
2. **Remember that the variable used to print the grade will be a string variable (e.g., G$).**
3. **Remember also that a value assigned to a string variable must be enclosed in quotes.**

6.4 On the first of each month except January of each year, a person deposits $100 into an account earning 12 percent interest compounded monthly. The account is opened February 1. How much money will be in the account on January 1 five years later? Assume that the interest is computed and added to the account on the last day of each month. Write a program that produces the following printed output, including the message that follows the table. The balance in the table is the balance on the last day of the month, after the interest for that month has been added to the account.

```
YEAR-MONTH              BALANCE ON LAST DAY

 1 - 1                        0.00
 1 - 2                      101.00
   .                           .
   .                           .
 1 - 12                   1,168.25

 2 - 1                    1,179.93
   .                           .
   .                           .

 5 - 12                   7,523.01

THE ACCOUNT BALANCE IS $7,523.01
ON JANUARY 1 FIVE YEARS LATER.
```

TIPS

1. **Look back at program 6C.**
2. **Try to make your program a series of steps that do what the bank does during each month.**

6.5 A young woman agrees to begin working for a company at a salary of one cent per day, with the condition that her daily salary would double each week (five work days each week). Write a program that will print a salary table as shown below. The table should end when the woman's salary exceeds $1,000 per week. Your program should print the message that follows the table below, using variables to print the salary and week number.

```
WEEK              SALARY

 1                 Ø.Ø5
 2                 Ø.1Ø
 3                 Ø.2Ø
 4                 Ø.4Ø
 5                 Ø.8Ø
 6                 1.6Ø
 .                  .
 .                  .
16             1,638.4Ø

THE YOUNG WOMAN'S SALARY WILL BE $1,638.4Ø
DURING WEEK NUMBER 16.
```

TIPS

1. **Remember that the salary is paid daily, but this daily salary doubles only once a week.**
2. **The salary shouldn't double until the end of the first week.**
3. **Use a loop to compute each week's salary and double the daily salary. Use an IF/THEN statement to terminate this loop.**
4. **Note that the weekly salary used in the IF/THEN statement that terminates the loop will be five times the daily salary.**

6.6 The Northern Lights Power Company has the following rate structure for electricity (KWHR = kilowatt-hours).

	Oct-May	June-Sept
Fixed charge each month, $	2.50	2.50
First 500 KWHR, $ per KWHR	0.0454	0.0454
Next 500 KWHR, $ per KWHR	0.0406	0.0454
Excess, per KWHR	0.0308	0.0454

Write a program that enters the number of the month (i.e., Jan = 1, etc.), the previous KWHR reading, the present KWHR reading, and prints the kilowatt-hours used and the monthly bill as shown below.

```
THE NUMBER OF THE MONTH IS: 3
THE PREVIOUS KWHR READING IS: 5973
THE PRESENT KWHR READING IS: 6623
THE KWHR USED IS 650
YOUR ELECTRICITY BILL IS $31.29
```

Your printed output should include one run for the summer months (June–Sept) and three runs for the winter months (Oct–May). The three winter runs must include one with KWHR less than 500, one with KWHR between 500 and 1,000, and one with KWHR greater than 1,000. Your printed output should also include a written calculation verifying each monthly bill.

TIPS

1. **This is a very difficult program. If you can do it, you are to be congratulated.**
2. **Write one part of your program that is executed only for summer months; it should be simple since there is only one rate.**
3. **Write another part that is executed only for winter months, with IF/THEN statements for each rate.**

CHAPTER 7

GETTING ARTISTIC

Printing Patterns with Subroutines

NEW CONCEPTS TAUGHT

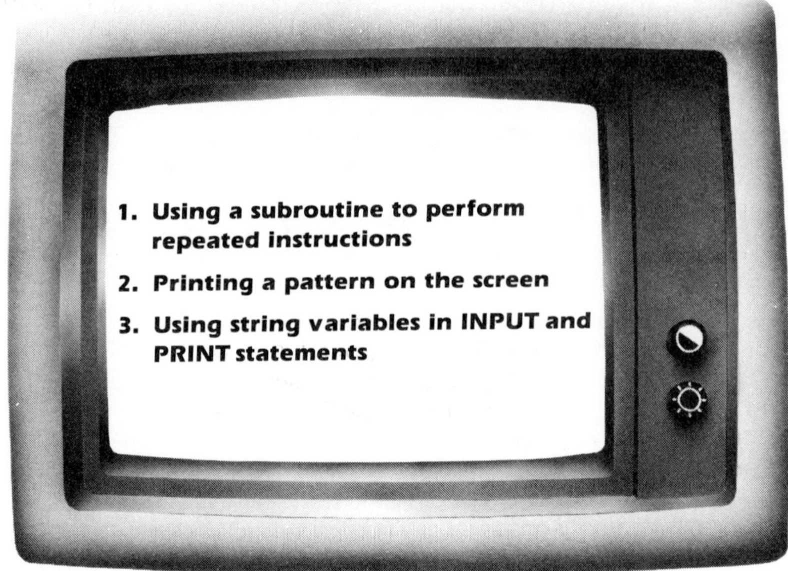

1. Using a subroutine to perform repeated instructions
2. Printing a pattern on the screen
3. Using string variables in INPUT and PRINT statements

THE SUBROUTINE

The subroutine is one of the most powerful tools in programming. It speeds the execution of programs, keeps us from having to type in repeated instructions over and over again, and makes programs easier to write and understand.

The concept of the subroutine is really very simple. A subroutine is a series of normal program lines located anywhere in the program that end with the word RETURN. We use the GOSUB command to begin execution of the subroutine and the RETURN command to end the subroutine. If we have a subroutine at line 1000 in a program, anytime in that program we need to have the subroutine performed, we insert the command GOSUB 1000. When the computer sees this, it makes a note of where it is in the program and then jumps to line 1000. It does whatever the lines following 1000 tell it to do, and when it comes to the RETURN statement, it returns to the first line *after* the GOSUB statement and continues with the program.

To make the program more readable, we have placed a line number followed by a single apostrophe (') at the end of each subroutine. Line 560, for example:

```
560 '
```

Such a line has no real effect on the execution of the program (except to slow it down by a few imperceptible microseconds). When the program is listed, these "null lines" help us to see the subroutine as a separate unit.

Complicated programs often have many subroutines, and in well-written professional programs almost all of the work is done by subroutines. This is part of what is referred to as structured programming. We will talk more about this concept later.

Pictures on the Screen

There are two basic programming techniques used to put a picture on the screen. One of these uses the built-in graphics commands of BASIC to plot points and draw lines on the screen. This technique is covered in chapter 11. The second method, sometimes called character graphics, is a little more primitive. Character graphics is done by simply printing letters or symbols from the keyboard onto the screen in such a way that they make a pattern. In this chapter you will use this technique to put a pattern of your own choice on the screen.

The Christmas Tree

Program 7A may be a little confusing at first. It has two subroutines: one at line 500, which prints spaces (how many spaces is determined by the current value of the variable S), and another at line 600 to print characters (the number of characters is determined by the value of the variable C, and the character printed is the value of C$). So, at any time in the program, we can print S spaces or C characters.

To understand how the program works, you must think of the Christmas tree as made up of eight horizontal lines. Each line has a row of spaces followed by a "*" (lines 2 through 5 have a row of spaces, one "*", a row of spaces, and another "*"). Notice that the DATA lines 301 to 308 are numbered to match the line number of the pattern and that the four lines that have the space, "*", space, "*" pattern (lines 2 through 5) have four values. By now you have probably figured out that the DATA values stand for number of spaces (S) and number of characters (C). So line 150 reads the first DATA value (19) from line 301 and then goes to the subroutine at line 500 and prints 19 spaces; the program then returns and reads the second DATA value (1) from line 301 and then goes to the subroutine at line 600, which prints one character. The PRINT statement at the end of line 150 causes a carriage return, and then we're ready to print the next line. This completes line 1 of the pattern (the single asterisk at the top of the tree). Notice how the numbers in the DATA statements correspond to the numbers on the right side of the planning grid in figure 7.1. Lines 160 to 180 print lines 2 to 5 of the pattern by reading DATA values and printing the spaces and characters. Lines 190 to 210 finish the tree by printing lines 6 to 8 of the pattern. The program then drops down to line 399 (the DATA statements are ignored unless referred to by a READ statement) and ends.

never jump out of a subroutine - don't use a goto

EXAMPLE 7A Christmas Tree

Problem Write a program that will print the outline of a Christmas tree as shown on the grid in figure 7.1. Use subroutines to print spaces and characters. Use READ/DATA statements to specify how often each subroutine will be performed.

Solution

FIGURE 7.1 Planning Grid for Christmas Tree

```
#1: 19, 1
#2: 18,1,1,1
#3: 17,1,3,1
#4: 16,1,5,1
#5: 15,1,7,1
#6: 14,11
#7: 19,1
#8: 17,5
```

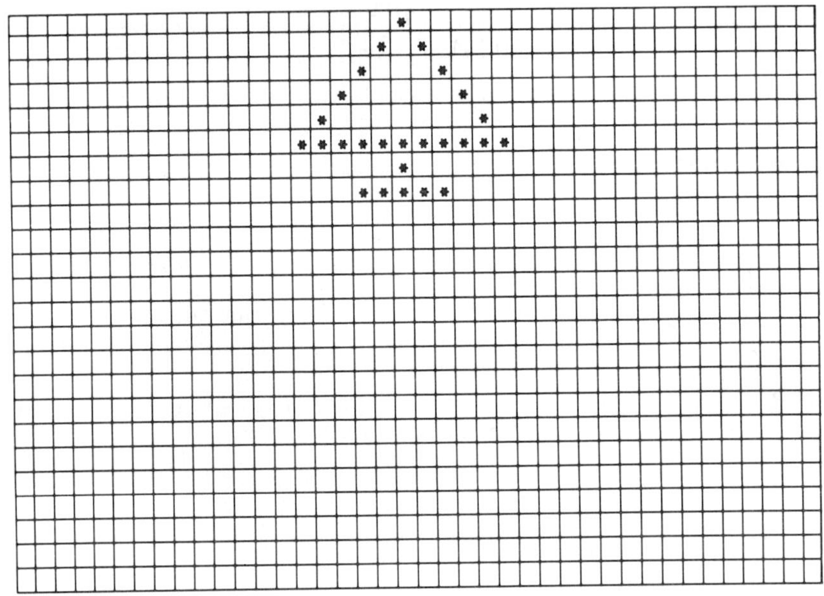

(Figure continued)

(Figure 7.1 continued)

```
LIST
1     PN$ = "P7A-TREE"
2     NA$ = "YOUR NAME"
3     DA$ = "ØØ/ØØ/ØØ"
1Ø    '  ===== VARIABLES =====
11    '  C$ = CHARACTER USED IN PATTERN
12    '  C = NUMBER OF CHARACTERS PRINTED AT ONE TIME
13    '  I = LOOP COUNTER FOR NUMBER OF SPACES OR CHARACTERS
14    '  LIN = LOOP COUNTER FOR NUMBER OF LINES
15    '  S = NUMBER OF SPACES
1ØØ   '  ===== MAIN PROGRAM =====
1Ø1   CLS : PRINT TAB(4Ø - (LEN (PN$) / 2)) PN$
11Ø   PRINT
12Ø   INPUT "TYPE THE CHARACTER TO BE USED: ", C$ : PRINT
13Ø   '  ===== PRINT THE PATTERN =====
14Ø   '  LIN = 1
15Ø   GOSUB 5ØØ : GOSUB 6ØØ : PRINT
16Ø   FOR LIN = 2 TO 5
17Ø      GOSUB 5ØØ : GOSUB 6ØØ : GOSUB 5ØØ : GOSUB 6ØØ : PRINT
18Ø   NEXT LIN
19Ø   FOR LIN  = 6 TO 8
2ØØ      GOSUB 5ØØ : GOSUB 6ØØ : PRINT
21Ø   NEXT LIN
3ØØ   '  ===== DATA SECTION =====
3Ø1   DATA  19,1
3Ø2   DATA  18,1,1,1
3Ø3   DATA  17,1,3,1
3Ø4   DATA  16,1,5,1
3Ø5   DATA  15,1,7,1
3Ø6   DATA  14,11
3Ø7   DATA  19,1
3Ø8   DATA  17,5
399   END : '  ==  END OF MAIN PROGRAM ==
5ØØ   '  ===== SUBROUTINE TO PRINT SPACES =====
51Ø   READ S
52Ø   FOR I = 1 TO S
53Ø      PRINT " ";
54Ø   NEXT I
55Ø   RETURN
56Ø   '
6ØØ   '  ===== SUBROUTINE TO PRINT CHARACTERS =====
61Ø   READ C
62Ø   FOR I = 1 TO C
63Ø      PRINT C$;
64Ø   NEXT I
65Ø   RETURN
66Ø   '
Ok
```

(Figure continued)

(Figure 7.1 continued)

RUN

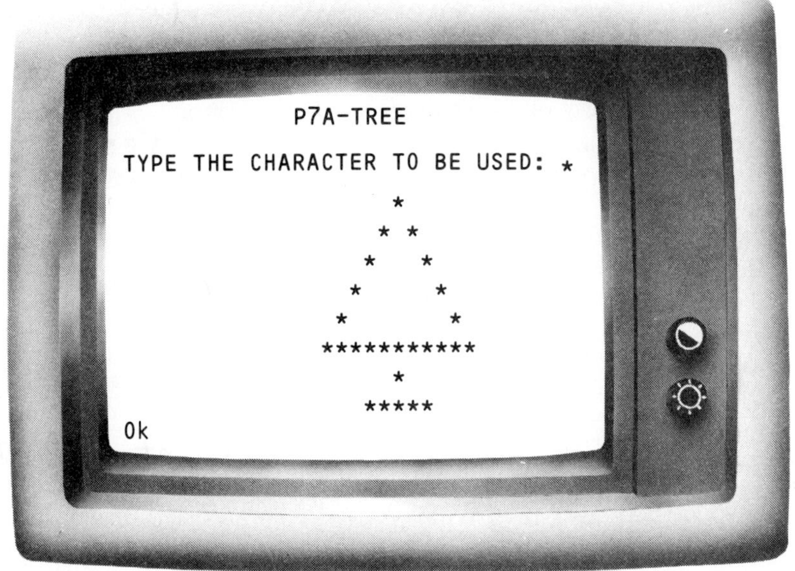
P7A-TREE
TYPE THE CHARACTER TO BE USED: *
*
* *
*   *
*   *
*   *
****
*
*****
Ok

GOSUB AND RETURN Sometimes you will find it necessary to use the same sequence of instructions in several places in your program. The GOSUB and RETURN statements allow you to write this sequence of instructions once as a subroutine. You use a GOSUB statement each time you need the subroutine, and then a RETURN statement in the subroutine transfers control back to the next statement in your main program.

Example:

```
1Ø FOR J = 1 TO 4
2Ø GOSUB 5ØØ
3Ø PRINT "*";
4Ø GOSUB 5ØØ
6Ø NEXT J
7Ø GOSUB 5ØØ
8Ø PRINT "*"
9Ø STOP
1ØØ DATA 15,7,16,5,17,3,18,1,19

5ØØ REM SUBROUTINE TO PRINT SPACES
51Ø READ S
52Ø FOR I = 1 TO S
53Ø PRINT " ";
54Ø NEXT I
55Ø RETURN
```

In the above example the GOSUB at line 20 transfers control to the subroutine at line 500, and the RETURN at line 550 transfers control back to line 30. The GOSUB at line 40 transfers control to the subroutine at line 500, and the RETURN at line 550 transfers control back to line 50. The GOSUB at line 70 transfers control to the subroutine, and the RETURN transfers control back to line 80. The result is the same as it would be if the three GOSUB statements were each replaced by lines 510, 520, 530, and 540.

```
RUN

               *       *
                *     *
                 *   *
                  * *
                   *
```

SELF-TESTING QUESTIONS

Step through the program in each question and write the output produced when the program runs.

7.1

```
110  LET C$ = "*"
120  FOR I = 1 TO 5
130      PRINT C$;
140  NEXT I
```

7.2

```
110 LET C$ = "*"
120 FOR I = 1 TO 5
130       PRINT C$
140 NEXT I
```

7.3

```
110  READ C$
120  FOR I = 1 TO 5
130      READ N
140      FOR J = 1 TO N
150          PRINT " ";
160      NEXT J
170      READ M
180      FOR J = 1 TO M
190          PRINT C$;
200      NEXT J
210      PRINT
220  NEXT I
230  DATA *,7,3,8,1,7,3,6,5,6,5
```

7.4 Same program as question 7.3, except change line 230 to the following:

```
230  DATA *,10,4,10,1,10,3,10,1,10,4
```

7.5 Same program as question 7.3, except change line 230 to the following:

```
230  DATA *,10,6,10,6,12,2,12,2,12,2
```

7.6 Same program as question 7.3, except change line 230 to the following:

```
230  DATA *,10,5,14,1,14,1,14,1,13,2
```

EXERCISES

Choose One of the Following

7.1 Use the grid provided to design a pattern of your own choosing in the same manner as the Christmas tree in the example. Write the main program and DATA statements that will produce your pattern. Use the subroutines and line numbers as in program 7A. Put your DATA statements between lines 300 to 399 and put the two subroutines at lines 500 and 600. Use the same variables as in program 7A. Use the blank grid in figure 7.2 to plan your pattern.

FIGURE 7.2 Planning Grid For Your Pattern

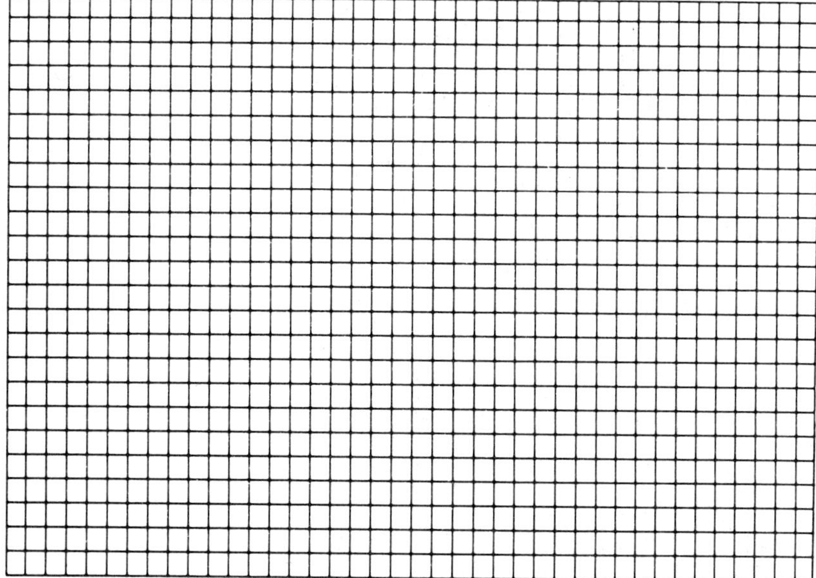

TIPS

1. **As in example 7A, number your DATA lines so that their line numbers are the same as the lines of your pattern.**
2. **Remember to put a semicolon (;) after the PRINT statement in the subroutines.**
3. **Remember to put exactly one space between the quotation marks in the subroutine to print spaces.**
4. **Keep the variable LIN equal to the line number of the pattern. Do not use LINE as a variable name; it is a reserved word.**
5. **Remember to finish each line of the pattern with a PRINT statement.**
6. **Don't make your pattern too complicated; this exercise is hard enough as it is.**

7.2 Write a program that will print a bar graph indicating the number of sales made by each member of a group of salespeople, based on a set of DATA statements like the following:

```
301  DATA  NORDGREN, 21
302  DATA  SIGFORD, 18
303  DATA  PETERSON, 13
  .
  .
  .
```

The program should produce a graph like the following:

```
NAME               NUMBER OF SALES
---------------------------------------------------------
NORDGREN           |=====================
SIGFORD            |==================
PETERSON           |=============
  .
  .
  .
```

TIPS

1. Use a subroutine like the one in the example to print the line of characters.
2. Use a TAB statement to position the vertical line (|). Make sure this is past the end of every name.
3. Make sure the pattern will not go off the right side of the screen. If you are ambitious, have the program check for this and make a correction.

7.3 A major design flaw of program 7A is that in order to print another pattern, the main program must be completely rewritten. Using subroutines to print characters and spaces, write a program that will print any pattern. The program should be written so that when a new pattern is to be printed, *only* the DATA statements will need to be changed. This means that all the information about the pattern will be contained in the DATA statements.

TIPS

1. **Follow the tips for exercise 7.1 (except for tip 4; the variable LIN should not be necessary).**
2. **In the DATA statements, use positive numbers to indicate characters, negative numbers to indicate spaces, zero to indicate the end of a line of the pattern, and 9999 to indicate the end of the whole pattern.**
3. **For example, the line:**

```
302  DATA -18, 1, -1, 1, Ø
```

   should print 18 spaces, 1 character, 1 space, 1 more character, and then a carriage return.
4. **Do not have any READ statements in the subroutines. There should be only one READ statement, and it should be in the main program.**
5. **Be sure to set the correct limit variable for each subroutine (C and S in the example) before calling it.**

CHAPTER 8

FUNCTIONING
Using Functions Properly

NEW CONCEPTS TAUGHT

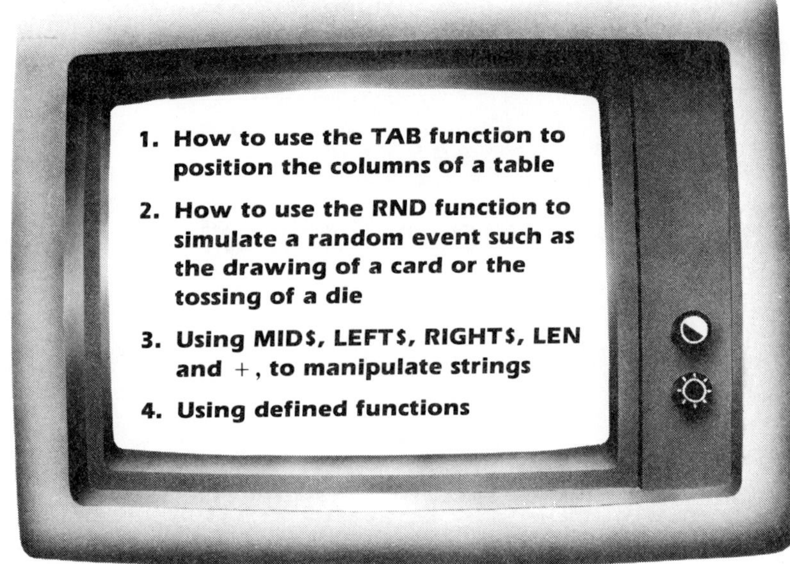

1. How to use the TAB function to position the columns of a table
2. How to use the RND function to simulate a random event such as the drawing of a card or the tossing of a die
3. Using MID$, LEFT$, RIGHT$, LEN and +, to manipulate strings
4. Using defined functions

WHAT IS A FUNCTION?

A function is a defined term that performs a specific job. Some functions are built into BASIC, such as the INT function; others are defined by the user, like the defined functions A, B, C, and D we use to round off in program 8A. In this chapter we will also look at several more built-in functions.

The TAB function positions the cursor to a particular spot on the screen and is useful for making output on the screen or printer look neat and orderly. The RND function is used to generate a random number and can be used to simulate a random event such as drawing a card, tossing a coin, or throwing a pair of dice. The string functions LEFT$, RIGHT$, MID$, LEN, and + are used for the manipulation of string variables.

Table of Square Roots

Program 8A in figure 8.1 uses the TAB function to print a table using TAB statements and a simple loop. The main program, from lines 100 to 130, is very straightforward.

```
100  '  ===== MAIN PROGRAM =====
101  CLS : PRINT TAB(40 - (LEN (PN$) / 2)) PN$
110  GOSUB 200 : '  PRINT HEADING
120  GOSUB 300 : '  PRINT TABLE
130  END
```

Line 101 prints the traditional heading centered on the screen. Line 110 calls the subroutine at line 200 that prints the headings. Line 220 calls the subroutine at line 1000 that prints the row of dashes under the headings. Line 120 calls the subroutine that does all of the hard work, printing the table.

A new feature of this program is the four defined functions we have added in lines 40 to 48.

```
40    '  ===== FUNCTIONS =====
41    '  ROUND TO WHOLE NUMBER WITH FN A(X)
42    DEF  FN A(X) = INT (1 * X + .5) / 1
43    '  ROUND TO ONE DECIMAL PLACE WITH FN B(X)
44    DEF  FN B(X) = INT (10 * X + .5) / 10
45    '  ROUND TO TWO DECIMAL PLACES WITH FN C(X)
46    DEF  FN C(X) = INT (100 * X + .5) / 100
47    '  ROUND TO THREE DECIMAL PLACES WITH FN D(X)
48    DEF  FN D(X) = INT (1000 * X + .5) / 1000
```

These functions are used for rounding off. Notice that the four rounding functions are labeled A, B, C, D. A rounds to whole numbers (no decimal places), B rounds to one decimal place, C to two, and D to three. Suppose you have a variable called X that has a current value of 3.6789 and you would like to round it off. If you have the defined functions entered in lines 40 to 48, you may use them to do this. As the program goes past lines 40 to 48, the computer makes a note of the functions so it will know what to do if you mention them later in the program. If you want to round your variable to two decimal places, you will use function C (notice that the remark statement in line 45 tells you this). All you need to do is put the following in the program:

```
LET X = FN C(X).
```

The computer first looks to the right of the equal sign. This part tells it to take whatever is in memory cell X and apply function C to it; it remembers function C from line 46. The computer does its work and then notes that the left side of the statement tells it to put this result back in the memory cell named X. When it is finished, if we add the command PRINT X, we will find that X is now 3.68. If this is a bit confusing, remember that to round any variable with these defined functions, all you really need to know is the following:

```
          LET variable name = FN function name (variable name)
                    ↓                  ↓               ↓
Example:      LET X         = FN       C              (X)
```

Variable name is the name of the variable you want to round off, and *function name* is the name of the rounding function (in this case, A, B, C, or D).

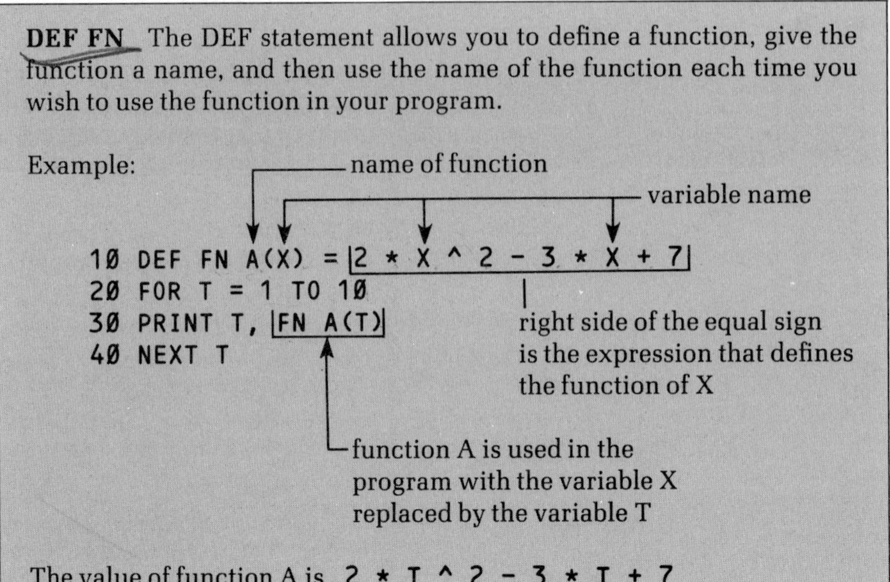

DEF FN The DEF statement allows you to define a function, give the function a name, and then use the name of the function each time you wish to use the function in your program.

Example:

```
10 DEF FN A(X) = 2 * X ^ 2 - 3 * X + 7
20 FOR T = 1 TO 10
30 PRINT T, FN A(T)
40 NEXT T
```

name of function
variable name
right side of the equal sign is the expression that defines the function of X
function A is used in the program with the variable X replaced by the variable T

The value of function A is `2 * T ^ 2 - 3 * T + 7`

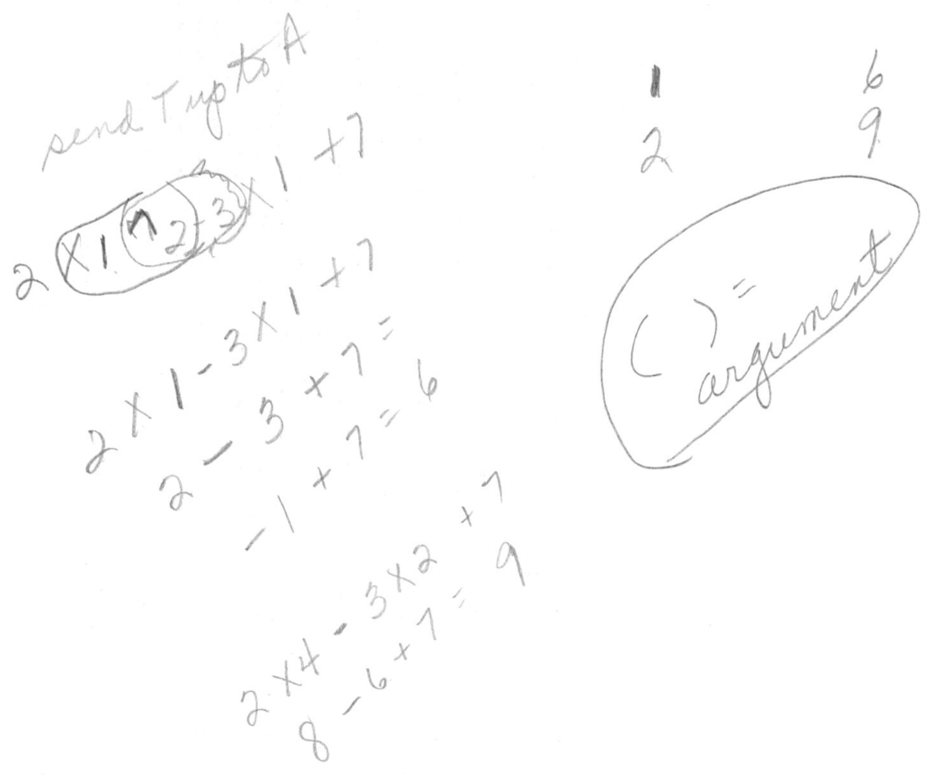
send T up to A
( ) = argument

TAB The TAB command is used in a PRINT statement to cause the display to begin in a particular column. The next item will be printed in the named column (counting from the left side of the display). TAB must be used in a PRINT statement and, unlike LOCATE, can cause movement only to the right of the current position.

The general form of TAB is:

line number `PRINT TAB(`*number or expression*`);` *Variable Name*

The value of the number or expression following the word TAB is the position on the line where the next character will be placed.

String variable names, expressions, numbers, and messages may be used where the variable name appears in the general form above.

Examples of the TAB command:

```
10 READ A,B,C,D,E,F
20 DATA 1,2,3,4,5,6
30 PRINT TAB(12);A;TAB(24);B;TAB(36);C;
40 PRINT TAB(48);D;TAB(60);E;TAB(72);F
```

The above instructions will produce the following printed output.

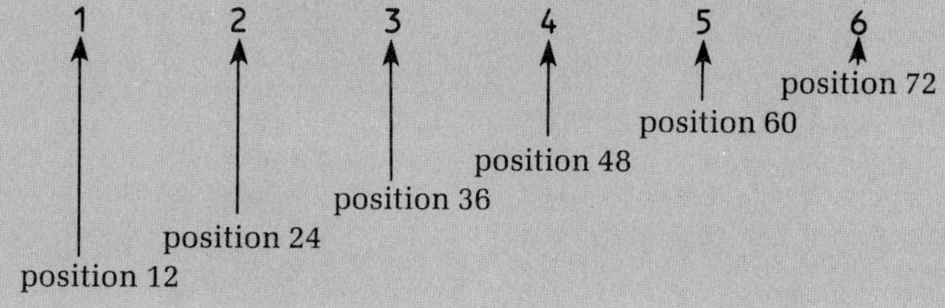

The loop in the subroutine at line 300 is fairly short (lines 310 to 360), and each time around it prints one line of the table.

```
310  FOR I = 1 TO 10
320       LET N  = I ^ .5
330       LET N1 = FN B(N)
340       LET N2 = FN C(N)
350       LET N3 = FN D(N)
360       PRINT I; TAB(8); N1; TAB(16); N2; TAB(24); N3
370  NEXT I
```

Line 320 sets N equal to the square root of N. Lines 330 to 350 use the rounding functions to set N1, N2, and N3. N1 is rounded to one decimal place with FN B; N2 is rounded to two decimal places with FN C; line 360 prints N, N1, N2, and N3 in four columns, under the headings printed above. After the table is printed, the program returns to the main program at 130 and ends.

EXAMPLE 8A Table of Square Roots

Problem Write a program that will print a table of square roots for the numbers 1,2,3, . . 10. The table should have four columns: one for the number itself and three for the square root of the number rounded to one, two, and three decimal places. Use the TAB function to put the three square roots at columns 8, 16, and 24.

Solution

FIGURE 8.1

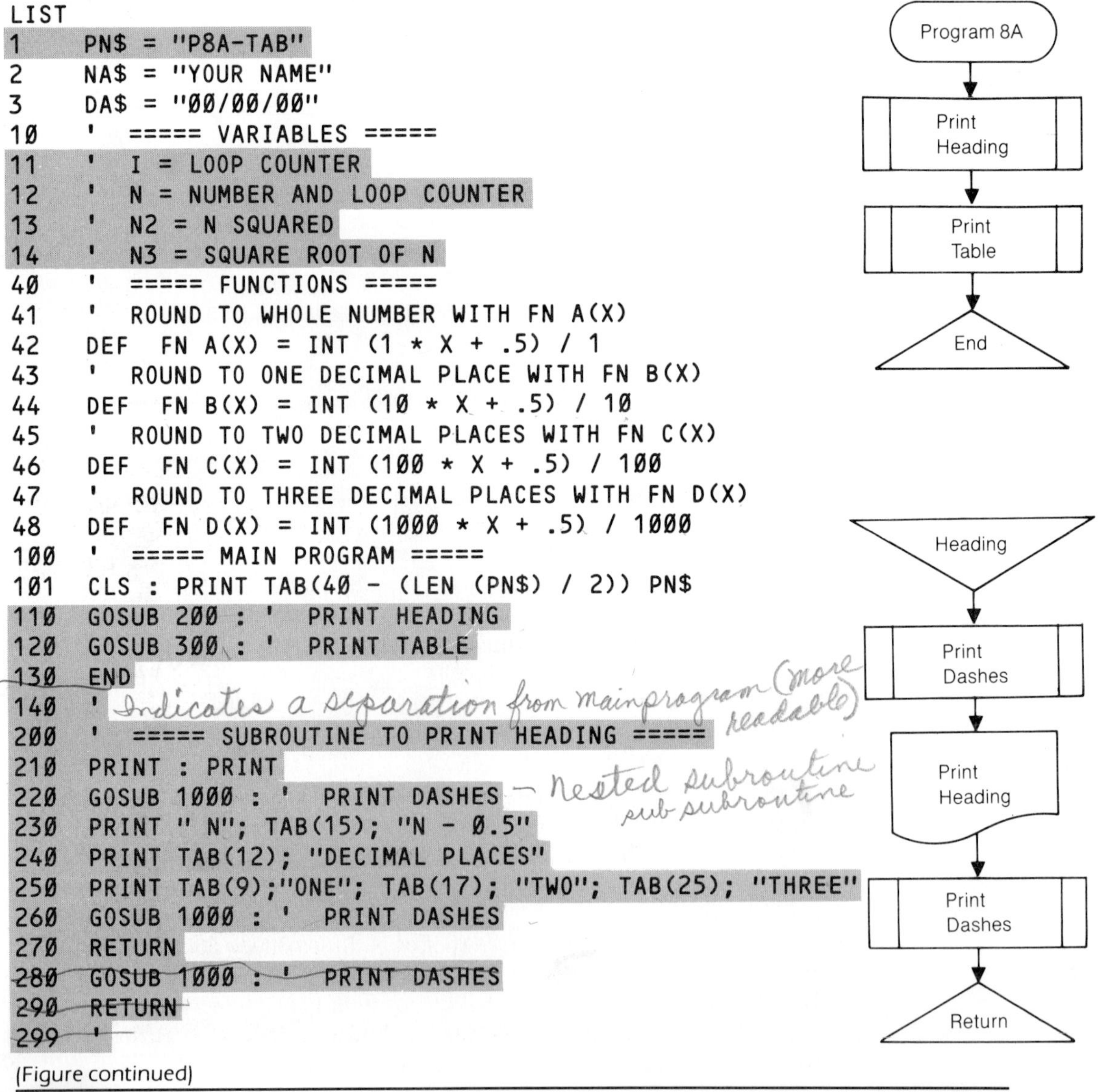

```
LIST
1     PN$ = "P8A-TAB"
2     NA$ = "YOUR NAME"
3     DA$ = "ØØ/ØØ/ØØ"
1Ø    '  ===== VARIABLES =====
11    '  I = LOOP COUNTER
12    '  N = NUMBER AND LOOP COUNTER
13    '  N2 = N SQUARED
14    '  N3 = SQUARE ROOT OF N
4Ø    '  ===== FUNCTIONS =====
41    '  ROUND TO WHOLE NUMBER WITH FN A(X)
42    DEF  FN A(X) = INT (1 * X + .5) / 1
43    '  ROUND TO ONE DECIMAL PLACE WITH FN B(X)
44    DEF  FN B(X) = INT (1Ø * X + .5) / 1Ø
45    '  ROUND TO TWO DECIMAL PLACES WITH FN C(X)
46    DEF  FN C(X) = INT (1ØØ * X + .5) / 1ØØ
47    '  ROUND TO THREE DECIMAL PLACES WITH FN D(X)
48    DEF  FN D(X) = INT (1ØØØ * X + .5) / 1ØØØ
1ØØ   '  ===== MAIN PROGRAM =====
1Ø1   CLS : PRINT TAB(4Ø - (LEN (PN$) / 2)) PN$
11Ø   GOSUB 2ØØ : '  PRINT HEADING
12Ø   GOSUB 3ØØ : '  PRINT TABLE
13Ø   END
14Ø   '
2ØØ   '  ===== SUBROUTINE TO PRINT HEADING =====
21Ø   PRINT : PRINT
22Ø   GOSUB 1ØØØ : '  PRINT DASHES
23Ø   PRINT " N"; TAB(15); "N - Ø.5"
24Ø   PRINT TAB(12); "DECIMAL PLACES"
25Ø   PRINT TAB(9);"ONE"; TAB(17); "TWO"; TAB(25); "THREE"
26Ø   GOSUB 1ØØØ : '  PRINT DASHES
27Ø   RETURN
28Ø   GOSUB 1ØØØ : '  PRINT DASHES
29Ø   RETURN
299   '
```


(Figure continued)

(Figure 8.1 continued)

```
300  '  ===== SUBROUTINE TO PRINT TABLE =====
310  FOR I = 1 TO 10
320      LET N  = I ^ .5
330      LET N1 = FN B(N)
340      LET N2 = FN C(N)
350      LET N3 = FN D(N)
360      PRINT I; TAB(8); N1; TAB(16); N2; TAB(24); N3
370  NEXT I
380  GOSUB 1000 : '  PRINT DASHES
390  RETURN
399  '
1000  '  SUBROUTINE TO PRINT ROW OF DASHES =====
1010  FOR I = 1 TO 29
1020      PRINT "-";
1030  NEXT I
1040  PRINT
1050  RETURN
1099  '
Ok
```

Print Table

N = 1 to 10

Compute Square Root

Print One Row of Table

N

Print Dashes

Return

RUN

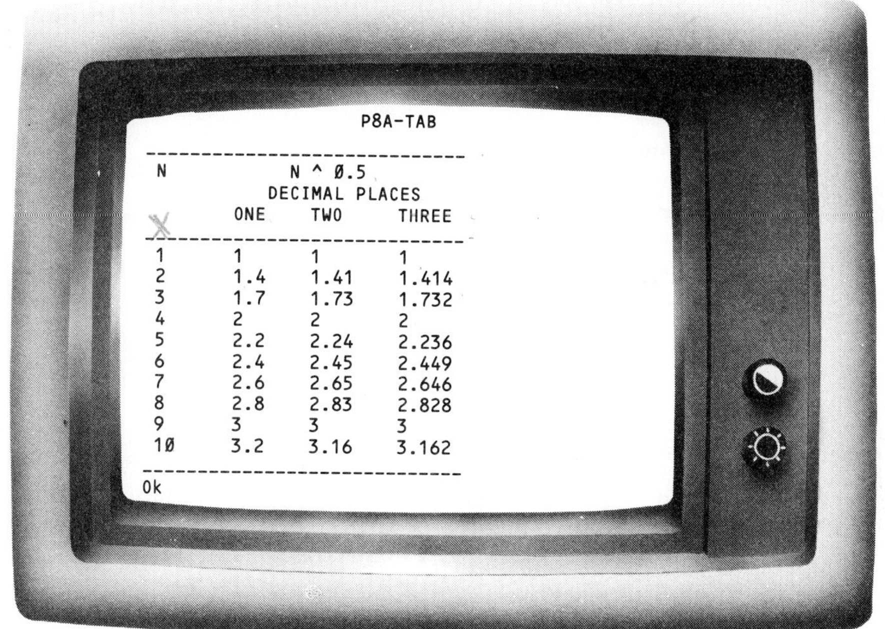
P8A-TAB

N	N ^ 0.5 DECIMAL PLACES ONE	TWO	THREE
1	1	1	1
2	1.4	1.41	1.414
3	1.7	1.73	1.732
4	2	2	2
5	2.2	2.24	2.236
6	2.4	2.45	2.449
7	2.6	2.65	2.646
8	2.8	2.83	2.828
9	3	3	3
10	3.2	3.16	3.162

Ok

Pick a Card

Program 8B introduces a very handy subroutine for picking a random number. The working parts of this subroutine are all on line 210.

```
21Ø  LET N = INT ( (UL + 1 - LL) * RND) + LL
```

We could substitute actual numbers for LL and UL, but doing it this way makes the subroutine more general and therefore more useful. Doing it this way means that in any program where we need a random number within a certain range, we can just set LL as the lower limit and UL as the upper limit and call this subroutine. We need it in this program because when picking a suit we need a number between 1 and 4, and when picking a card we need a number between 1 and 13.

If we used the random function alone to get random numbers, the program would pick the same sequence of random numbers each time it ran. To avoid this, we need to use the RANDOMIZE statement to *reseed* the random number generator at the beginning of the program. This is the function of line 102. The RANDOMIZE statement reseeds the random number generator so that it produces a new sequence of random numbers. If you use just RANDOMIZE by itself, the program will stop and ask the user to enter a number to reseed the random number generator. It would be better if the program did not bother the user in this way, and fortunately, this can be avoided by following the RANDOMIZE statement with a number to be used (e.g., RANDOMIZE 123). The trouble with this is that if we use the same number each time, the same sequence of numbers will be picked. To avoid this, line 102 uses the computer's internal clock to pick the number. This way the number is likely to be different each time the program runs. IBM BASIC has a built-in variable TIME$ that holds the current time. Try typing:

```
PRINT TIME$
```

to see how the time is formatted. Notice that the two numbers on the right are hundredths of a second. Since these change very often, they are useful for reseeding the random number generator. Looking at line 102 from the inside out, we first get the two right-hand digits of TIME$ with RIGHT$(TIME$,2). The RIGHT$ function is described later in this chapter. Now we have the hundredths of a second, but they are in the form of a string and we need a number to use with the RANDOMIZE statement. So we use the VAL( ) function to convert the string to a number. We do this all on one line with:

```
1Ø2  RANDOMIZE VAL(RIGHT$(TIME$,2))
```

In the main program we set LL and UL in line 110, and in line 120 we call the subroutine. The subroutine returns the random number N, which will be a number from 1 to 4. Here we must use another variable (S) and set it equal to N (line 130), because the next time we call the subroutine N will change.

Now that we have the suit number, we need to get a card number. The process is exactly the same, so we reset LL and UL and call the subroutine again, then in line 160 we set C equal to N. Since we now have S and C, the suit and card numbers, we go to subroutines 300 and 400 to get the suit and card names. All that's left to do is to print the results in line 190 and end.

RND and RANDOMIZE The RND function gives a random number that is greater than or equal to 0 and less than 1.

Example:

```
10   LET X = RND
```

To get a random number between 1 and a certain number *n*, use:

```
10   LET X = INT(RND * n) + 1
```

RND can be followed by a number in parentheses (e.g., RND(1)), but this is seldom done since RND is almost always used to get a new random number between 0 and 1 and this is the result when RND is used with no number.

The RANDOMIZE statement is used to reseed the random number generator. Without this, a program will produce the same sequence of random numbers each time it is run. If the RANDOMIZE program is used without a number following it, the program will stop and ask the user for a number to be used to reseed the generator. The following example shows how to reseed the random number generator using the current value of hundredths of a second on the system clock. This will reseed the generator without bothering the user and will produce a new sequence of random numbers each time the program is run:

```
102  RANDOMIZE VAL(RIGHT$(TIME$,2))
```

EXAMPLE 8B Pick a Card

Problem Write a program that simulates the drawing of a card from a full deck. Use S$ for the suit and C$ for the name of the card. Your program should print the following message if C$ = KING and S$ = HEARTS:

```
THE CARD DRAWN IS THE KING OF HEARTS
```

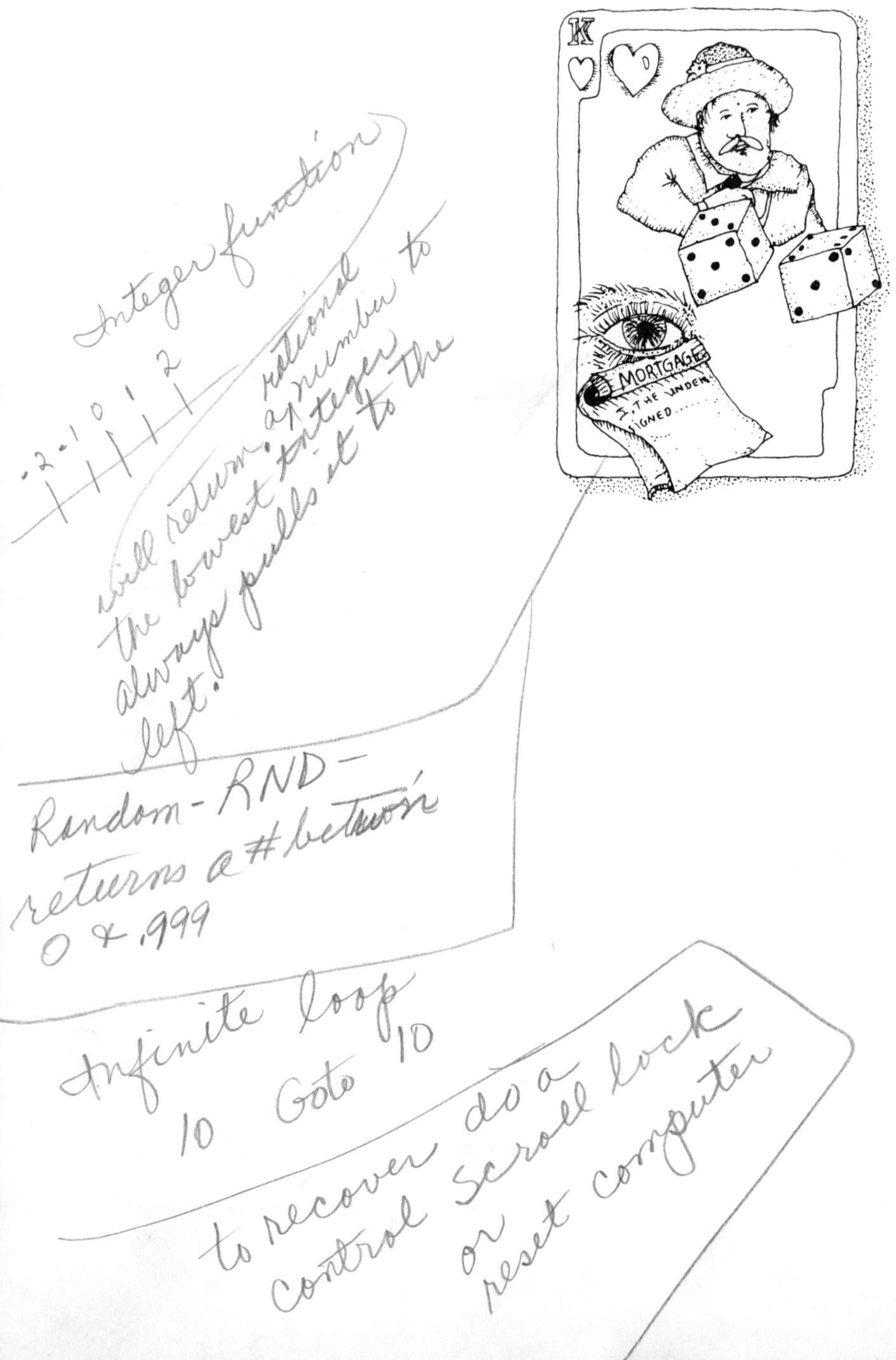

Solution

FIGURE 8.2

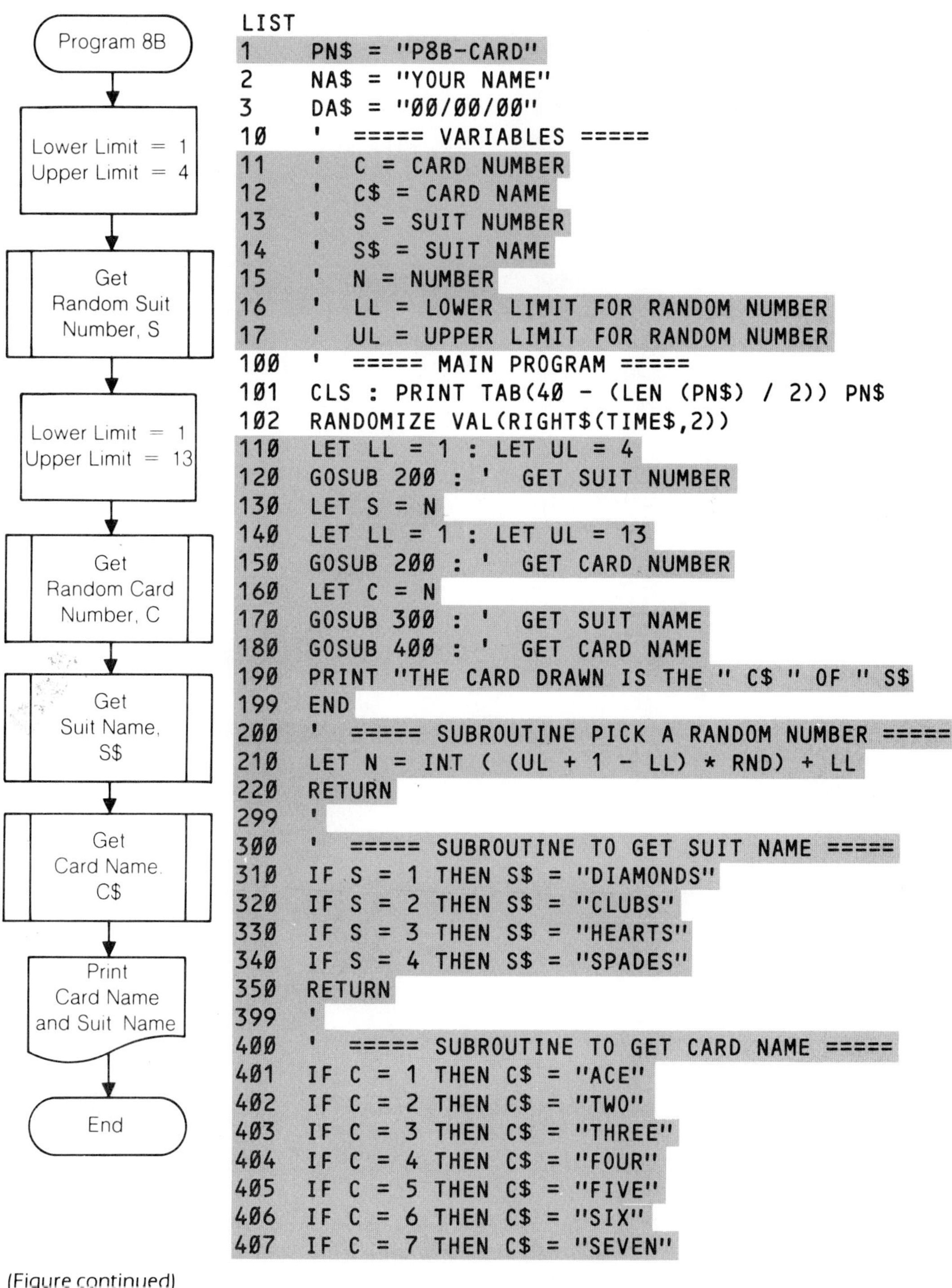


```
LIST
1     PN$ = "P8B-CARD"
2     NA$ = "YOUR NAME"
3     DA$ = "00/00/00"
10    '  ===== VARIABLES =====
11    '  C = CARD NUMBER
12    '  C$ = CARD NAME
13    '  S = SUIT NUMBER
14    '  S$ = SUIT NAME
15    '  N = NUMBER
16    '  LL = LOWER LIMIT FOR RANDOM NUMBER
17    '  UL = UPPER LIMIT FOR RANDOM NUMBER
100   '  ===== MAIN PROGRAM =====
101   CLS : PRINT TAB(40 - (LEN (PN$) / 2)) PN$
102   RANDOMIZE VAL(RIGHT$(TIME$,2))
110   LET LL = 1 : LET UL = 4
120   GOSUB 200 : '  GET SUIT NUMBER
130   LET S = N
140   LET LL = 1 : LET UL = 13
150   GOSUB 200 : '  GET CARD NUMBER
160   LET C = N
170   GOSUB 300 : '  GET SUIT NAME
180   GOSUB 400 : '  GET CARD NAME
190   PRINT "THE CARD DRAWN IS THE " C$ " OF " S$
199   END
200   '  ===== SUBROUTINE PICK A RANDOM NUMBER =====
210   LET N = INT ( (UL + 1 - LL) * RND) + LL
220   RETURN
299   '
300   '  ===== SUBROUTINE TO GET SUIT NAME =====
310   IF S = 1 THEN S$ = "DIAMONDS"
320   IF S = 2 THEN S$ = "CLUBS"
330   IF S = 3 THEN S$ = "HEARTS"
340   IF S = 4 THEN S$ = "SPADES"
350   RETURN
399   '
400   '  ===== SUBROUTINE TO GET CARD NAME =====
401   IF C = 1 THEN C$ = "ACE"
402   IF C = 2 THEN C$ = "TWO"
403   IF C = 3 THEN C$ = "THREE"
404   IF C = 4 THEN C$ = "FOUR"
405   IF C = 5 THEN C$ = "FIVE"
406   IF C = 6 THEN C$ = "SIX"
407   IF C = 7 THEN C$ = "SEVEN"
```

(Figure continued)

(Figure 8.2 continued)

```
408  IF C = 8 THEN C$ = "EIGHT"
409  IF C = 9 THEN C$ = "NINE"
410  IF C = 10 THEN C$ = "TEN"
411  IF C = 11 THEN C$ = "JACK"
412  IF C = 12 THEN C$ = "QUEEN"
413  IF C = 13 THEN C$ = "KING"
420  RETURN
Ok
```

RUN

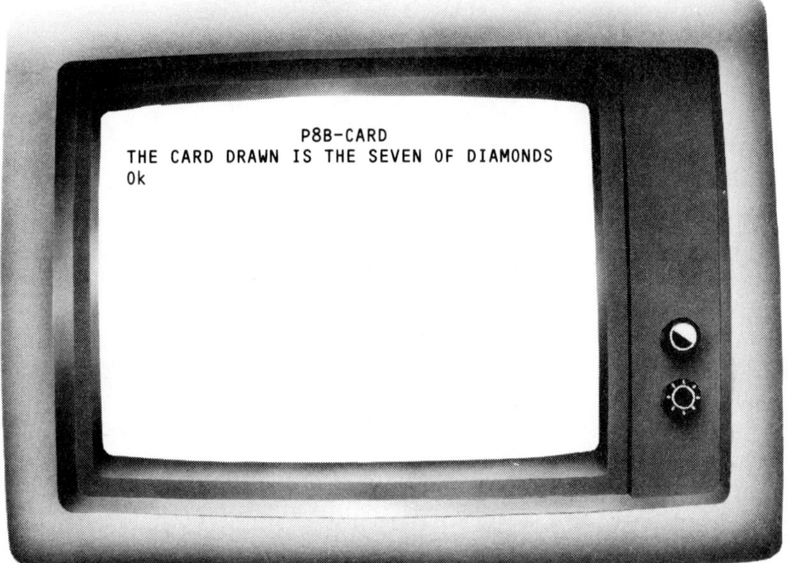

P8B-CARD
THE CARD DRAWN IS THE SEVEN OF DIAMONDS
Ok

RUN

P8B-CARD
THE CARD DRAWN IS THE NINE OF HEARTS
Ok

Multiplication Table

Program 8C is much like program 8A, but with a few twists. For one thing, it uses a nested loop to print the table. This means that we have put a loop inside a loop. Another difference is that unlike earlier programs, this one will not “fit” on a 40 column screen. We have added the WIDTH statement in line 101 to make sure the screen is set to 80 columns.

In the subroutine at line 400, we print the column headings for the table.

```
400  '  ===== SUBROUTINE TO PRINT COLUMN HEADINGS =====
410  FOR J = 1 TO N
420       LET P = L + W * (J - 1)
430       PRINT TAB(P);J;
440  NEXT J
450  PRINT
460  RETURN
499  '
```

The variable P is the position on the screen where the next character will be printed. In lines 120 and 130, L is set equal to 15, the column where the table starts (L for left side), and W is set equal to 5, the width of each column. In the loop in subroutine 400, each time through the loop, P is set to L plus the column number minus 1 (J − 1) times the width of each column (W). We use J − 1 because the first time through the loop, we want P to equal L + 0.

The subroutine at line 600 contains a typical nested loop used to print a table.

```
600  '  ===== SUBROUTINE TO PRINT ROW HEADING & ROW =====
610  FOR I = 1 TO N
620       PRINT TAB(6);I; TAB(11);"!";
630       FOR J = 1 TO N
640            LET P = L + W * (J - 1)
650            PRINT TAB(P); I * J;
660       NEXT J
670       PRINT
680  NEXT I
690  RETURN
699  '
```

Each time the inner loop (lines 640 to 650) executes, it prints one number (I * J). Each time the outer loop (lines 620 to 670) executes, it prints one row of the table. Notice that lines 640 and 650 print each row of the table in the same manner as lines 420 and 430 print the headings.

EXAMPLE 8C Multiplication Table

Problem Write a program that generates a multiplication table from 1 to 12 and prints the table with column and row headings. Allow five spaces for each column.

Solution

FIGURE 8.3

```
LIST
1     PN$ = "P8C-MULT"
2     NA$ = "YOUR NAME"
3     DA$ = "00/00/00"
10    '  ===== VARIABLES =====
11    '  I = LOOP COUNTER FOR ROWS
12    '  J = LOOP COUNTER FOR COLUMNS
13    '  L = FIRST TAB POSITION
14    '  N = # OF COLUMNS AND # OF ROWS
15    '  P = TAB POSITION
16    '  W = # OF SPACES IN EACH COLUMN
100   '  ===== MAIN PROGRAM =====
101   WIDTH 80 : CLS : PRINT TAB(40 - (LEN (PN$) / 2)) PN$
110   PRINT : PRINT
120   LET L = 15
130   LET W = 5
140   LET N = 12
150   GOSUB 400 : '  PRINT COLUMN HEADINGS
160   GOSUB 500 : '  PRINT DASHES
170   GOSUB 600 : '  PRINT TABLE
180   END
400   '  ===== SUBROUTINE TO PRINT COLUMN HEADINGS =====
410   FOR J = 1 TO N
420       LET P = L + W * (J - 1)
430       PRINT TAB(P);J;
440   NEXT J
450   PRINT
460   RETURN
499   '
500   '  ===== SUBROUTINE TO PRINT DASHES =====
510   PRINT TAB(11);
520   FOR I = 11 TO 75
530       PRINT "-";
540   NEXT I
550   PRINT
560   RETURN
599   '
```

(Figure continued)

(Figure 8.3 continued)

```
600  ' ===== SUBROUTINE TO PRINT ROW HEADING & ROW =====
610  FOR I = 1 TO N
620      PRINT TAB(6);I; TAB(11);"!";
630      FOR J = 1 TO N
640          LET P = L + W * (J - 1)
650          PRINT TAB(P); I * J;
660      NEXT J
670      PRINT
680  NEXT I
690  RETURN
699  '
Ok
```

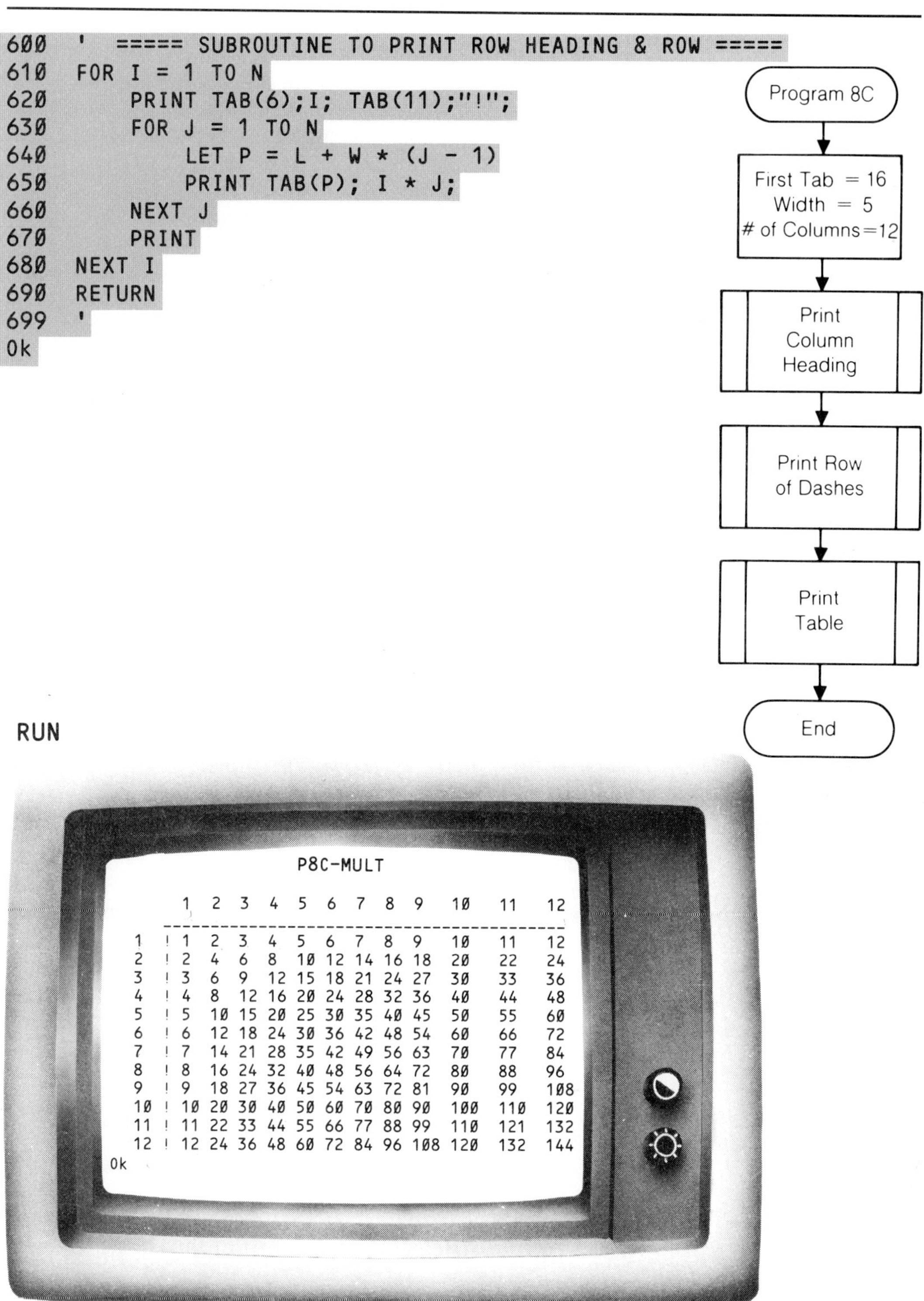

RUN

```
                     P8C-MULT

         1  2  3  4  5  6  7  8  9   10   11   12
     ---------------------------------------------
 1   ! 1  2  3  4  5  6  7  8  9   10   11   12
 2   ! 2  4  6  8  10 12 14 16 18  20   22   24
 3   ! 3  6  9  12 15 18 21 24 27  30   33   36
 4   ! 4  8  12 16 20 24 28 32 36  40   44   48
 5   ! 5  10 15 20 25 30 35 40 45  50   55   60
 6   ! 6  12 18 24 30 36 42 48 54  60   66   72
 7   ! 7  14 21 28 35 42 49 56 63  70   77   84
 8   ! 8  16 24 32 40 48 56 64 72  80   88   96
 9   ! 9  18 27 36 45 54 63 72 81  90   99   108
 10  ! 10 20 30 40 50 60 70 80 90  100  110  120
 11  ! 11 22 33 44 55 66 77 88 99  110  121  132
 12  ! 12 24 36 48 60 72 84 96 108 120  132  144
Ok
```

NAME SWAP

Program 8D in figure 8.4 demonstrates the use of the string functions, which allow us to do almost anything we can think of with string variables. In this program we use them to reverse a group of names and add a comma in the middle of each name. Line 120 READs a single name from the DATA section. If it is "9999," it means the program is done and we end. If not, the program continues.

How Long? In line 140 we use the LEN function to set L to the number of characters in NM$.

```
140  LET L = LEN(NM$) : '  L IS LENGTH OF NAME
```

We have used this function many times before; for example, in line 101 it is used to help center the title of each program. Here we want to know how many characters are in NM$ because some of the subroutines need to know the length of the string they're dealing with.

Finding the Space Once we know the length of the name, we call the subroutine at line 400 to split the name into two parts. Since we want to split the name at the space between the first and last name, line 410 calls the subroutine at line 500 to find the space.

```
500  '  ===== SUBROUTINE TO FIND SPACE =====
510  FOR I = 1 TO L
520       IF MID$ (NM$, I, 1) = " " THEN RETURN
530  NEXT I
540  PRINT "NO SPACE IN THIS NAME" : STOP
550  '
```

The loop in lines 510 to 530 uses the MID$ function to find the space. The MID$ function in line 520 uses the three pieces of information in the parentheses (called "arguments"): the first, in this case NM$, is the string referred to; the second, in this case I, is the position of the beginning character; and the third, in this case 1, is the number of characters referred to. So each time through the loop this line checks to see if the Ith character of NM$ is a space. When the space is found, I must be the position of the space in NM$. For example, if NM$ is JANE SANCHEZ, the first time through the loop, I will be 1 and MID$ (NM$, I, 1) will be "J." When I is 5 (the fifth time through the loop), MID$ (NM$, I, 1) will be a space and the program will RETURN and continue with line 420. If the name has no space, the program falls through to line 540, prints the error message, and stops.

We should mention that the second and third arguments (items in the parentheses) of the MID$ function can be either numbers or variables and can have any value up to 255. Instead of looking for a single character, as we do here, it is also possible to search for a string of characters in a larger string.

Left and Right If the FIND SPACE subroutine has been successful, line 420 uses the LEFT$ function to set LF$ to I − 1 characters from the left side of NM$.

```
420  LET LF$ = LEFT$ (NM$, I - 1) : '  FIRST NAME
430  LET RT$ = RIGHT$ (NM$, L - I) : '  LAST NAME
```

To use our example of JANE JONES, since I is 5, LF$ will be the left four (5 – 1) characters of NM$, or "JANE."

In line 430 we do something similar using the RIGHT$ function. Earlier we used the LEN function to set L to the length of NM$. For the name JANE SANCHEZ, L is 12 (the space counts). So, RT$ is set to 7 characters from the right side of NM$, or "SANCHEZ." Notice that with LEFT$ and RIGHT$, we have captured the first and last name (but not the space) in separate variables. When this has been accomplished, the program returns to the main section.

Left $(Var, Char)
Right $ (Var, char)
Mid $ (Var, Start Char, no. of char.)

LEFT$, RIGHT$, and MID$ These functions allow the programmer to alter, manipulate, and create strings from parts of other strings.

The string function **LEFT$** has the general form:

LEFT$(*string variable name, n*)

This expression refers to the leftmost *n* characters of the variable named.

```
10 LET C$ = "PETER PAN"
20 LET L$ = LEFT$ (C$, 7)
```

sets L$ to "PETER P"

The **RIGHT$** function is exactly like the LEFT$ function, except that it refers to the rightmost *n* characters of the variable named.

```
10 LET C$ = "PETER PAN"
20 LET R$ = RIGHT$ (C$, 7)
```

sets R$ to "TER PAN"

The **MID$** function is similar to the LEFT$ and RIGHT$ functions but has three arguments in the parentheses: the first is the name of the string variable referred to, the second is the starting position of the substring, and the third is the number of characters in the substring.

```
10 LET C$ = "PETER PAN"
20 LET M$ = MID$ (C$, 5, 3)
```

sets M$ to "R P"

MID$ may also be used on the left side of the equal sign to change the value of part of a string. In this case the first variable following MID$ is the name of the string variable to be changed, and the second is the position of the character in that string where the changing is to start. The following example shows how MID$ can be used to change the value of part of a string:

```
10  C$ = "MY FEET ARE HURTING ME"
20  MID$(C$,13) = "KILL"
30  PRINT C$

RUN
MY FEET ARE KILLING ME
```

LEN The string function LEN has the general form:

```
LEN (string variable name)
```

This function gives the number of characters in the string variable named.

Example:

```
10 LET C$ = "PETER PAN"
20 LET N = LEN(C$)
```

The above instruction sets N to 9.

Wrapping Things Up Back in the MAIN PROGRAM, line 160 uses the + function to put the name back together in reverse order and add the comma (and put the space back in). Putting strings together this way is called "concatenation."

```
160  LET NM$ = RT$ + ", " + LF$
```

Since we want to print only this reversed version of the name, we use NM$ here. If, for some reason, we wanted to preserve the unreversed version, we could use some other variable here (like EMAN$). Once the name has been printed, the program loops back to line 120 to READ another name. This process continues until all the names have been read. When NM$ is "9999," the program ends.

EXAMPLE 8D Name Swap

Problem Write a program that takes people's names from a series of DATA statements, turns them around, inserts a comma, and prints them as a list. For example:

```
301  DATA "MIKE BOSSARD"
302  DATA "ESTHER PETERSON"
303  DATA "JESSICA RAYGOR"
```

would be printed out as follows:

```
BOSSARD, MIKE
PETERSON, ESTHER
RAYGOR, JESSICA
```

Solution

FIGURE 8.4

```
LIST
1     PN$ = "P8D-NAME"
2     NA$ = "YOUR NAME"
3     DA$ = "00/00/00"
10    '  ===== VARIABLES =====
11    '  I = LOOP COUNTER
12    '  L = LENGTH OF NAME
13    '  NM$ = FULL NAME
14    '  LF$ = FIRST NAME
15    '  RT$ = LAST NAME
100   '  ===== MAIN PROGRAM =====
101   CLS : PRINT TAB(40 - (LEN (PN$) / 2)) PN$
110   PRINT : PRINT
120   READ NM$
130   IF NM$ = "9999" THEN END
140   LET L = LEN(NM$) : '  L IS LENGTH OF NAME
150   GOSUB 400 : '  SPLIT NAME
160   LET NM$ = RT$ + ", " + LF$
170   PRINT NM$
180   GOTO 120
190   '  END OF MAIN PROGRAM
195   '
300   '  ===== DATA SECTION =====
301   DATA  "LON CHANEY"
302   DATA  "PETER CUSHING"
303   DATA  "BORIS KARLOFF"
304   DATA  "CHRISTOPHER LEE"
305   DATA  "PETER LORRE"
306   DATA  "BELA LUGOSI"
307   DATA  "9999"
390   '
400   '  ===== SUBROUTINE TO SPLIT NAMES =====
410   GOSUB 500 : '  FIND SPACE (I IS LOCATION OF SPACE)
420   LET LF$ = LEFT$ (NM$, I - 1) : '  FIRST NAME
430   LET RT$ = RIGHT$ (NM$, L - I) :'  LAST NAME
440   RETURN
450   '
500   '  ===== SUBROUTINE TO FIND SPACE =====
510   FOR I = 1 TO L
520       IF MID$ (NM$, I, 1) = " " THEN RETURN
530   NEXT I
540   PRINT "NO SPACE IN THIS NAME" : STOP
550   '
Ok
```

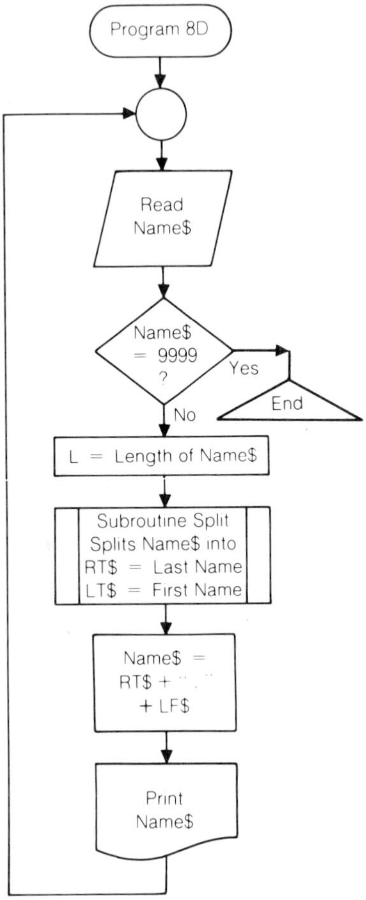

Program 8D
Read Name$
Name$ = 9999 ?
Yes
End
No
L = Length of Name$
Subroutine Split
Splits Name$ into
RT$ = Last Name
LT$ = First Name
Name$ = RT$ + ", " + LF$
Print Name$

(Figure continued)

(Figure 8.4 continued)

RUN

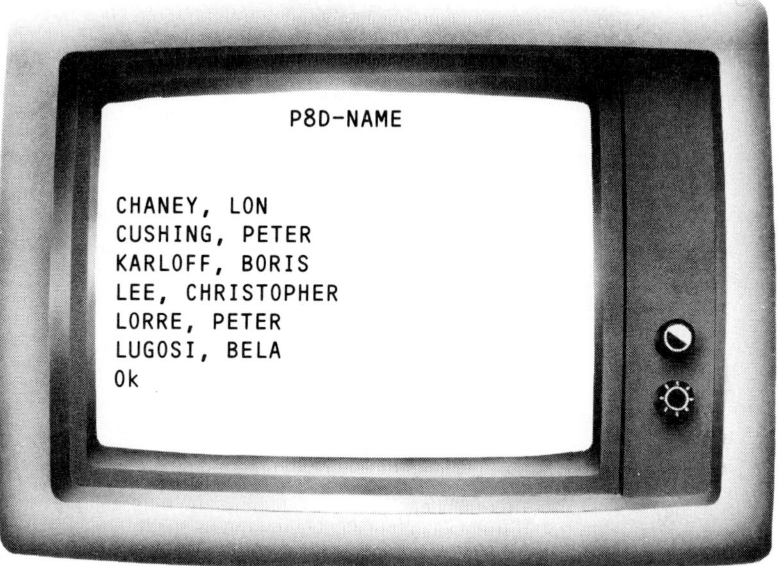

P8D-NAME
CHANEY, LON
CUSHING, PETER
KARLOFF, BORIS
LEE, CHRISTOPHER
LORRE, PETER
LUGOSI, BELA
Ok

SELF-TESTING QUESTIONS

8.1 List the set of possible numbers produced by each of the following functions:

```
a) INT (4 *  RND (1))
b) INT (4 *  RND (1)) + 1
c) INT (4 *  RND (1)) + 11
d) INT (13 *  RND (1)) + 1
e) INT (6 *  RND (1)) + 1
```

Step through the program in each question and write the output produced when the program runs.

8.2

```
110  LET C$ = "*"
120  LET N = 6
130  FOR I = N TO 11
140     PRINT TAB(N);C$
150  NEXT I
160  END
```

8.3

```
110  LET C$ = "*"
120  LET N = 6
130  FOR I = 13 TO 18
140     PRINT TAB(I);C$;
150  NEXT I
```

8.4

```
110  LET C$ = "*"
120  LET N = 6
130  FOR I = N TO 11
140     PRINT TAB(I);C$
150  NEXT I
```

8.5

```
110  LET C$ =  "*"
120  LET N = 6
130  FOR I = 1 TO N
140     PRINT TAB(3 * I);C$;
150  NEXT I
```

8.6

```
110  LET C$ = "*"
120  LET N = 6
130  FOR I = Ø TO 5
140     PRINT TAB(N - I);C$
150  NEXT I
```

8.7

```
100 LET S$ = "ALL PUMA RINGS TO GO"
110 LET L = LEN (S$)
120 LET L$ = MID$ (S$,14,1) + MID$ (S$,16,1)
130 LET L$ = L$ + MID$ (S$,10,4)
140 LET R$ = MID$ (S$,7,2) + MID$ (S$,12,1)
150 LET R$ = R$ + MID$ (S$,11,1) + MID$ (S$,5,2)
160 LET R$ = R$ + "L" + LEFT$ (S$,1) + MID$ (S$,L-4,1)
170 LET R$ = R$ + MID$ (S$,11,1) + RIGHT$ (S$,1)
180 LET R$ = R$ + MID$ (S$,12,1)
190 LET FINAL$ = L$ + " " + R$
200 PRINT FINAL$
```

EXERCISES

Choose One of the Following

8.1 Write a program that will produce the following table of X, X ^ 2, X ^ 3, and X ^ 0.5 for the values of X from 1 to 10. Use the TAB function to produce a table with four columns. Round the numbers to the nearest thousandth.

```
X           X^2         X^3         X^Ø.5
------------------------------------------
1           1           1           1
2           4           8           1.414
3           9           27          1.732
.           .           .           .
.           .           .           .
1Ø          1ØØ         1ØØØ        3.162
```

TIPS

1. **Use a single loop.**
2. **Use X as the counter for the loop (FOR X = 1 TO 10).**
3. **Print the four values inside the loop.**

8.2 In an earlier problem, an airline was preparing a booklet that included an altitude conversion table. The booklet was popular with U.S. passengers, but foreign passengers wanted the altitude in meters. Some passengers also asked about the outside air pressure. Write a program that will produce a four-column table as shown below. Use TAB statements to format the table. Round miles and pressure to the nearest hundredth. Round meters to the nearest integer. The relative air pressure is approximated by the following equation:

```
P = Ø.ØØØ2984 * (F/1ØØØ)^2 - Ø.Ø3262 * (F/1ØØØ) + 1
```

where: P = relative air pressure in atmospheres (sea level pressure is one atmosphere)
F = altitude in feet
The conversion to meters is: METERS = FEET/3.281
The conversion to miles is: MILES = FEET/5280

```
ALTITUDE ALTITUDE  ALTITUDE  RELATIVE
IN FEET  IN MILES  IN METERS PRESSURE
--------------------------------------
       Ø     Ø.ØØ          Ø     1.ØØ
   1,ØØØ     Ø.19        3Ø5     Ø.97
       .        .          .        .
       .        .          .        .
  5Ø,ØØØ     9.47     15,239     Ø.11
```

TIPS

1. **Use a single loop.**
2. **Use FEET to stand for altitude in feet and to serve as the loop counter, e.g., (FOR FEET = 0 TO 50000! STEP 1000).**
3. **Use METERS for altitude in meters, MILES for altitude in miles, and PRESSURE for relative pressure.**
4. **Print the four values inside the loop.**
5. **Use PRINT USING and TAB to print the table as follows:**

```
19Ø  PRINT USING "##,###" ; FEET;
2ØØ  PRINT TAB(11);: PRINT USING"##.##"; MILES;
21Ø  PRINT TAB(21);: PRINT USING ....
22Ø  PRINT TAB(31);: PRINT USING ....
```

8.3 A $45,000 home mortgage has a principal-plus-interest payment of $650 per month. The interest rate is 15 percent per year (1.25 percent per month). Write a program that will produce the following four-column table for the first five years. Use TAB statements to format the table. Round the numbers to the nearest cent.

```
YEAR-MONTH INTEREST PRINCIPAL BALANCE
-------------------------------------

 1 - 1      562.50     87.50     44,912.50
 1 - 2      561.41     88.59     44,823.91
 .            .          .          .
 .            .          .          .
 5 - 12       .          .          .
```

TIPS

1. **Use nested loops with MONTH as the counter for the inner loop and YEAR as the counter for the outer loop.**
2. **Inside the inner loop, try to do what the bank does—calculate the interest, calculate the principal, get the new balance, and print the four values.**
3. **Use PRINT USING and TAB to print the table as follows:**

```
220  PRINT Y" - "M; TAB(12);: PRINT USING"###.##";I;
230  PRINT TAB(21);: PRINT USING"###.##";P;
240  PRINT TAB(31);: PRINT USING ....
```

8.4 Write a program that will produce the following table based on tossing three dice ten times. Use TAB statements to format the table. Use the RANDOMIZE statement to reseed the random number generator.

```
DIE #1     DIE #2     DIE #3     TOTAL
------------------------------------
4          1          3          8
1          6          5          12
.          .          .          .
.          .          .          .
4          2          6          12
```

TIPS

1. **Use the subroutine from example 8B for picking a random number.**
2. **Use D1, D2, and D3 as the variables for the three dice.**
3. **Use a single loop to print the values and totals, e.g., (FOR I = 1 TO 10).**

8.5 Write a program that will produce the table below based on randomly drawing three cards. Use TAB statements to format the table. Use the subroutines from program 8B to pick and recognize the cards. Use IF statements to make sure that cards two and three have not been picked before. Use the RANDOMIZE statement to reseed the random number generator.

```
CARD #      ONE         TWO         THREE
-----------------------------------------
            QUEEN       SEVEN       FOUR
            OF          OF          OF
            SPADES      DIAMONDS    HEARTS
```

TIPS

1. **Use S1$, S2$, S3$, as the variables for the suit names.**
2. **Use C1$, C2$, C3$, as the variables for the card names.**
3. **Set all the variables before you try to print the table.**
4. **Don't use a loop to print the table; do it as five separate lines.**

8.6 You are having a dinner party and would like place cards for each guest. Write a program that will take names from DATA statements like the following:

```
301  DATA  "JOHNSON, SUE"
302  DATA  "GREEN, BILL"
```

and produce place cards like the one below:

```
*******************************************************
*                                                     *
*                                                     *
*                                                     *
*                                                     *
*                                                     *
*                                                     *
*                                                     *
*******************************************************
*                                                     *
*                                                     *
*                                                     *
*                     SUE JOHNSON                     *
*                                                     *
*                                                     *
*                                                     *
*******************************************************
```

The name should be first name first, and should be centered on the card. The card should be at least 50 columns wide. Use TAB statements to position the right-hand set of stars and the name.

TIPS

1. **Write a separate subroutine to find the comma.**
2. **Use another subroutine to remove the comma. Then swap the two names as in example 8D.**
3. **Use a subroutine to print the card.**
4. **In the main program, call the subroutine to remove the comma, then the subroutine to split the name, and then the subroutine to print the card.**

8.7 Same as 8.6, except that the names have middle initials.

```
301  DATA  "JOHNSON, SUE L."
```

This should be printed on the card as SUE JOHNSON.

TIPS

1. **See the tips for exercise 8.6.**
2. **Remember, you will have to find both spaces.**
3. **This is a very difficult program.**

8.8 Same as 8.7, except that only *some* of the names should have middle initials. The program will have to detect the presence or absence of the middle initial and act accordingly.

TIPS

1. **Write a subroutine that detects the middle initial by using the MID$ function to look for two separate spaces.**
2. **Use different loop counters for each loop to avoid side effects.**
3. **This is an extremely difficult program.**

CHAPTER 9

KEEPING TRACK

Using Subscripts and Sorting

NEW CONCEPTS TAUGHT

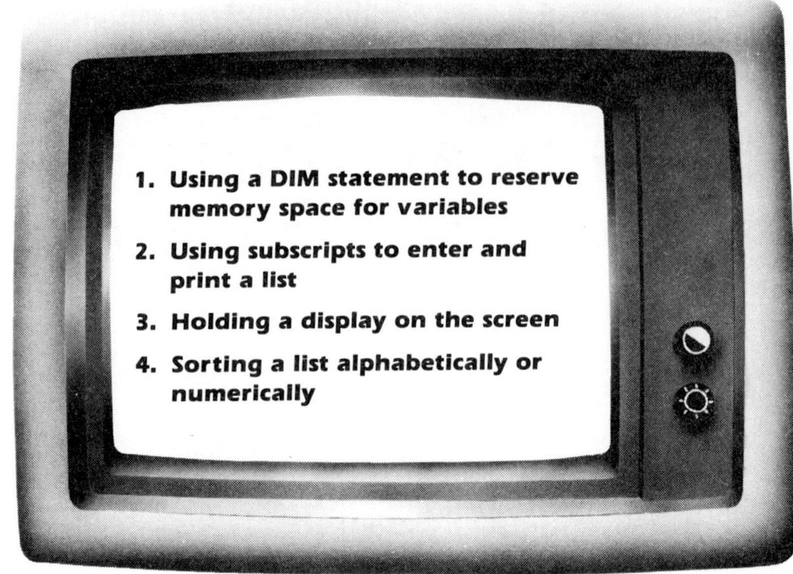

1. Using a DIM statement to reserve memory space for variables
2. Using subscripts to enter and print a list
3. Holding a display on the screen
4. Sorting a list alphabetically or numerically

NOTE ON THE PROGRAM

The line numbers for program 9A in figure 9.1 may look a little strange to you. We used the line numbers we did so that the subroutines of this program would be compatible with the example and exercises in chapter 10. We suggest that you use these same line numbers in writing your program or programs for this chapter. That way some of your subroutines may fit easily into the program you will write for chapter 10.

Store lists in arrays or matrix

let [Cards $(1)] = "one"
subscripted variable

FOR I = 1 to 13
READ CD$
LET CARD $(I) = CD$
NEXT I
DATA "one," "two," etc.
do you need paras

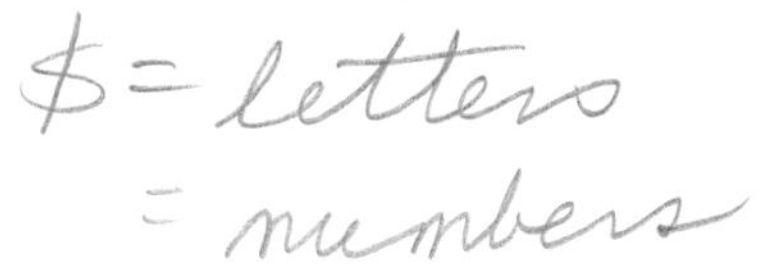

SUBSCRIPTS

Subscripts are reference numbers we can give to numeric or string variables that let us use a single variable name to store a list of names or numbers. For example, in this program, when we specify the bowlers' names, instead of the variable NM$ we use NM$(N), where N is some number. This way we can have NM$(1), NM$(2), NM$(3), and so on. In fact we can have as many as we have room for in memory.

Using NM$, the representation in memory might be thought of as looking like this:

NM$ | FRED |

With subscripts, it might be thought of as looking like this:

NM$(1) | SUE |

NM$(2) | JOE |

NM$(3) | ALICE |

If we put the subscripted variable inside a loop and use the loop counter inside the parentheses, we can create a very useful list of variables.

Example:

```
10 FOR I = 1 TO 10
20     LET T(I) = I
30 NEXT I
```

This way, T(1) would be 1, T(2) would be 2, and so on up to 10. Subscripts are also very handy for entering, sorting, and printing data. A list of subscripted variables is called an array and is used very often in programming.

You might think about how some of the earlier programs in this book could be written using subscripted variables. For example, the temperature conversion and miles per gallon programs could have allowed the user to enter input values as an array of subscripted variables and then looped through them to print the results.

Subscripted Variables The subscripted variable makes it more convenient for us to use a group of memory cells to store a list or table of names or numbers. By using a subscripted variable, we give the same name to every memory cell in the group and use the subscript value to distinguish between the memory cells in the group. This is a distinct advantage, because it is much easier to change the subscript value in a program than it is to change a variable name. A list of subscripted variables is called an array.

A subscripted variable name consists of a variable name followed by a subscript enclosed in parentheses. The subscript may be a number, a variable name, or an arithmetic expression.

Examples:

```
A(1)
B$(2)
C2(I)
SUM(J + 2 * I)
F3$(3 * I)
```

The DIM Statement

When using a subscripted variable, we need to tell the computer how much memory to set aside for the variable list. This is done with a DIM statement. The DIM statement reserves memory space that cannot be used for anything but the specified list of variables.

If you will never have a subscript over 10 in the list, the DIM statement is not necessary since the computer automatically dimensions to 10 when it sees a subscripted variable for the first time. When you do use a DIM statement, it must come before any appearance of the subscripted variable in the program, otherwise a "Duplicate Definition" error will occur. Having the program execute a DIM statement more than once will also cause this error, so be careful not to put a DIM statement inside a loop.

In program 9A in figure 9.1, we ask how many names will be entered in line 2020 and then dimension the variables for name and score in line 2030. This way the program does not reserve any more memory space for the variables than is necessary.

```
2020  INPUT "HOW MANY NAMES: ",N
2030  DIM NM$(N), SC(N)
```

Entering Data

In lines 2040 through 2080, we see subscripts used to enter the list of names and scores. The first time through the loop, I is 1, so we are entering NM$(1) and SC(1). Each time through the loop, we enter a new name and score without losing the previous names and scores. When we're finished with the loop, we have the list of names and scores in memory and can do what we want with them.

```
2040  FOR I = 1 TO N
2050      PRINT
2060      PRINT I;: LINE INPUT "  ENTER NAME: ",NM$(I)
2070      INPUT "             SCORE: ",SC(I)
2080  NEXT I
```

LINE INPUT The LINE INPUT statement is used to read an entire line into a string variable, including delimiters such as the comma. For example, if we wanted to assign the string "Jones, John" to the variable NM$, we could use the following LINE INPUT statement:

```
60  LINE INPUT "ENTER NAME:", NM$
```

When the prompt ENTER NAME appears on the screen, we would simply type: JONES, JOHN and press the Enter key. The name JONES, JOHN would be stored in the variable NM$, comma and all.

The INPUT statement can also be used to enter a string including delimiters by enclosing the string in quotation marks. For example, we could use the following INPUT statement:

```
60 INPUT "ENTER NAME:", NM$
```

When the prompt ENTER NAME appears on the screen, we would type: "JONES, JOHN" and press the Enter key. The name JONES, JOHN would be stored in the variable NM$, comma and all.

The LINE INPUT statement eliminates the necessity of enclosing the name JONES, JOHN in quotes. However, the LINE INPUT statement can also be used to include the quotation marks as part of the string. For example, we could use the following INPUT statement to enter a quotation:

```
220 LINE INPUT "ENTER QUOTE:", Q$
```

When the prompt ENTER QUOTE appears on the screen, we could type: "MARY HAD A LITTLE LAMB." and press the Enter key. The entire line, including the quotes and the period, would be stored in the variable Q$.

Printing a Table

One thing we want to do with the list of names and scores is to print a table. In the loop in lines 5670 to 5690, we simply print the names and scores in two columns. Notice that the score for each bowler will be printed on the same line as his or her name.

```
5600  '  === SUBROUTINE TO PRINT TABLE ===
5610  LN$ = "----------------------"
5620  CLS
5630  PRINT "BOWLING TEAM SCORES" : PRINT MESSAGE$
5640  PRINT LN$
5650  PRINT "NAME","SCORE"
5660  PRINT LN$
5670  FOR I = 1 TO N
5680      PRINT NM$(I),SC(I)
5690  NEXT I
5700  PRINT LN$
5710  GOSUB 6200: '  HOLD SCREEN
5720  RETURN
```

If you look at the main section of the program following line 100, you will see that we use the subroutine to print the table three times. First we print the names in the order they were entered; next we sort by name and print a table that is sorted alphabetically; finally we sort by score and print a table with the bowlers listed in rank order, the best bowlers on top. The use of well-designed subroutines, like this one, by several parts of a program is sometimes called "modular" or "structured" programming. We will talk more about this in chapter 10. For now, you might think about how much easier (and more understandable) it is to write the program in this way than to have three separate parts of the program to print the three tables.

```
100  '  ===== MAIN PROGRAM =====
110  GOSUB 2000: ' GET NAMES AND SCORES
120  MESSAGE$ = "UNSORTED"
130  GOSUB 5600: '  PRINT TABLE
140  GOSUB 2200: '  SORT BY NAME
150  MESSAGE$ = "SORTED BY NAME"
160  GOSUB 5600: '  PRINT TABLE
170  GOSUB 2600: '  SORT BY SCORE
180  MESSAGE$ = "SORTED BY SCORE"
190  GOSUB 5600: '  PRINT TABLE
199  END
```

Hold Screen

If we did not have this subroutine, the tables would flash on the screen too quickly to be read. The way we have done it here, as soon as the table is printed on the screen, the program jumps (in line 5710) to the subroutine at line 6200, which does nothing more than position the cursor at line 21, column 1, and print the message "PRESS ENTER TO CONTINUE" and wait for an input. Since the program will not continue until the user types ⟨Enter⟩, this effectively "freezes" the table on the screen until the user is ready to have the program continue.

```
6200  '  ======== HOLD SCREEN ========
6210  LOCATE 21,1
6220  INPUT "PRESS ENTER TO CONTINUE",C$
6230  RETURN
```

Sorting Alphabetically

Sorting is a very common computer procedure. It is something computers do very quickly and accurately compared to humans (the computer also enjoys it more). There are many ways to sort; the sorting technique we are using here (we call it the "simple sort") is a very slow one. We have chosen it because it is easy to understand. Since we don't have a lot of items to sort, speed is not that important.

```
2200  '  === SUBROUTINE TO SORT BY NAME ===
2205  IF N < = 1 THEN RETURN : '  NO SORTING NEEDED
2210  FOR I = 1 TO N - 1
2220      FOR J = (I + 1) TO N
2230          IF NM$(I) > NM$(J) THEN  GOSUB 2800: '  SWAP
2240      NEXT J
2250  NEXT I
2260  RETURN
```

The principle of this type of sort is really fairly simple. We have a nested loop in lines 2210 to 2250. The first time through the outer loop, I is 1. In the inner loop the first name, NM$(1), is compared to every other name in the list as J goes from 2 to N. The computer takes "⟨" and "⟩" to mean earlier and later in the alphabet when dealing with string variables. If the first name is later in the alphabet than the Jth name, the two are swapped (in the subroutine at line 2800). After the outer loop has executed once (and the inner loop N − 1 times), the earliest name (alphabetically) is at the head of the list as NM$(1). The second time through the outer loop, the second name is compared with all those that follow it and swapped if necessary so that at the end of this pass the second name, NM$(2) is the second lowest in the alphabet. This continues until the whole list is in alphabetical order.

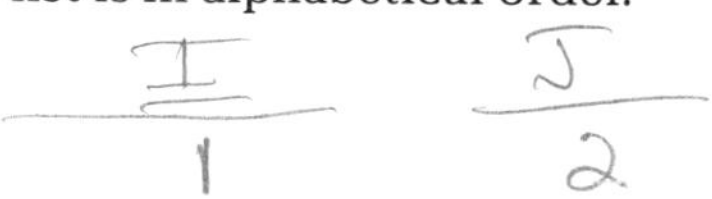

Notice that when the names are swapped in the subroutine at line 2800, the score is carried along with the name so that, no matter how many swaps occur, each bowler still has his or her own score. For example, the number stored in SC(5) will always be the correct score for the bowler whose name is stored in NM$(5).

```
2800  '  === SUBROUTINE TO SWAP NAMES AND SCORES ===
2810  SWAP NM$(I),NM$(J)
2820  SWAP SC(I),SC(J)
2830  RETURN
```

An interesting exercise here is to put a counter, like LET SW = SW + 1, in the swap subroutine at line 2800 and see how many swaps actually occur with various numbers of names entered during the program. This is done by typing PRINT SW after the program ends. With a more efficient sorting routine, there would be fewer swaps.

Sorting by Number

Sorting by number is exactly the same as sorting alphabetically, except that the line that checks to see if the names and scores need to be swapped (line 2630) compares scores instead of names. We have also turned the comparison sign around (> has become <), since with the names we wanted the lowest (alphabetically) at the top of the list, while here we want the bowler with the highest score at the top.

```
2600  '  === SUBROUTINE TO SORT BY SCORE ===
2605  IF N < = 1 THEN RETURN : '  NO SORTING NEEDED
2610  FOR I = 1 TO N - 1
2620      FOR J = (I + 1) TO N
2630          IF SC(I) < SC(J) THEN  GOSUB 2800: '  SWAP
2640      NEXT J
2650  NEXT I
2660  RETURN
```

EXAMPLE 9A Bowling Team

Problem You are the manager of a bowling team. Write a program that prompts you to enter the bowlers' names and scores and prints three tables: first, with the names and scores in the order they were entered; second, sorted alphabetically by name; and third, sorted by score with the best bowlers at the top. Each table should have a heading identifying it as unsorted, sorted by name, or sorted by number and should stay on the screen until the user presses the Enter key. The program should produce tables like the one below:

```
BOWLING TEAM SCORES
SORTED BY NAME
--------------------
NAME           SCORE
--------------------
ADAMS          18Ø
  .             .
  .             .
SANCHEZ        19Ø
--------------------
```

Solution

FIGURE 9.1

```
LIST
1     PN$ = "P9A-BT"
2     NA$ = "YOUR NAME"
3     DA$ = "00/00/00"
10    '  ===== VARIABLES =====
11    '  C$ = DUMMY VARIABLE FOR INPUT
12    '  I = LOOP COUNTER
13    '  J = LOOP COUNTER
14    '  LN$ = ROW OF DASHES
15    '  MESSAGE$ = PART OF HEADER FOR TABLE
16    '  NM$(I) = LIST OF BOWLERS" NAMES
17    '  SC(I) = LIST OF BOWLERS" SCORES
100   '  ===== MAIN PROGRAM =====
110   GOSUB 2000: ' GET NAMES AND SCORES
120   MESSAGE$ = "UNSORTED"
130   GOSUB 5600: '  PRINT TABLE
140   GOSUB 2200: '  SORT BY NAME
150   MESSAGE$ = "SORTED BY NAME"
160   GOSUB 5600: '  PRINT TABLE
170   GOSUB 2600: '  SORT BY SCORE
180   MESSAGE$ = "SORTED BY SCORE"
190   GOSUB 5600: '  PRINT TABLE
199   END
2000   '  ==== SUBROUTINE TO ENTER NAMES AND SCORES ====
2010   CLS
2020   INPUT "HOW MANY NAMES: ",N
2030   DIM NM$(N), SC(N)
2040   FOR I = 1 TO N
2050       PRINT
2060       PRINT I;: LINE INPUT "  ENTER NAME: ",NM$(I)
2070       INPUT  "             SCORE: ",SC(I)
2080   NEXT I
2090   RETURN
2099   '
2200   '  === SUBROUTINE TO SORT BY NAME ===
2205   IF N < = 1 THEN RETURN : '  NO SORTING NEEDED
2210   FOR I = 1 TO N - 1
2220       FOR J = (I + 1) TO N
2230           IF NM$(I)  NM$(J) THEN  GOSUB 2800: '  SWAP
2240       NEXT J
2250   NEXT I
2260   RETURN
2270   '
```

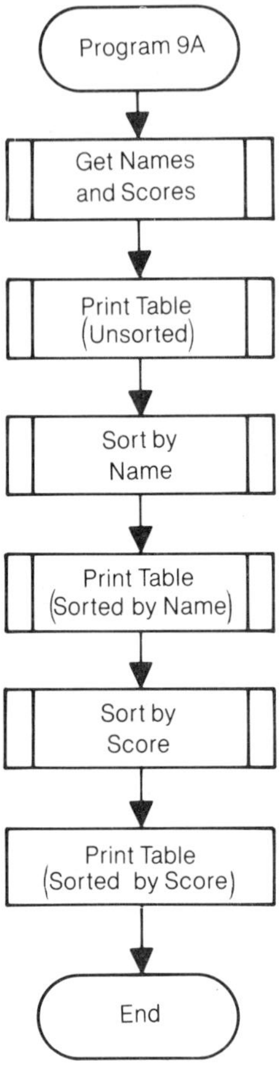

Program 9A

Get Names and Scores

Print Table (Unsorted)

Sort by Name

Print Table (Sorted by Name)

Sort by Score

Print Table (Sorted by Score)

End

(Figure continued)

(Figure 9.1 continued)

```
2600  ' === SUBROUTINE TO SORT BY SCORE ===
2605  IF N < = 1 THEN RETURN : '  NO SORTING NEEDED
2610  FOR I = 1 TO N - 1
2620      FOR J = (I + 1) TO N
2630          IF SC(I) < SC(J) THEN  GOSUB 2800: '  SWAP
2640      NEXT J
2650  NEXT I
2660  RETURN
2670  '
2800  ' === SUBROUTINE TO SWAP NAMES AND SCORES ===
2810  SWAP NM$(I),NM$(J)
2820  SWAP SC(I),SC(J)
2830  RETURN
2840  '
5600  ' === SUBROUTINE TO PRINT TABLE ===
5610  LN$ = "--------------------"
5620  CLS
5630  PRINT "BOWLING TEAM SCORES" : PRINT MESSAGE$
5640  PRINT LN$
5650  PRINT "NAME","SCORE"
5660  PRINT LN$
5670  FOR I = 1 TO N
5680      PRINT NM$(I),SC(I)
5690  NEXT I
5700  PRINT LN$
5710  GOSUB 6200: '  HOLD SCREEN
5720  RETURN
5730  '
6200  ' ======== HOLD SCREEN ========
6210  LOCATE 21,1
6220  INPUT "PRESS ENTER TO CONTINUE",C$
6230  RETURN
Ok
```

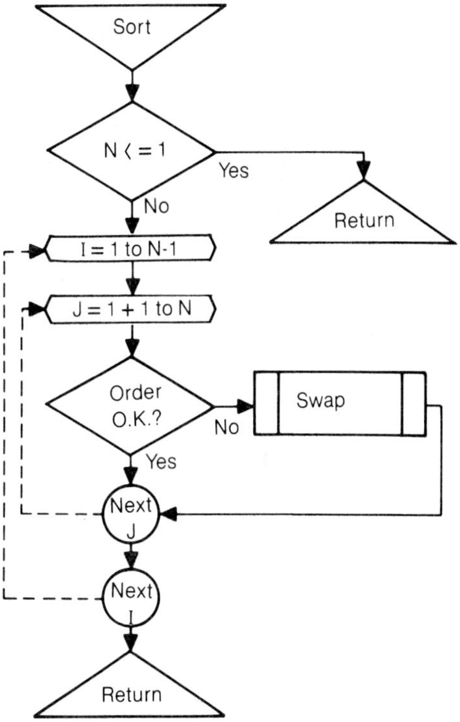

(Figure continued)

(Figure 9.1 continued)

RUN (Screen #1)

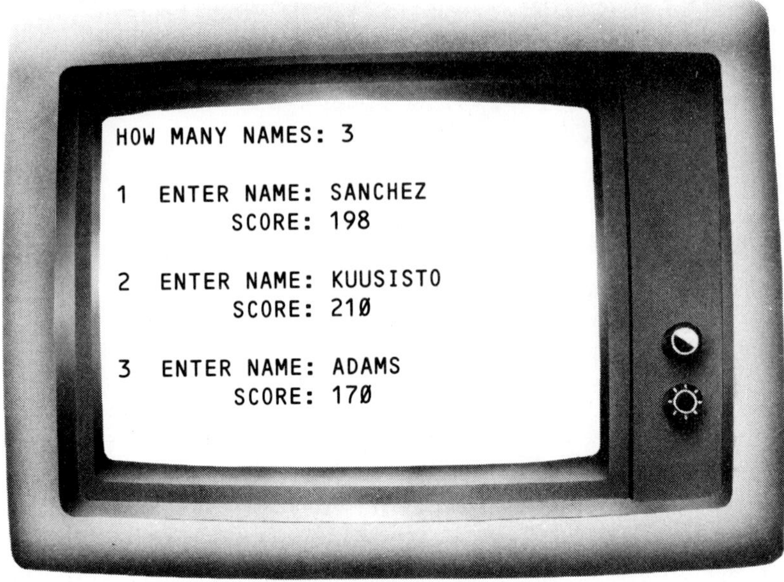

HOW MANY NAMES: 3
1 ENTER NAME: SANCHEZ
SCORE: 198
2 ENTER NAME: KUUSISTO
SCORE: 210
3 ENTER NAME: ADAMS
SCORE: 170

RUN (Screen #2)

BOWLING TEAM SCORES
UNSORTED

NAME SCORE

SANCHEZ 198
KUUSISTO 210
ADAMS 170

PRESS ENTER TO CONTINUE

(Figure continued)

(Figure 9.1 continued)

RUN (Screen #3)

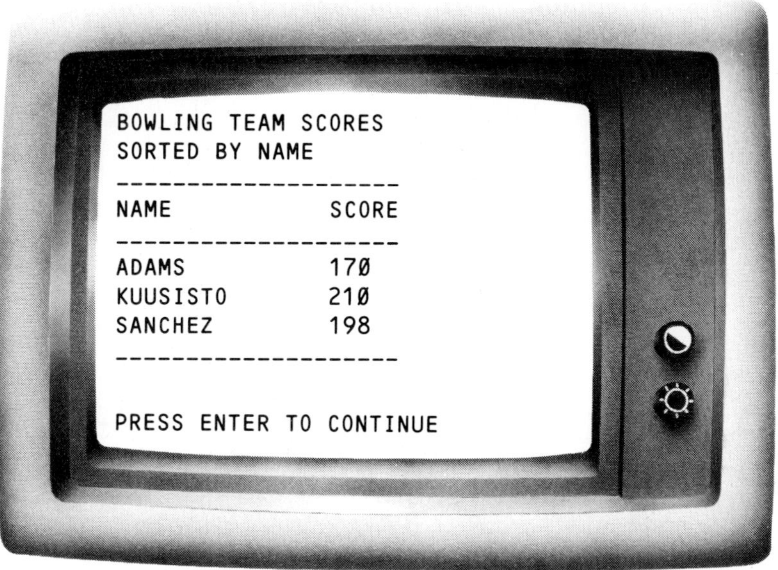

BOWLING TEAM SCORES
SORTED BY NAME

NAME SCORE

ADAMS 170
KUUSISTO 210
SANCHEZ 198

PRESS ENTER TO CONTINUE

RUN (Screen #4)

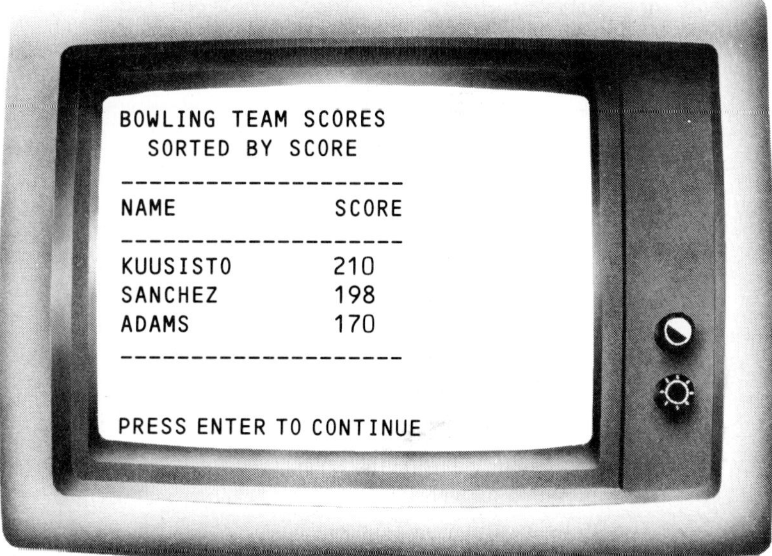

BOWLING TEAM SCORES
SORTED BY SCORE

NAME SCORE

KUUSISTO 210
SANCHEZ 198
ADAMS 170

PRESS ENTER TO CONTINUE

SELF-TESTING QUESTIONS

Step through the program in each question and write the output produced when the program runs.

9.1
```
110  FOR I = 1 TO 5
120     READ A(I)
130  NEXT I
140  DATA 8,7,5,4,3
150  FOR I = 1 TO 5
160     PRINT A(I);" ";
170  NEXT I
```

9.2
```
110  FOR I = 1 TO 5
120     READ A(I)
130  NEXT I
140  DATA 7,2,4,8,3
150  FOR I = 5 TO 1 STEP -1
160     PRINT A(I);" ";
170  NEXT I
```

9.3 Lines 110 to 140 apply to (a) and (b).

```
110  FOR I = 1 to 4
120     READ N$(I), S(I)
130  NEXT I
140  DATA JANE,80, DAVE,82, CAROL,90, FRANK,88
```

(a)
```
150  FOR I = 1 TO 4
160     PRINT N$(I);TAB(10);S(I)
170  NEXT I
```

(b)
```
150  FOR I = 1 TO 4
160     PRINT N$(I);TAB(8 * I);
170  NEXT I
180  PRINT
190  FOR I = 1 TO 4
200     PRINT S(I);TAB(8 * I);
210  NEXT I
```

9.4 Lines 110 through 180 apply to (a) through (e).

```
110  FOR I = 1 TO 3
120     FOR J = 1 TO 3
130        READ A(I,J)
140     NEXT J
150  NEXT I
160  DATA 8, 14, 15
170  DATA 21, 3, 7
180  DATA 19, 2, 9
```

(a)
```
190  FOR I = 1 TO 3
200     FOR J = 1 TO 3
210        PRINT A(I,J);" ";
220     NEXT J
230     PRINT
240  NEXT I
```

(b)
```
190  FOR J = 1 TO 3
200     FOR I = 1 TO 3
210        PRINT A(I,J);" ";
220     NEXT I
230     PRINT
240  NEXT J
```

(c)
```
190  FOR I = 1 TO 3
200     PRINT A(I,I);" ";
210  NEXT I
```

(d)
```
190  FOR I = 1 TO 3
200     FOR J = 1 TO 3
210        PRINT A(J,I);" ";
220     NEXT J
230     PRINT
240  NEXT I
```

(e)
```
190  FOR I = 3 TO 1 STEP -1
200     FOR J = 3 TO 1 STEP -1
210        PRINT A(I,J);" ";
220     NEXT J
230     PRINT
240  NEXT I
```

9.5 Lines 110 through 190 apply to (a) through (e).

```
110  FOR I = 1 TO 3
120     READ N$(I)
130     FOR J = 1 TO 3
140        READ S(I,J)
150     NEXT J
160  NEXT I
170  DATA TERRY, 82, 78, 90
180  DATA CARL, 88, 80, 85
190  DATA JUNE, 86, 90, 84
```

(a)
```
200  FOR I = 1 TO 3
210     PRINT N$(I);
220     FOR J = 1 TO 3
230        PRINT TAB(8 * J); S(I,J);
240     NEXT J
250     PRINT
260  NEXT I
```

(b)
```
200  FOR I = 1 TO 3
210     PRINT N$(I);TAB(8 * I);
220  NEXT I
230  PRINT
240  FOR J = 1 TO 3
250     FOR I = 1 TO 3
260        PRINT S(I,J);TAB(8 * I);
270     NEXT I
280     PRINT
290  NEXT J
```

(c)
```
200  FOR I = 1 TO 3
210     PRINT N$(I);TAB(10);S(I,3)
220  NEXT I
```

(d)
```
200  FOR I = 1 TO 3
210     LET T(I) = 0
220     FOR J = 1 TO 3
230        LET T(I) = T(I) + S(I,J)
240     NEXT J
250     PRINT N$(I);TAB(10);T(I)
260  NEXT I
```

(e)
```
200  FOR I = 1 TO 3
210     LET T(I) = 0
220     FOR J = 1 TO 3
230        LET T(I) = T(I) + S(I,J)
240     NEXT J
250     LET A(I) = INT (T(I) / 3 + .5)
260     PRINT N$(I); TAB(10);A(I)
270  NEXT I
```

9.6 Lines 110 through 160 apply to (a) and (b).

```
110  FOR I = 1 TO 3
120     READ N$(I), S(I)
130  NEXT I
140  DATA TERRY, 78
150  DATA CARL, 64
160  DATA JUNE, 76
```

(a)
```
170  FOR I = 1 TO 2
180     FOR J = I + 1 TO 3
190        IF N$(I) < N$(J) GOTO 230
200        LET T$ = N$(I)
210        LET N$(I) = N$(J)
220        LET N$(J) = T$
230     NEXT J
240  NEXT I
250  FOR I = 1 TO 3
260     PRINT N$(I);TAB(10);S(I)
270  NEXT I
```

(b)
```
170  FOR I = 1 TO 2
180     FOR J = I + 1 TO 3
190        IF S(I) < S(J) GOTO 230
200        LET T = S(I)
210        LET S(I) = S(J)
220        LET S(J) = T
230     NEXT J
240  NEXT I
250  FOR I = 1 TO 3
260     PRINT N$(I);TAB(10);S(I)
270  NEXT I
```

(c) Correct the instructions in (a) so that the scores will not be mixed up.

(d) Correct the instructions in (b) so that the names will not be mixed up.

EXERCISES

Choose One of the Following

We **strongly** advise you to use the same line numbers for your program as those in program 9A so that you can use some of the subroutines you write for this program in chapter 10.

9.1 You manage a team of salespeople and need a program to print out their sales for the current week. Use subscripts and INPUT statements to enter the names and sales figures for the salespeople. Print three tables: one in the order the names were entered, one sorted alphabetically by name, and one sorted by sales with the best salesperson on top. Round all numbers to the nearest whole dollar. Arrange the table as shown below. Use TAB statements or PRINT USING to format the table. As in example 9A, each table should have a title that tells how it is sorted. Use the following variables:

```
N = NUMBER OF EMPLOYEES
NM$(I) = NAME OF SALESPERSON
SALES(I) = SALES FOR THE WEEK
```

```
WEEKLY SALES
UNSORTED
----------------
NAME       SALES
----------------
SANCHEZ    416
  .          .
  .          .
WILSON     51Ø
----------------
```

9.2 You are the owner of a hardware store and would like a program to print an inventory statement. Use subscripts and INPUT statements to enter the name, price, and quantity of each item. Print three tables: one in the order the items were entered, one sorted alphabetically by item, and one sorted by price with the most expensive item on top. Use TAB statements or PRINT USING to format your table. Round all dollar amounts to the nearest cent. As in example 9A, each table should have a title that tells how it was sorted. Your program should produce a table like the one shown below.

Use the following variables:

```
N = NUMBER OF ITEMS
NM$(I) = NAME OF ITEM
PRICE(I) = PRICE OF ITEM
QUANTITY(I) = NUMBER ON HAND
```

```
HARDWARE INVENTORY
UNSORTED
-------------------------------
NAME          PRICE   QUANTITY
-------------------------------
HAMMER         9.5      35
 .              .        .
 .              .        .
CHAIN SAW      285      12
-------------------------------
```

9.3 You manage a baseball team and need to keep track of the players' statistics. Use subscripts and INPUT statements to enter the names, hits, and at-bats for each player and have the program calculate each player's batting average (hits/at-bats). Print three tables: one in the order the names were entered, one sorted alphabetically by name, and one sorted by batting average with the best hitter on top. Batting averages are rounded to the nearest thousandth. Arrange the table as shown below. Use TAB statements or PRINT USING to format your table. As in example 9A, each table should have a title that tells how it was sorted.

Use the following variables:

```
N = NUMBER OF PLAYERS
NM$(I) = NAME OF EACH PLAYER
BA(I) = CURRENT BATTING AVERAGE
HITS(I) = TOTAL HITS
AB(I) = TOTAL AT-BATS
```

```
BASEBALL STATISTICS
UNSORTED
-------------------------------------
              BATTING TOTAL   TOTAL
NAME          AVERAGE HITS    AT-BATS
-------------------------------------
BABBAGE        .3Ø8    37      12Ø
   .            .       .       .
   .            .       .       .
WOZNIAK        .333    45      135
-------------------------------------
```

9.4 Your employees are paid by the week. Use subscripts and INPUT statements to enter the names, wage rates, and hours worked this week for each employee and have the program calculate their pay. Print three tables: one in the order the names were entered, one sorted alphabetically by name, and one sorted by pay with the highest-paid employee on top. Use time and a half for overtime (hours > 40). Round all dollar amounts to the nearest cent. Arrange the table as shown below. Use TAB statements or PRINT USING to format your table. As in example 9A, each table should have a title that tells how it was sorted.

Use the following variables:

```
N = NUMBER OF EMPLOYEES
NM$(I) = NAME OF EACH EMPLOYEE
WAGE(I) = WAGE RATE FOR EACH EMPLOYEE
HOURS(I) = HOURS FOR EACH EMPLOYEE
PAY(I) = PAY FOR CURRENT WEEK
```

```
PAYROLL
UNSORTED
----------------------------
EMPLOYEE     WAGE     PAY
NAME         RATE     FOR WEEK
----------------------------
ARBOGAST     5.22     210.80
 .            .        .
 .            .        .
ZELNIK       7.81     312.40
----------------------------
```

9.5 You need a gradebook program to print out your students' grades. All your exams are worth 100 points. Use subscripts and INPUT statements to enter the names and exam scores for the students. Print three tables: one in the order the names were entered, one sorted by name, and one sorted by score (with the A's on top, of course). Use TAB statements or PRINT USING to format your table. As in example 9A, each table should have a title that tells how it was sorted. The grades are given as follows:

95 and over = A
85 to 94 = B
70 to 84 = C
60 to 69 = D
under 60 = F

Use the following variables:

```
N = NUMBER OF STUDENTS
NM$(I) = NAME OF EACH STUDENT
MARK(I) = THIS WEEK'S SCORE
G$(I) = CURRENT GRADE
```

```
GRADES
UNSORTED
-------------------------
NAME          SCORE   GRADE
-------------------------
ANTON          77       C
  .             .       .
  .             .       .
WESTON         86       B
-------------------------
```

CHAPTER 10

THE BIG ONE
Writing a Major Program

NEW CONCEPTS TAUGHT

1. Using a menu to make a large program more structured and user friendly
2. Using sequential files to store information on the disk
3. Error trapping, catching user mistakes before they cause trouble
4. Using a delay loop to keep a display on the screen for a certain amount of time

WRITING A LARGE PROGRAM

Our programming standards have to become a little stricter when writing a large and complex program like program 10A in figure 10.1. The program must have a logical structure so that we can write it, debug it, and generally find our way around in it. One way of structuring a program is to use a menu. This gives the user a number of choices and makes the program more "user friendly." It also divides the program into logical units that we can work with one at a time. In program 10A the menu divides the program into five basic parts; these are the main routines that start at line 1100.

At line 2000 and following, we have the supporting routines. These do the actual work for the main routines. If you look at the main routines, you can see that they don't actually *do* anything except call the supporting subroutines. At line 6000 are the two utility routines (to be discussed later).

By dividing the program into these sections, we not only make it easier to understand, but we also break this fairly large task into smaller jobs that are much easier to tackle. We have also made the program "modular" by planning the supporting routines so that they can be used by several of the main routines. For example, the routine that reads the file (at line 5400) is used by four of the five main routines. This kind of programming not only makes the program easier to write and understand, it also saves memory. The methods we have described here are generally called "structured-programming techniques" and are absolutely required for good programming. Although BASIC is often accused of being an "unstructured" language, programs in BASIC can be as well structured as you want to make them.

We recommend that you make a list with the name of each subroutine of the program and its line number and that you keep this list handy at all times.

SUBSCRIPTS

The subscripts in this program are used just as they were in chapter 9. They are used to enter data, print tables, and sort. In addition, they are used in program 10A to read and write data on the disk and to set all the scores to zero.

INITIALIZATION

This is a new section of code we haven't seen before. In larger programs there are often many variables that keep the same value throughout the program. We have already seen this with PN$ for the program name. In the initialization section of program 10A in figure 10.1 (following line 50), we are dealing with file variables.

```
50    '  ========= INITIALIZATION ===========
51    '  SET UP MAJOR VARIABLES
52    LET F$ = "BOWLING": '  FILE NAME
53    DIM NM$(100), T(100), AVG(100)
59    '
```

F$ as the Filename

A new feature of this program is that it stores information on the disk in what is called a "data file" or "text file." The program will need to refer to this file by name in the commands that read and write the file. We could refer to the file by name, but, to make it easier and to protect against spelling errors, we set F$ to the file name in line 52; that way we can read the file by having a line like the following:

```
5420  OPEN  F$ FOR INPUT AS #1
```

which is the equivalent of:

```
5420 OPEN "BOWLING" FOR INPUT AS #1
```

The DIM Statement

We have put the dimension statement here (line 53) to make sure that it is executed only once (otherwise a "Duplicate Definition" error would occur). Make sure when you write your program that this is the only DIM statement in it, or you will get this error. In line 53 we dimension all of the subscripted variables we will need in the program. Since we don't know for sure how many bowlers will be on the team, we dimension all the variables to 100, which should be more than enough.

THE MENU

We have put the menu at line 100, since it is the heart of the program. A menu is a list of choices the user can make to direct the operation of the program. This program always comes back to the menu, and what the program does is determined by the user in making a menu choice. The section of program that prints the menu and gets the user's response is pretty straightforward, with two exceptions.

Error Trapping

At the end of the menu section, you may be able to see some of the techniques commonly used to catch user mistakes and respond to them before everything goes boom. If we had only the menu and the INPUT statement at the end of it, what would happen if the user entered 22 as the menu choice? How about 2.2, or just hitting ⟨Enter⟩ without making a choice? In any good program, user input is checked *before* it is acted upon, and if something is wrong, the program tries to recover gracefully. This is called "error trapping."

In line 190 we use C$ for the variable to be inputted and convert it to the numeric variable C in line 200, using the VAL function.

```
200  LET C =  VAL (C$)
```

We do this because if we input C and the user enters a letter instead of a number, the program will issue a "Redo from start" command. This is messy, and it also scrolls the menu off the top of the screen (one line at a time). So in line 210 the user has typed a number (C); it still may not match one of the menu choices. This is what line 220 is for.

```
220  IF C > 0 AND C < 7 AND INT(C) = C THEN GOTO 260
```

If C is between 1 and 6 (inclusive) and C is an integer, everything is fine and the program jumps to line 260, which we'll discuss in a minute. If not, the number is not a legal menu choice and in line 230 the user is informed as gently as possible that a mistake has been made.

```
230  PRINT "I RESPOND ONLY TO INTEGERS FROM 1 TO 6"
240  FOR TIME = 1 TO 1000: NEXT TIME
250  GOTO 100
```

Line 240 has the job of doing nothing 1000 times so that the message of line 230 ("I respond only to integers from 1 to 6") will stay on the screen long enough for the user to read it. When the time is up, line 250 sends the program back to line 100, where the screen is cleared and the menu is started fresh. This process is repeated until the user has entered a legal menu choice.

ON/GOSUB

When the user enters a legitimate menu choice, line 260 is executed. The ON/GOSUB command is a somewhat fancy branching statement.

```
260   ON C GOSUB 1100,1200,1300,1400,1500,300
```

It represents a whole string of IF/THEN statements (like IF C = 1 THEN GOSUB 1100). Notice that in line 260 there are six line numbers corresponding to the five main routines and the end. The statement ON C GOSUB means that if C is 1, the program should go to the first subroutine in the list (in this case the one at line 1100); if C is 2, it will go to the second one on the list, and so on. Since it is a GOSUB command, after the subroutine is finished the program will return to the next line *after* the line with the ON/GOSUB command. This is line 270, which sends the user back to the menu (unless the user has picked choice 6, in which case the program goes to line 300 and ends). BASIC also has the ON/GOTO command, but its use is usually considered to be a bad programming practice and makes programs hard to understand.

UTILITIES

Option Not Available Subroutine (line 6000)

This subroutine is one that will not be used when the program is finished. It allows us to test the menu section without writing the whole program. If we set things up so that each of the main routines contains nothing but a call to this subroutine and a RETURN statement, then every legal menu choice (except number 6) should produce the SORRY, THIS OPTION IS NOT AVAILABLE YET message.

```
6000  '  === SUBROUTINE TO PRINT NOT AVAILABLE ===
6010  CLS : LOCATE 20,10
6020  PRINT "SORRY, THIS OPTION IS NOT AVAILABLE YET"
6030  FOR TIME = 1 TO 1000: NEXT TIME: '  TIME DELAY
6040  RETURN
6050  '
```

Later, when each main routine is written, the GOSUB 6000 will be removed. These subroutines that don't really do anything but test other parts of a program are called "dummy subroutines," or "stubs."

Hold Screen Subroutine (line 6200)

In chapter 9 we saw how to use this subroutine to keep a display on the screen as long as the user wants it there; we are using it the same way here.

THE MAIN ROUTINES

The following five main routines correspond to the first five menu choices. We will discuss what each one does and then talk about the supporting subroutines that they call.

Enter Names and Start New File (line 1100)

This routine gets things started. The names are entered and sorted and the scores set to zero.

```
1100  ' ==== ENTER NAMES & START NEW FILE ====
1110  GOSUB 2000: '  ENTER NAMES
1120  GOSUB 2200: '  SORT NAMES
1130  GOSUB 5000: '  ZERO SCORES
1140  GOSUB 5200: '  WRITE FILE ON DISK
1150  GOSUB 5600: '  PRINT TABLE
1160  GOSUB 6200: '  HOLD SCREEN
1170  RETURN :    '  RETURN TO MENU
1180  '
```

Then the file is written to the disk and the table printed on the screen and held until the user is ready to return to the menu.

Read File and Print Table (line 1200)

Now that there is a file on the disk, we can read it and print the file on the screen (sorted alphabetically by name) and hold it there.

```
1200  ' ======= READ FILE & PRINT TABLE =======
1210  GOSUB 5400: '  READ FILE FROM DISK
1220  GOSUB 5600: '  PRINT TABLE
1230  GOSUB 6200: '  HOLD SCREEN
1240  RETURN :    '  RETURN TO MENU
1250  '
```

At first the file and the table will have all the scores set to zero. This will be true until the file is updated the first time.

Enter Scores and Update File (line 1300)

Every week new bowling scores are entered for each player, and the total scores and the new averages are written into the file on the disk.

```
1300  '  ===== ENTER SCORES & UPDATE FILE ======
1310  GOSUB 5400: '  READ FILE FROM DISK
1320  GOSUB 2400: '  ENTER SCORES & UPDATE FILE
1330  GOSUB 5200: '  WRITE UPDATED FILE ON DISK
1340  GOSUB 5600: '  PRINT TABLE
1350  GOSUB 6200: '  HOLD SCREEN
1360  RETURN :    '  RETURN TO MENU
1370  '
```

First the current information must be read from the disk. Then the new information is entered, the new data are written to the disk, and a new table is printed and held on the screen.

Zero Scores and Write File (line 1400)

This option is used when things get goofed up and you need to start over.

```
1400  '  === ZERO SCORES & WRITE FILE ===
1410  GOSUB 5400: '  READ FILE FROM DISK
1420  GOSUB 5000: '  ZERO SCORES
1430  GOSUB 5200: '  WRITE ZEROED FILE ON DISK
1440  GOSUB 5600: '  PRINT TABLE
1450  GOSUB 6200: '  HOLD SCREEN
1460  RETURN :    '  RETURN TO MENU
1470  '
```

Suppose that you have successfully written the routines that read and write the file and they work fine. Now you try to write the update part of the program, and it not only doesn't work, it messes up the file on the disk. Now even if you fix the update routine, it won't work right (and neither will the read file routine) because the file is messed up. You need a convenient way to get the file back in shape without having to enter the names all over again. When you run it, you lose all the scores, but at least the names don't have to be reentered. Another use for this routine would be to start a new season for the team and set all scores and averages to zero.

Sort by Score and Print Table (line 1500)

Because the enter names routine sorts the names alphabetically, they remain so in the file and any table will be printed that way unless resorted.

```
1500  '  ===== SORT BY SCORE & PRINT TABLE =====
1510  GOSUB 5400: '  READ FILE FROM DISK
1520  GOSUB 2600: '  SORT BY SCORE
1530  GOSUB 5600: '  PRINT TABLE
1540  GOSUB 6200: '  HOLD SCREEN
1550  RETURN :    '  RETURN TO MENU
1560  '
```

This subroutine might be used to print a table each week sorted by total score so that whoever has the highest total score would be at the top of the list. It first reads the file, then sorts it, then prints the table (sorted by score) and holds it on the screen. This routine has no effect on the file, since the newly sorted scores are not written back to the disk.

End (line 300)

This one is pretty obvious.

SUPPORTING ROUTINES

As mentioned before, these supporting routines do the actual work of the program and are written as "modules" that can be used by various main routines (and by other programs as well).

Enter Names (line 2000)

This subroutine does nothing but prompt the user to enter the names of the bowlers that are stored in the array NM$(I).

```
2000  '  ====== SUBROUTINE TO ENTER NAMES ======
2010  CLS
2020  PRINT "ENTER NAMES FOR NEW FILE"
2030  PRINT : PRINT
2040  INPUT "HOW MANY NAMES WILL YOU ENTER? ",N
2050  LET WEEK = 0
2060  PRINT
2070  FOR I = 1 TO N
2080      PRINT I; :  LINE INPUT"    ";NM$(I)
2090  NEXT I
2100  RETURN
```

As in chapter 9, we use the LINE INPUT statement in case the user enters a name with a comma in it.

Sort by Name (line 2200)

This is like the alphabetical sorting we did in chapter 9.

Enter Scores and Update Numbers (line 2400)

This subroutine prompts the user with the name of each bowler and gets his or her score (S) for the current week.

```
2400  '  == SUBROUTINE TO ENTER SCORES & UPDATE ==
2410  CLS
2420  LET WEEK = WEEK + 1
2430  PRINT : PRINT "ENTER THE SCORE FOR EACH PLAYER": PRIN
2440  FOR I = 1 TO N
2450      PRINT NM$(I); TAB(15);: INPUT S
2460      LET T(I) = T(I) + S
2470      LET AVG(I) =  T(I)/WEEK
2480  NEXT I
2490  RETURN
2500  '
```

First, WEEK is increased by 1 since it is a new week. Then S is entered by the user and added to T(I) to get the new total. In line 2470 the new average is computed by dividing the new total by the number of weeks.

Sort by Score (line 2600)

This is a slightly more complicated sort than the one in chapter 9. Here we need to carry each bowler's total score and average along with their name. Otherwise we might have some pretty angry bowlers on our hands.

```
2600  '  ===== SUBROUTINE TO SORT BY SCORE =====
2610  FOR I = 1 TO N - 1
2620      FOR J = I + 1 TO N
2630          IF T(I) < T(J) THEN GOSUB 2800 : '  SWAP
2640      NEXT J
2650  NEXT I
2660  RETURN
2670  '
```

The structure of this subroutine is exactly the same as the one to sort by name. The only difference is in which variables are compared in the decision of when to swap names and scores.

Swap Names and Scores (line 2800)

This is the same subroutine we used in chapter 9, with the addition of another variable.

```
2800  '  === SUBROUTINE TO SWAP NAMES AND SCORES ===
2810  SWAP NM$(I),NM$(J)
2820  SWAP T(I),T(J)
2830  SWAP AVG(I),AVG(J)
2840  RETURN
2850  '
```

The third variable is needed, since here we have a three-column table with two sets of scores.

Zero Scores (line 5000)

This subroutine is nothing but a simple loop that sets each bowler's total score and average to zero.

```
5000  '  ====== SUBROUTINE TO ZERO SCORES ======
5010  FOR I = 1 TO N
5020      LET T(I) = 0
5030      LET AVG(I) = 0
5040  NEXT I
5050  LET WEEK = 0
5060  RETURN
5070  '
```

It allows us to zero the scores without reentering the names.

Write File to Disk (line 5200)

This subroutine does the important job of storing the information we have collected in a permanent file on the disk.

```
5200  '  == SUBROUTINE TO WRITE FILE ON DISK ==
5210  CLS : LOCATE 10,10 : PRINT "WRITING FILE TO DISK"
5220  OPEN F$ FOR OUTPUT AS #1
5230  PRINT#1, N
5240  PRINT#1,  WEEK
5250  FOR I = 1 TO N
5260      PRINT#1, NM$(I)
5270      PRINT#1, T(I)
5280      PRINT#1, AVG(I)
5290  NEXT I
5300  CLOSE #1
5310  RETURN
5320  '
```

Since the writing of the file to the disk is invisible to the user, we first print the message in line 5210 telling the user what is going on.

Line 5220 opens the file. Before any file can be read or written to, it must first be opened. This tells the system to set aside a buffer in memory for data going to or from the file and to find the beginning of the file. The buffer holds 256 characters (letters, digits, symbols, or spaces). When writing to a file, the information is not actually written to the disk until the buffer is full or the file is closed. This is one reason why it's important to remember to close a file after writing to it.

OPEN The OPEN command tells the computer that we want to read from or print to a disk file. When opening a file, we must specify whether we plan to use the file for input, output, or appending. The most common form of the OPEN statement is:

line number `OPEN` *filename* `FOR` *mode* `AS` `#`*filenum*

where *mode* is INPUT, OUTPUT, or APPEND and *filenum* is the number we intend to refer to the file by.

The following opens the file "DATAFILE" for input:

```
10  OPEN "DATAFILE" FOR INPUT AS #1
```

The number 1 is the file number and can be any number from 1 to the maximum number of allowable open files (usually 3 or 4). The file number is used in other BASIC commands that read from or print to the file.

CLOSE Information to be written to a file is not always written to the file right away. It is stored in a buffer and is often written to the file only when the buffer is full. The CLOSE command makes sure everything is written properly to the file and also releases the file number for use by another file. Files should always be closed when you are through with them.

Example:

```
10 CLOSE#1
```

Using CLOSE with no file number causes all open files to be closed.

PRINT# and PRINT# USING These are the same as the PRINT and PRINT USING statements, except that they print the information to a file rather than to the screen. See appendix A, section 3.22 for more information.

Example:

```
10  OPEN "DATAFILE" FOR OUTPUT AS #1
20  PRINT#1, "HELLO"
30  PRINT#1 USING "##.##"; A
```

Line 20 prints the word HELLO in the DATAFILE disk file.

In line 5230 we print N, the number of bowlers on the team, and in line 5240 we print the week number. In the loop from line 5260 to line 5280, we print their name, total score, and average. The "#" in the PRINT# statement tells the computer that we want to print the information to file #1 rather than to the screen.

If, after three weeks, we could look at the file for two bowlers, it might look like this:

```
2
3
ADAMS
300
100
SMITH
450
150
```

Actually, you can look at the file as it is being written by changing F$ in line 5220 to "SCRN:"

```
5220  OPEN "SCRN:" FOR OUTPUT AS #1
```

This will cause the output to go to the screen rather than to the file. You will have to put a pause at the end of this subroutine

```
5305  INPUT Q$
```

or the screen will be cleared before you can read the information. If you use this technique, remember that the information is being written to the screen, **NOT TO THE FILE**. The contents of the file will not change. Once you are confident that the right information is being written, change "SCRN:" back to F$.

Read File from Disk (line 5400)

This subroutine is exactly the same as the one to write the file, except that instead of the PRINT# command, we use the INPUT# command.

```
5400  '  ======= SUBROUTINE TO READ FILE =======
5410  CLS : LOCATE 10,9 : PRINT "READING FILE FROM DISK"
5420  OPEN  F$ FOR INPUT AS #1
5430  INPUT#1, N
5440  INPUT#1, WEEK
5450  FOR I = 1 TO N
5460      LINE INPUT#1, NM$(I)
5470      INPUT#1, T(I)
5480      INPUT#1, AVG(I)
5490  NEXT I
5500  CLOSE #1
5510  RETURN
5520  '
```

The # following the INPUT statement tells the computer that the INPUT statement should read data from the disk instead of from the keyboard. If you try to read more items than there are in a file, an "Input past end" error results.

INPUT# and LINE INPUT# These commands work just like the INPUT and LINE INPUT commands, except that they get their input from a file rather than from the keyboard. See appendix A for more information about these commands.

Examples:

```
10  OPEN "DATAFILE" FOR INPUT AS #1
20  INPUT#1, A$
30  LINE INPUT#1, B$
```

Print Table (line 5600)

This is a standard subroutine that uses a FOR/NEXT loop to print a table of results.

```
5600  '  ====== SUBROUTINE TO PRINT TABLE ======
5610  LET LN$ = "-------------------------------------"
5620  CLS
5630  PRINT  TAB(10);"BOWLING TEAM SCORES"
5640  PRINT  TAB(14);"FOR WEEK #";WEEK
5650  PRINT LN$
5660  PRINT "NAME"; TAB(19);"TOTAL"; TAB(30);"AVERAGE"
5670  PRINT  TAB(19);"SCORE"; TAB(30);"SCORE"
5680  PRINT LN$
5690  FOR I = 1 TO N
5700    PRINT USING"\       \####       ###.##";NM$(I),T(I),AVG(I)
5710  NEXT I
5720  PRINT LN$
5730  RETURN
5740  '
```

Notice the use of the backslash "\" in the PRINT USING statement. This symbol is used rather than the "#" to format a string variable. The "\ \" in line 5700 tells the computer to set aside 16 spaces for the variable NM$. NM$ will be printed at the left of this space and the remaining spaces left blank.

EXAMPLE 10A Bowling Team

Problem Write a program that keeps track of the records of a bowling team. Use INPUT statements to enter the names of the bowlers. Use a sequential file to record the names, total scores, and average scores on the disk. In the file the bowlers should be in alphabetical order. Each week the file should be updated by having the user enter the bowlers' scores for that week. Print a table showing each bowler's name, total score, and average score so far. You should have the option to print a table sorted by total score or to print a table based on the alphabetical file on the disk. The program should produce a table like the one below:

```
           BOWLING TEAM SCORES
               FOR WEEK # 3

 ------------------------------------
 NAME              TOTAL      AVERAGE
                   SCORE      SCORE
 ------------------------------------
 ADAMS             300        100.00
  .                 .            .
  .                 .            .
 SMITH             450        150.00
 ------------------------------------
```

Solution

FIGURE 10.1

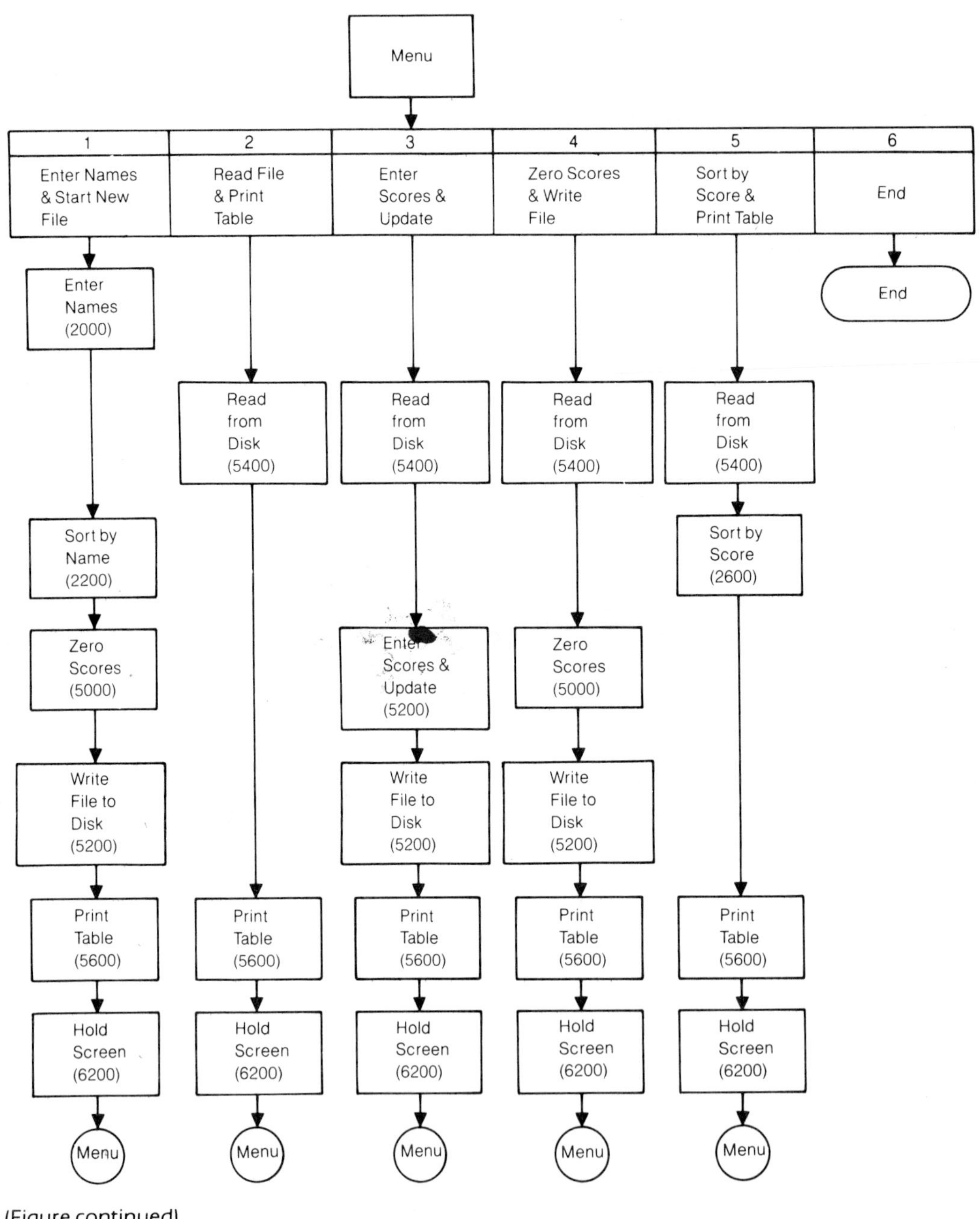

(Figure continued)

(Figure 10.1 continued)

```
LIST
1     LET PN$ = "P10A-BT"
2     LET NA$ = "YOUR NAME"
3     LET DA$ = "00/00/00"
10    '  =========== MENU VARIABLES ============
11    '  C$ = MENU RETURN AND INPUT CHARACTER
12    '  C = MENU CHOICE NUMBER
13    '  TIME = TIME DELAY COUNTER
20    '  =========== FILE VARIABLES ============
21    '  N = NUMBER OF NAMES IN THE FILE
22    '  WEEK = WEEK NUMBER
23    '  NM$(I) = LIST OF NAMES
24    '  T(I) = LIST OF TOTAL SCORES
25    '  AVG(I) = LIST OF AVERAGE SCORES
30    '  ========== UTILITY VARIABLES ==========
31    '  I = LOOP COUNTER
32    '  J = LOOP COUNTER
33    '  LN$ = A ROW OF DASHES
34    '  S = VARIABLE USED TO ENTER CURRENT WEEK'S SCORE
50    '  ========= INITIALIZATION ===========
51    '  SET UP MAJOR VARIABLES
52    LET F$ = "BOWLING": '  FILE NAME
53    DIM NM$(100), T(100), AVG(100)
59    '
100   '  ================ MENU =================
101   CLS : PRINT TAB(40 - (LEN (PN$) / 2)) PN$
110   PRINT  TAB(18);"MENU"
120   PRINT : PRINT "1.  ENTER NAMES & START NEW FILE"
130   PRINT : PRINT "2.  READ FILE & PRINT TABLE"
140   PRINT : PRINT "3.  ENTER SCORES & UPDATE FILE"
150   PRINT : PRINT "4.  ZERO SCORES & WRITE FILE"
160   PRINT : PRINT "5.  SORT BY SCORE & PRINT TABLE"
170   PRINT : PRINT "6.  END PROGRAM"
180   PRINT : PRINT : PRINT
190   INPUT "ENTER THE NUMBER OF YOUR CHOICE  ",C$
200   LET C =  VAL (C$)
210   PRINT : PRINT
220   IF C > 0 AND C < 7 AND  INT (C) = C THEN  GOTO 260
230   PRINT "I RESPOND ONLY TO INTEGERS FROM 1 TO 6"
240   FOR TIME = 1 TO 1000: NEXT TIME
250   GOTO 100
260   ON C GOSUB 1100,1200,1300,1400,1500,300
270   GOTO 100
300   PRINT "GOODBYE" : END
310   '
```

(Figure continued)

(Figure 10.1 continued)

```
1100  '  ==== ENTER NAMES & START NEW FILE ====
1110  GOSUB 2000: '  ENTER NAMES
1120  GOSUB 2200: '  SORT NAMES
1130  GOSUB 5000: '  ZERO SCORES
1140  GOSUB 5200: '  WRITE FILE ON DISK
1150  GOSUB 5600: '  PRINT TABLE
1160  GOSUB 6200: '  HOLD SCREEN
1170  RETURN :    '  RETURN TO MENU
1180  '
1200  '  ======= READ FILE & PRINT TABLE =======
1210  GOSUB 5400: '  READ FILE FROM DISK
1220  GOSUB 5600: '  PRINT TABLE
1230  GOSUB 6200: '  HOLD SCREEN
1240  RETURN :    '  RETURN TO MENU
1250  '
1300  '  ===== ENTER SCORES & UPDATE FILE ======
1310  GOSUB 5400: '  READ FILE FROM DISK
1320  GOSUB 2400: '  ENTER SCORES & UPDATE FILE
1330  GOSUB 5200: '  WRITE UPDATED FILE ON DISK
1340  GOSUB 5600: '  PRINT TABLE
1350  GOSUB 6200: '  HOLD SCREEN
1360  RETURN :    '  RETURN TO MENU
1370  '
1400  '  === ZERO SCORES & WRITE FILE ===
1410  GOSUB 5400: '  READ FILE FROM DISK
1420  GOSUB 5000: '  ZERO SCORES
1430  GOSUB 5200: '  WRITE ZEROED FILE ON DISK
1440  GOSUB 5600: '  PRINT TABLE
1450  GOSUB 6200: '  HOLD SCREEN
1460  RETURN :    '  RETURN TO MENU
1470  '
1500  '  ===== SORT BY SCORE & PRINT TABLE =====
1510  GOSUB 5400: '  READ FILE FROM DISK
1520  GOSUB 2600: '  SORT BY SCORE
1530  GOSUB 5600: '  PRINT TABLE
1540  GOSUB 6200: '  HOLD SCREEN
1550  RETURN :    '  RETURN TO MENU
1560  '
2000  '  ====== SUBROUTINE TO ENTER NAMES ======
2010  CLS
2020  PRINT "ENTER NAMES FOR NEW FILE"
2030  PRINT : PRINT
2040  INPUT "HOW MANY NAMES WILL YOU ENTER? ",N
2050  LET WEEK = 0
2060  PRINT
2070  FOR I = 1 TO N
```

(Figure continued)

(Figure 10.1 continued)

```
2080      PRINT I; : LINE INPUT"   ";NM$(I)
2090  NEXT I
2100  RETURN
2110  '
2200  '  ===== SUBROUTINE TO SORT BY NAME ======
2205  IF N <= 1 THEN RETURN : ' NO SORTING NEEDED
2210  FOR I = 1 TO N - 1
2220      FOR J = I + 1 TO N
2230          IF NM$(I) > NM$(J) THEN GOSUB 2800 : '  SWAP
2240      NEXT J
2250  NEXT I
2260  RETURN
2270  '
2400  '  == SUBROUTINE TO ENTER SCORES & UPDATE ==
2410  CLS
2420  LET WEEK = WEEK + 1
2430  PRINT : PRINT "ENTER THE SCORE FOR EACH PLAYER": PRINT
2440  FOR I = 1 TO N
2450      PRINT NM$(I); TAB(15);: INPUT S
2460      LET T(I) = T(I) + S
2470      LET AVG(I) =  T(I)/WEEK
2480  NEXT I
2490  RETURN
2500  '
2600  '  ===== SUBROUTINE TO SORT BY SCORE =====
2610  FOR I = 1 TO N - 1
2620      FOR J = I + 1 TO N
2630          IF T(I) < T(J) THEN GOSUB 2800 : '  SWAP
2640      NEXT J
2650  NEXT I
2660  RETURN
2670  '
2800  '  === SUBROUTINE TO SWAP NAMES AND SCORES ===
2810  SWAP NM$(I),NM$(J)
2820  SWAP T(I),T(J)
2830  SWAP AVG(I),AVG(J)
2840  RETURN
2850  '
5000  '  ====== SUBROUTINE TO ZERO SCORES ======
5010  FOR I = 1 TO N
5020      LET T(I) = 0
5030      LET AVG(I) = 0
5040  NEXT I
5050  LET WEEK = 0
5060  RETURN
5070  '
```

(Figure continued)

(Figure 10.1 continued)

```
5200  ' == SUBROUTINE TO WRITE FILE ON DISK ==
5210  CLS : LOCATE 10,10 : PRINT "WRITING FILE TO DISK"
5220  OPEN F$ FOR OUTPUT AS #1
5230  PRINT#1, N
5240  PRINT#1,  WEEK
5250  FOR I = 1 TO N
5260      PRINT#1, NM$(I)
5270      PRINT#1, T(I)
5280      PRINT#1, AVG(I)
5290  NEXT I
5300  CLOSE #1
5310  RETURN
5320  '
5400  '  ======= SUBROUTINE TO READ FILE =======
5410  CLS : LOCATE 10,9 : PRINT "READING FILE FROM DISK"
5420  OPEN  F$ FOR INPUT AS #1
5430  INPUT#1, N
5440  INPUT#1, WEEK
5450  FOR I = 1 TO N
5460      LINE INPUT#1, NM$(I)
5470      INPUT#1, T(I)
5480      INPUT#1, AVG(I)
5490  NEXT I
5500  CLOSE #1
5510  RETURN
5520  '
5600  '  ====== SUBROUTINE TO PRINT TABLE ======
5610  LET LN$ = "----------------------------------------"
5620  CLS
5630  PRINT  TAB(10);"BOWLING TEAM SCORES"
5640  PRINT  TAB(14);"FOR WEEK #";WEEK
5650  PRINT LN$
5660  PRINT "NAME"; TAB(19);"TOTAL"; TAB(30);"AVERAGE"
5670  PRINT  TAB(19);"SCORE"; TAB(30);"SCORE"
5680  PRINT LN$
5690  FOR I = 1 TO N
5700  PRINT USING"\              \####       ###.##";NM$(I),T(I),AVG(I)
5710  NEXT I
5720  PRINT LN$
5730  RETURN
5740  '
6000  '  === SUBROUTINE TO PRINT NOT AVAILABLE ===
6010  CLS : LOCATE 20,10
6020  PRINT "SORRY, THIS OPTION IS NOT AVAILABLE YET"
6030  FOR TIME = 1 TO 1000: NEXT TIME: '  TIME DELAY
6040  RETURN
```

(Figure continued)

(Figure 10.1 continued)

```
6050  '
6200  '  ======= HOLD SCREEN ========
6210  LOCATE 23,8
6220  INPUT "PRESS ENTER TO CONTINUE",C$
6230  RETURN
6240  '
Ok
```

RUN (Screen 1)

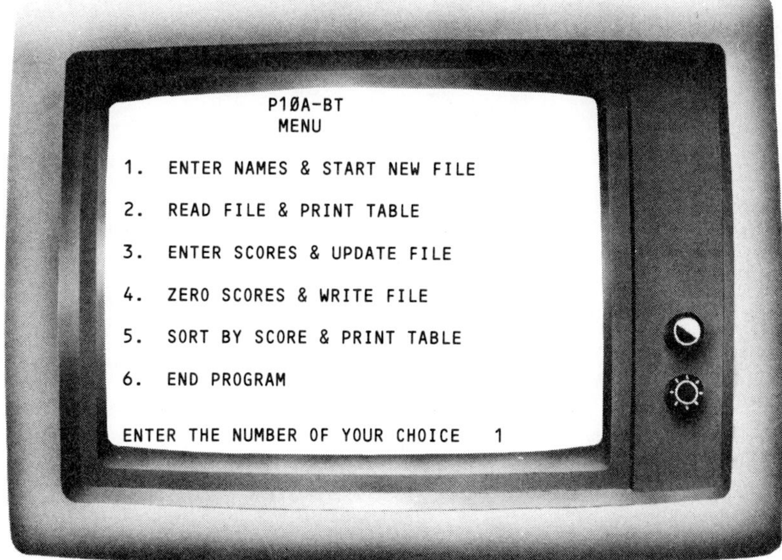

RUN (Screen 2)

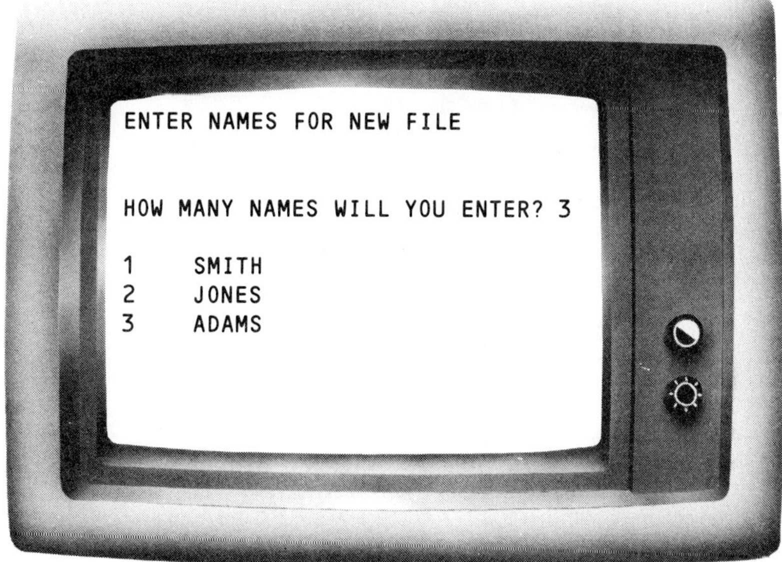

(Figure continued)

(Figure 10.1 continued)

RUN (Screen 3)

RUN (Screen 4)

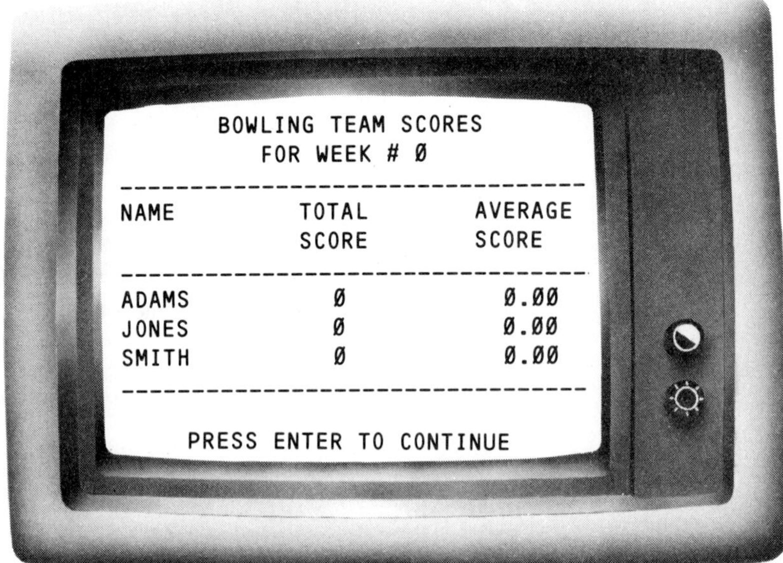

BOWLING TEAM SCORES
FOR WEEK # Ø
NAME TOTAL AVERAGE
SCORE SCORE
ADAMS Ø Ø.ØØ
JONES Ø Ø.ØØ
SMITH Ø Ø.ØØ
PRESS ENTER TO CONTINUE

(Figure continued)

SELF-TESTING QUESTIONS

10.1 Lines 110 through 140 apply to (a), (b), and (c). Write the output produced by each part if the file named NUMBERS has the content shown below.

```
110  LET F$ = "NUMBERS"
120  OPEN F$ FOR INPUT AS #1
130  INPUT#1, N
140  FOR I = 1 TO N
```

CONTENTS OF "NUMBERS" FILE:

```
3
12
8
71
47
63
21
18
4
7
```

(a)

```
170  INPUT#1, A(I)
180  INPUT#1, B(I)
190  INPUT#1, C(I)
200  NEXT I
210  CLOSE #1
220  FOR I = 1 TO N
230  PRINT B(I);" ";
240  NEXT I
```

(b)

```
170  INPUT#1, A(I)
180  INPUT#1, B(I)
190  INPUT#1, B(I + 3)
200  NEXT I
210  CLOSE #1
220  FOR I = N - 1 TO N + 1
230  PRINT B(I);" ";
240  NEXT I
```

(c)

```
170  FOR J = 1 TO 3
180  INPUT#1, A(I,J)
190  NEXT J
200  NEXT I
210  CLOSE #1
220  FOR I = 1 TO 3
230  FOR J = 1 TO 3
240  PRINT A(J,I);" ";
250  NEXT J
260  PRINT
270  NEXT I
```

10.2 Lines 110 through 120 and line 210 apply to (a), (b), and (c).

```
110  LET F$ = "STUDENTS"
120  OPEN F$ FOR OUTPUT AS #1

210  CLOSE #1
```

Assume the following values have been entered in a previous section of the program.

```
N = 3              L = 4
N$(1) = "TERRY"    N$(2) = "CARL"   N$(3) = "JUNE"
S(1) = 92          S(2) = 88        S(3) = 84
```

Write the content of the file made by each of the three versions of a write file program given in (a), (b), and (c).

(a)
```
150  PRINT#1, N
160  PRINT#1, L
170  FOR I = 1 TO N
180  PRINT#1, N$(I)
190  PRINT#1, S(I)
200  NEXT I
```

(b)
```
150  PRINT#1, N
160  FOR I = 1 TO N
170  PRINT#1, L
180  PRINT#1, N$(I)
190  PRINT#1, S(I)
200  NEXT I
```

(c)
```
150  PRINT#1, N
160  FOR I = 1 TO N
170  PRINT#1, N$(I)
180  PRINT#1, S(I)
190  NEXT I
200  PRINT#1, L
```

DIRECTIONS FOR EXERCISES

Because this is a large and impressive program, the exercises for chapter 10 will take a slightly different form than earlier exercises. Although it may look extremely difficult and complex at first, we think you will find that it can be done in small, relatively easy steps. The trick is to concentrate on one step at a time; don't proceed to the next step until you are satisfied that the current version of your program is working properly.

We suggest that you keep a second "backup" copy of this program as you write it. Whenever the current version is working properly, back it up by saving it again under another name (like P10A.BAK). That way you'll have something to fall back on if you accidentally destroy your main version.

In program 10A we have presented a menu-driven program that keeps a file of scores for a bowling team on the disk. In the exercise assignments that follow, you will find that you can write programs that are, in many ways, exactly like the example program (many parts of it you can copy line for line). Some parts will vary because of differences in the information being stored. For example, the batting average program records the name of each player, batting average, total hits, and total at-bats; this takes four columns of data rather than three. This means that the parts of the program that actually handle the data—such as the sorting, file-writing, and table-printing subroutines—will be slightly different (another variable will need to be dimensioned in the DIM statement also). Another difference is that the formula for batting average is different from the one for bowling average. Once you have figured out these differences, however, we think you'll find that your program will look very much like program 10A.

Your assignment is to pick one of the exercises that follow (10.1 to 10.5) and follow the general instructions presented here. Because of the length of the program, it is **essential** that you follow these directions to the letter. It is also absolutely necessary that you use the same beginning line numbers for the subroutines as those used in program 10A (it will also be a lot easier if you use the same line numbers within as many subroutines as possible). Some of the subroutines from the program you wrote for chapter 9 will be useful to you here; some may be used as they are, others may have to be modified.

Step 1:

1.1 Load STARTER and change the program name in line 1.

1.2 Type in the utility subroutines at lines 6000 and 6200 from program 10A exactly as they are written.

1.3 Type in the menu section from program 10A exactly as it is written.

1.4 For all of the main routines (lines 1100, 1200, 1300, 1400, 1500), type in the remark statement with the name of the routine as it appears in program 10A. After the remark statement, add a line like the following:

```
1101 GOSUB 6000 : RETURN
```

1.5 At this point the program should run and the menu should work without crashing (although it won't really do anything), and it should handle things when you enter an illegal number or a letter as a menu choice (try it). If it won't, correct any errors and, when it runs properly, save it as VERSION1 and make a backup.

Step 2:

2.1 Add the routine at line 1100 of program 10A to your program (get rid of the GOSUB 6000 : RETURN line). Insert a ' at the beginning of lines 1120 and 1140 (the calls to the subroutines to sort and write the file) so that they won't execute; you will add these functions later.

2.2 Modify the subroutines to enter names (2000), zero scores (5000), and print table (5600) to fit your application, and add them to the program.

2.3 Now option 1 of the menu should work, letting you enter the names, and should print the table (unsorted) with zero for all the amounts. Depending on which exercise you choose, you should change the word "SCORE" to whatever makes sense throughout the program (e.g., "QUANTITY" or "SALES").

2.4 When this part runs properly, save it as VERSION2 and make a backup.

2.5 Modify the subroutines at lines 2200 and 2800 and add them to your program. Then remove the ' from line 1120 so that it calls the sort subroutine; then get the sort subroutine to work. It should print the table in alphabetical order no matter which names are entered first.

Step 3:

3.1 When the sort is working, modify and add the subroutines to read and write the file (they should be almost identical). Remove the ' from line 1140 that calls the subroutine that writes the file, and remove the GOSUB 6000 : RETURN from line 1201.

3.2 Add the initialization section at line 50. Be sure to modify the DIM statement to fit your application (it may need more variables) and change F$.

3.3 Get menu options 1 and 2 to work completely. In order to find out what is going on with the files, use the OPEN "SCRN:" method discussed earlier in the write file subroutine. Don't forget to change it back to F$ later.

3.4 This should make menu options 1, 2, and 4 fully functional (once you take out the GOSUB 6000 : RETURN line). If not, make the necessary corrections and save this as VERSION3 and make a backup.

Step 4:

4.1 Modify and add the subroutine from program 10A to enter scores (or whatever) and update the file (at line 2400).

4.2 When you have the update working, modify and add the subroutine to sort the scores by number.

4.3 This should make the program fully functional. Try all the menu options. Make any corrections necessary to make them all work properly; save this as VERSION4 and start celebrating. Congratulations!

EXERCISES

Choose One and Follow the Steps Given

10.1 You manage a team of salespeople and need a program to keep track of their sales for the current week and the total sales they have earned so far this year. Start the file by using INPUT statements to enter the names of the salespeople. Each week (in option 3, update) you will enter their weekly sales and calculate their total sales. The names should be alphabetical in the file, but option 5 should print a table sorted by this week's sales so that bonuses can be given to the week's top salespeople. Print all numbers rounded to the nearest whole dollar. Arrange the table as shown below.

Use the following file variables:

```
F$ = "SALES"
N = NUMBER OF EMPLOYEES
WEEK = WEEK #
NM$(I) = NAME OF SALESPERSON
WSAL(I) = SALES FOR CURRENT WEEK
TSAL(I) = TOTAL SALES
```

```
                 SALES
               WEEK # 11
-------------------------------------
NAME        WEEKLY SALES    TOTAL SALES
-------------------------------------
SMITH      $416.ØØ         $71467.ØØ
  .            .                .
  .            .                .
WILSON     $51Ø.ØØ         $98275.ØØ
-------------------------------------
```

10.2 You are the owner of a hardware store and would like a program to help you keep track of your inventory. Start the file by using INPUT statements to enter the name of each item. The items should be sorted alphabetically by name for placement in the file. Option 5 of the menu should allow you to sort the items and print the table so they are sorted by price with the most expensive at the top of the list. In your update option (option 3), you should be able to enter the quantity on hand and the current price of each item, and have the program print the table with the current price and value (quantity * price) and update the file. Arrange the table as shown below.

Use the following file variables:

```
F$ = "HARDWARE"
N = NUMBER OF ITEMS
WEEK = WEEK #
NM$(I) = NAME OF ITEM
PRICE(I) = PRICE OF ITEM
QUANTITY(I) = NUMBER ON HAND
VALUE(I) = VALUE OF EACH ITEM
```

```
                 HARDWARE INVENTORY
                      WEEK # 1
---------------------------------------
NAME             PRICE   QUANTITY  VALUE
---------------------------------------
HAMMER           $9.50   35      $333.00
  .                .      .          .
  .                .      .          .
CHAIN SAW      $285.00   12     $3420.00
---------------------------------------
```

10.3 You manage a baseball team and need to keep track of the players' statistics. You start the file by simply entering the players' names (using INPUT statements). Each week (in option 3, update) you enter the number of at-bats and hits for each player for that week, and the program updates their total hits and total at-bats and calculates their current batting average (hits/at-bats). Batting averages are rounded to the nearest thousandth. The file should be alphabetical by player's name. Option 5 should allow you to print a table for the local newspaper sorted by current batting average. Arrange the table as shown below.

Use the following file variables:

```
F$ = "BASEBALL"
N = NUMBER OF PLAYERS
NM$(I) = NAME OF EACH PLAYER
BA(I) = CURRENT BATTING AVERAGE
HITS(I) = TOTAL HITS
AB(I) = TOTAL AT-BATS
```

```
          BASEBALL STATISTICS
               WEEK # 11
-------------------------------------
              BATTING TOTAL   TOTAL
NAME          AVERAGE HITS    AT-BATS
-------------------------------------
BABBAGE       .3Ø8    37      12Ø
  .            .       .       .
  .            .       .       .
WOZNIAK       .333    45      135
-------------------------------------
```

10.4 Your employees are paid by the week. To create the file, you enter their names and wage rates (different for each employee). Each week, using option 3 (update), you will enter the number of hours each employee worked this week. You need to know how much they should be paid this week and need to keep a record of their total pay for the year. Option 5 should allow you to print the table sorted by this week's pay with this week's hardest workers on top. Use time and a half for overtime (hours > 40). Round all dollar amounts to the nearest cent. Arrange the table as shown below.

Use the following file variables:

```
F$ = "PAYROLL"
N = NUMBER OF EMPLOYEES
WEEK = WEEK #
NM$(I) = NAME OF EACH EMPLOYEE
WAGERATE(I) = WAGE RATE FOR EACH EMPLOYEE
WEEKLYPAY(I) = PAY FOR CURRENT WEEK
TOTALPAY(I) = TOTAL PAY FOR YEAR
```

```
                  PAYROLL
                  WEEK # 7
----------------------------------------
EMPLOYEE    WAGE     PAY          PAY
NAME        RATE     FOR WEEK     FOR YEAR
----------------------------------------
ARBOGAST   $5.22    $21Ø.8       $1475.6
 .            .         .             .
 .            .         .             .
ZELNIK     $7.81    $312.4       $2186.8
----------------------------------------
```

10.5 You need a gradebook program to keep track of your students' grades. All your exams are worth 100 points. You start the file by entering just the names of the students. Every week you give another exam and enter each student's score (using option 3, update). The file contains the score for the week, the total score so far, and the letter grade so far. The file should be alphabetical by student, but option 5 should print the table sorted by total score (with the A's on top, of course). The grades are given as follows:

95 and over	=	A
85 to 94	=	B
70 to 84	=	C
60 to 69	=	D
under 60	=	F

Round off average scores to the nearest tenth.

Use the following file variables:

```
F$ = "GRADES"
N = NUMBER OF STUDENTS
WEEK = WEEK #
NM$(I) = NAME OF EACH STUDENT
WEEKLYSCORE(I) = THIS WEEK'S SCORE
TOTALSCORE(I) = TOTAL SCORE SO FAR
LETTERGRADE$(I) = CURRENT GRADE
```

```
              GRADES
             WEEK # 3
------------------------------------
             WEEKLY  AVERAGE
NAME         SCORE   SCORE      GRADE
------------------------------------
ANTON        87      83.5       C
  .           .        .        .
  .           .        .        .
WESTON       66      88.5       B
------------------------------------
```

NOTE: This program is harder than it looks.

CHAPTER 11

FLYING SAUCERS

Using Sound and Graphics

NEW CONCEPTS TAUGHT

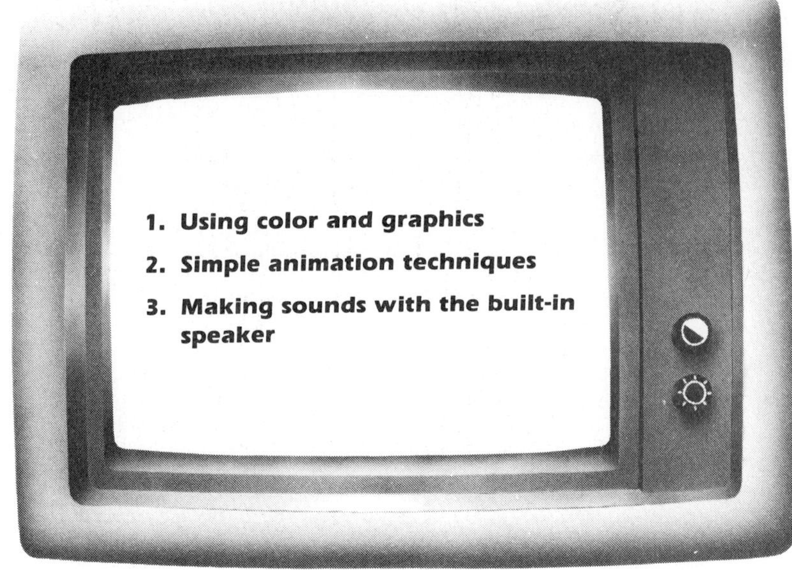

1. Using color and graphics
2. Simple animation techniques
3. Making sounds with the built-in speaker

GRAPHICS

No book on microcomputers would be complete without some discussion of graphics. Because of the complexity of the past few programs, we have tried to make this one a little more fun.

As we mentioned earlier, there are several ways of doing graphics on the computer. In this chapter we combine character graphics and medium-resolution graphics to produce a simple arcade-style game. This program comes in two versions: P11A–COL for computers with a color graphics adapter, and P11A–MON for computers with a monochrome display adapter.

The IBM has a special set of commands for graphics operations. The command SCREEN 1,0 puts the computer into the graphics mode and tells it we want to use color. Once in this mode, other commands can be used to change color, plot a line, or draw a filled or empty box on the screen. The commands are simple; they tell the computer the location of the things to be drawn and the color to use.

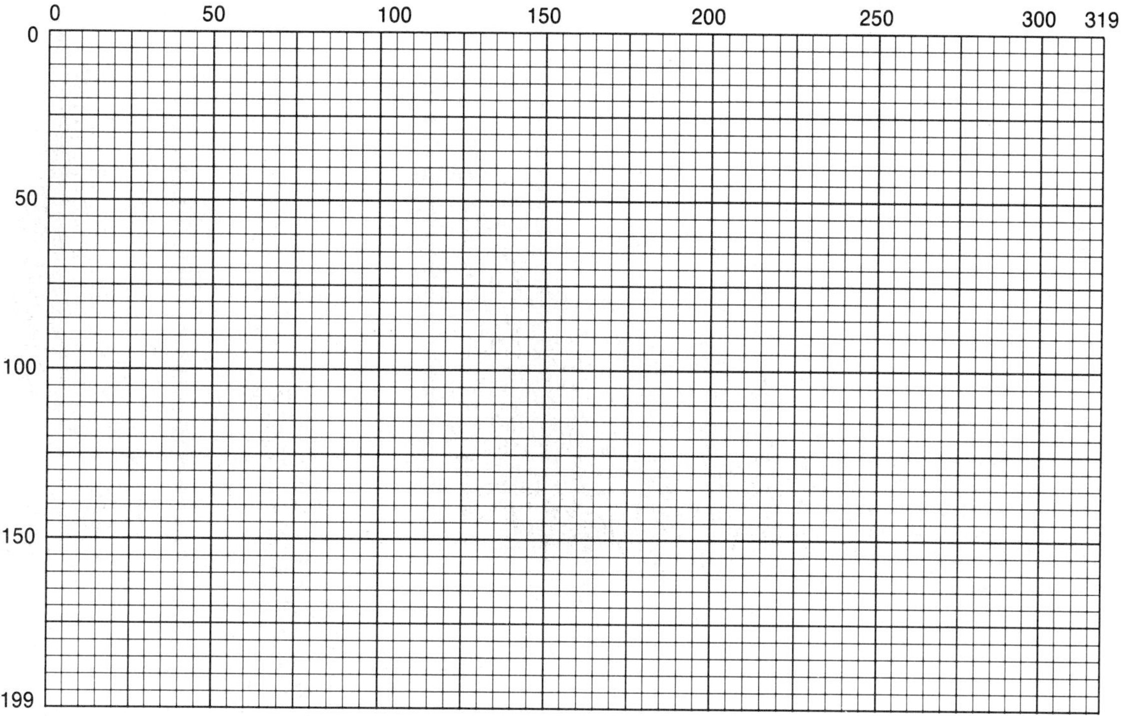

The graphics screen can be thought of as a grid of little squares just like the planning grid we used in chapter 7, except that it has many more points. It is 320 squares wide and 200 squares high. Some of the graphics commands require information about points on this grid. Although the grid is 320 X 200, the columns are numbered from 0 to 319 and the rows from 0 to 199. The LINE statement shows how these locations are expressed:

```
LINE  (Ø,Ø) - (319,199)
```

will draw a diagonal line from the upper left corner to the lower right corner of the screen;

```
LINE  (319,Ø) - (Ø,199)
```

will draw a line from the upper right corner to the lower left corner. The LINE statement can be used to perform a number of different functions. Each pair of numbers in parentheses specifies a single point on the screen (x,y), where x is the column or horizontal position on the screen and y is the row or vertical position on the screen. The simplest form of the LINE statement is:

```
LINE  -(x,y)
```

This draws a line from the last point referenced to the point specified by (x,y). The form used above:

```
LINE  (x1,y1)  -  (x2,y2)
```

draws a line between the two points specified by (x1,y1) and (x2,y2). The line command may also be followed by a comma and a color number, which will cause the line to be drawn in color.

```
LINE  (2Ø,2Ø)  -  (3Ø,3Ø),2
```

will draw a line at the upper left of the screen in color 2. If the color number is followed by a comma and B or BF, a colored box will be drawn instead of a line, using the two points specified as the corners of the box. B causes an empty box to be drawn, and BF causes the box to be filled. If the color number is left out, the box will be drawn in the current foreground color:

```
LINE  (2Ø,2Ø)  -  (3Ø,3Ø),,BF
```

Both commas must be present.

If you have a color graphics adapter but don't have a color monitor, you will still see some difference in the shading of the various colors.

The graphics commands will work in the immediate mode, so you can try them directly even when no program is running. Try typing SCREEN 1,0 ⟨Enter⟩. This puts the computer into the medium-resolution graphics mode. Next, type COLOR 1,1. This should give you white letters on a blue background. You can restore the screen to white letters on a black background by typing:

```
COLOR Ø,1
```

This is a good thing to remember, as some color combinations make text on the screen almost impossible to read.

The LINE statement also works when typed directly with no line number, but before you try it, read the next section on setting colors.

Getting the Color You Want

Trying to get the IBM to present the colors you want can be a frustrating experience. There are two tables of color codes and several color graphics modes. The parts of certain screen commands mean different things in different screen modes. To simplify the problem somewhat, we have confined ourselves to a small set of graphics statements and to screen mode 1 (medium-resolution color graphics).

In order for the graphics statements in this chapter to work, a

```
SCREEN 1,Ø
```

command must be given either directly or in a program line. The 1 sets graphics mode 1, and the 0 allows the use of color.

In table 11.1, the fifteen color numbers can be used to set the background color of the screen using the COLOR statement:

```
COLOR background, palette
```

where *background* is a number from 1 to 15 chosen from table 11.1 and *palette* is either 1 or 0. The palette determines which of the two palettes of three colors each shown in table 11.2 will be used.

TABLE 11.1

COLOR CODES

CODE	COLOR	CODE	COLOR
0	BLACK	8	GRAY
1	BLUE	9	LIGHT BLUE
2	GREEN	10	LIGHT GREEN
3	CYAN	11	LIGHT CYAN
4	RED	12	LIGHT RED
5	MAGENTA	13	LIGHT MAGENTA
6	BROWN	14	YELLOW
7	WHITE	15	HIGH-INTENSITY WHITE

Table 11.2 shows the two color palettes we can choose from in graphics mode 1.

```
10 COLOR 4,1
```

tells the computer to use color 4 from table 11.1 as the background color (red) and to select palette number 1. The palette selected determines what color will be used in certain graphics statements (PSET, PRESET, LINE, CIRCLE, PAINT, VIEW, and DRAW). We will be using just the LINE statement. We have found that palette 1 usually gives the best results when text and graphics are mixed.

TABLE 11.2

PALETTES

COLOR	PALETTE 0	PALETTE 1
1	GREEN	CYAN
2	RED	MAGENTA
3	BROWN	WHITE

Look at the following example:

```
5   CLS
10  SCREEN 1,0
20  COLOR 2,1
30  LINE (20,20) - (90,90),2,BF
```

Line 10 selects medium-resolution graphics mode 1 and allows the use of color. Line 20 selects color 2 (green) from table 11.1 as the background color and selects palette 1. Line 30 draws a filled box in palette color 2. Notice that with palette 1, table 11.2 shows palette color 2 to be magenta, so this is the color the box will be drawn in.

We recommend that you type in the simple program we have just discussed and experiment with it until you feel you understand how to get the colors you want for objects on the screen. This will save you a great deal of time and trouble when it comes to the exercise for this chapter.

SOUND

The simplest way to make the computer sound off is to type or PRINT a ⟨Ctrl-G⟩ (try it). The same result can be obtained with the BEEP statement. BEEP can be used in immediate mode or in a program line.

A more sophisticated way of creating sounds is to use the SOUND statement. The simple form of the SOUND statement is:

SOUND *f,d*

where *f* is the frequency of the sound in hertz (cycles/second) and *d* is the duration. Legal values for frequency are from 37 to 32767. Duration is measured in clock ticks. Clock ticks occur 18.2 times per second, so a duration of 18 means the sound lasts about a second. Legal values for duration range from .0015 to 65535. If you use a large value for duration, you may have to listen to the sound for quite a while.

In the program for this chapter, we are using a loop in BASIC to make the speaker do more than just beep. In the subroutine in line 600, we alternate a beep and a sound three times to produce the kind of sound a flying saucer makes when hit.

FLYING SAUCERS

Air Attack

In program 11A in figure 11.1, we have set up a simple arcade-type game, since this provides the best way to learn about graphics and animation. In this program a target moves back and forth at the top of the screen. When the space bar is pressed, a shot is fired from the cannonlike gun at the bottom of the screen. If the shell fired from the gun hits the target, the screen flashes, some noises are made, and the shooter's score goes up.

As we explained earlier, there are two versions of this program: P11A-COL for computers with color capabilities, and P11A-MON for those with only the monochrome adapter. The monochrome version uses character graphics, which we covered in chapter 7. The color version uses medium-resolution graphics, which is the focus of this chapter. Therefore, the following discussion will cover the color version.

Lines 101 to 120 perform some preliminary actions necessary to the program.

```
101  KEY OFF
102  SCREEN 1,0 :                  '  SET GRAPHICS MODE 1 IN COLOR
110  GOSUB 200 :                   '  SET UP TARGET
120  CLS
```

Line 101 turns off the function key display at the bottom of the screen. Line 102 selects medium-resolution graphics mode 1 and tells the computer we want color. Line 110 calls a subroutine at line 200 that sets the speed, width, and shape of the flying saucer.

```
200  ' =========== SET UP TARGET ==========
210  S = 2 :                                 '  SET SPEED
220  W = 3 :                                 '  WIDTH OF TARGET
230  SIDE$ = CHR$(21)
240  MIDDLE$ = STRING$(W-2,23)
250  SHIP$ = SIDE$ + MIDDLE$ + SIDE$ :'  DEFINE TARGET
260  RETURN
270  '
```

Line 120 clears the screen. In line 130 the game begins, giving the player five shots at the saucer.

```
130  GOSUB 300:                    '  DRAW GUN
140  FOR SHOT = 1 TO 5
150     GOSUB 400:                 '  SHOW TARGET
160     GOSUB 500:                 '  FIRE SHOT & CHECK FOR HIT
170  NEXT SHOT
180  GOSUB 1000:                   '  GIVE RESULTS
190  END
```

The Gun

The subroutine at line 300 draws the gun at the bottom of the graphics screen. In line 120 of the main part of the program, we entered the graphics mode and then took off (in line 130) for the subroutine at line 300.

```
300  '  ===== DRAW GUN =====
310  COLOR 1,1
320  LINE (97,165)-(202,175),1,B
330  LINE (142,130)-(153,170),1,BF
340  LOCATE 24, 8
350  PRINT "PRESS SPACE BAR TO FIRE";
360  RETURN
370  '
```

After the color is set in line 310 to give a blue background and select palette 1, line 320 draws the base of the gun as an empty box in color 1. Since palette 1 has been selected, color 1 is cyan, a greenish blue. Next, line 330 draws the barrel pointing up in the air as a filled box, also in cyan. Line 350 prints the message in at the bottom of the screen, and the program returns to the main section.

Shooting

The loop started at line 140 will execute five times (giving the player five shots). For each shot, the program goes to the subroutine at line 400, which moves the target back and forth at the top of the screen until the space bar is pressed, and then returns (more about this later). The fact that the space bar has been pressed means that the player wants to fire, so line 160 sends the program to the subroutine at line 500, which shows the shell coming out of the gun and traveling to the top of the screen. This subroutine checks for a hit and, if there is one, calls the hit subroutine at line 600, which flashes the screen, makes noise, and increases the player's score (number of hits).

```
130  GOSUB 300:                    '  DRAW GUN
140  FOR SHOT = 1 TO 5
150      GOSUB 400:                '  SHOW TARGET
160      GOSUB 500:                '  FIRE SHOT & CHECK FOR HIT
170  NEXT SHOT
180  GOSUB 1000:                   '  GIVE RESULTS
190  END
```

Then the program returns to the main section and the loop is done five times. When the player's five shots are up, results are given by the subroutine at line 1000.

Firing a Shot

The animation of the target in this program is relatively simple. One new concept is animating the target in such a way that pressing the space bar will initiate a shot. If we used a simple loop to animate the target and an INPUT statement to allow the user to press the space bar, then when the program got to the INPUT statement, the animation would stop. To solve this problem, we use the INKEY$ variable, which gives information about the keyboard. INKEY$ is a variable that holds the value of a key pressed on the keyboard. It allows us to "look" at the keyboard to see if any key has been pressed without stopping execution of the program. Thus, in the subroutine at line 400, every time we move the target (lines 440 and 470), we check to see if the space bar has been pressed (lines 445 and 475).

```
430  '                                 '  MOVE TARGET TO RIGHT
435  FOR A = 1 TO 35 STEP S
440     LOCATE 1,A : PRINT SHIP$ :     '    DRAW TARGET
445     IF INKEY$ = " " THEN RETURN :  '    RETURN IF SHOT FIRED
450     LOCATE 1,A : PRINT SPACE$(W) :'    ERASE PREVIOUS TARGET
455  NEXT A
460  '                                 '  MOVE TARGET TO LEFT
465  FOR A = 35 TO 1 STEP -S
470     LOCATE 1,A : PRINT SHIP$ :     '    DRAW TARGET
475     IF INKEY$ = " " THEN RETURN :  '    RETURN IF SHOT FIRED
480     LOCATE 1,A : PRINT SPACE$(W) :'    ERASE PREVIOUS TARGET
485  NEXT A
490  GOTO 430
```

When we first enter this subroutine, we clear the keyboard with

```
405  IF INKEY$ <> "" THEN GOTO 405
```

This is in case the player accidentally presses a key before the target is displayed. The program stays on line 405 until the keyboard buffer is empty. If we did not do this, the program might detect a "shot" when we didn't want it to.

Animating the Target

The subroutine at line 400 is really two different routines lumped together: one to move the target to the right (lines 430 to 455), and one to move it to the left (lines 460 to 485). We could put these in separate subroutines, but it would slow down the animation slightly.

In order to animate an object on the screen, two things have to happen. First, we need to "draw" the object (in this case the saucer) at a number of new locations on the screen. Second, we have to "erase" the object at the old locations; otherwise, in this program, we would soon have a solid line of ships across the top of the screen.

The function of the loop in lines 430 to 455 is to move the saucer to the right across the top of the screen. We define the saucer in lines 230 to 255:

```
230  SIDE$ = CHR$(21)
240  MIDDLE$ = STRING$(W-2,23)
250  SHIP$ = SIDE$ + MIDDLE$ + SIDE$ :'  DEFINE TARGET
```

This sets the ship to be a combination of characters from the IBM's extended character set. Each time through the loop, a ship will be drawn one column to the right of where it was drawn the previous time through the loop (in line 440). As we said above, if all we did were draw saucers, we would soon have a solid line of them across the top of the screen that would stay there for the rest of the program. To avoid this, every time through the loop we not only draw the saucer, but we also erase it (in line 450). What appears on the screen seems to be a single ship, moving from left to right across the screen.

Moving the target to the left is exactly the same, except that the limits in the FOR statement are reversed and the STEP is negative instead of positive. By the way, we could speed up the apparent motion of the target by increasing the size of the step, which is set in line 210. We could also increase the width of the target, which is set in line 220.

Notice that the two FOR/NEXT loops that move the target back and forth are inside of a simple GOTO loop (lines 420 to 490). This loop is endless, so that if no shot is fired, the target will move back and forth at the top of the screen forever.

Animating the Shell

Since the shell is only a single square on the screen, we use character graphics to draw it in the subroutine at line 500. Otherwise, the process is the same as that of animating the target. At each position along its path, we first draw the shell, and then erase it. When the loop is finished, the shell is at the top of the screen and may or may not have hit the target; the player has scored a hit if the shell location is on the target. Since the shell is always on column 19, it will be a hit if the left square of the target (A) is less than or equal to 19 *and* the right square of the target (A + W) is greater than or equal to 19. If the shot is a hit, we go to the subroutine at line 600 to make the sound and increment the number of hits. If the shot is not a hit, we don't have to do anything.

```
500  ' ============ SHOOT ============
510  FOR I = 15 TO 1 STEP -1
520     LOCATE I,19: PRINT CHR$(24) : '  DRAW SHELL
530     LOCATE I,19: PRINT " " :      '  ERASE SHELL
540  NEXT I
550  IF A <= 19 AND A + W - 1 >= 19 THEN GOSUB 600 : '  HIT
560  RETURN
570  '
```

Sounding Off

The subroutine at line 600 executes every time there is a hit. It flashes a red background and makes the two sounds (three times each), then increments the number of hits.

```
600  ' =========== HIT ===========
610  FOR I = 1 TO 3
620     COLOR 4,1 : COLOR 1,1
630     BEEP : SOUND 220,1
640  NEXT I
650  LET HITS = HITS + 1
660  RETURN
670  '
```

EXAMPLE 11A Flying Saucers

Problem Write a program that will use medium-resolution graphics and sound to simulate an antiaircraft gun shooting at a flying saucer. The saucer should move back and forth at the top of the screen, and the gun should be stationary at the center of the lower part of the screen. When the space bar is pressed, a shell should come out of the gun and move up to the top of the screen. If the shell hits the saucer, sounds should be made and the player's score (number of hits) should increase by one. Each run should give the player five shots and then print the results.

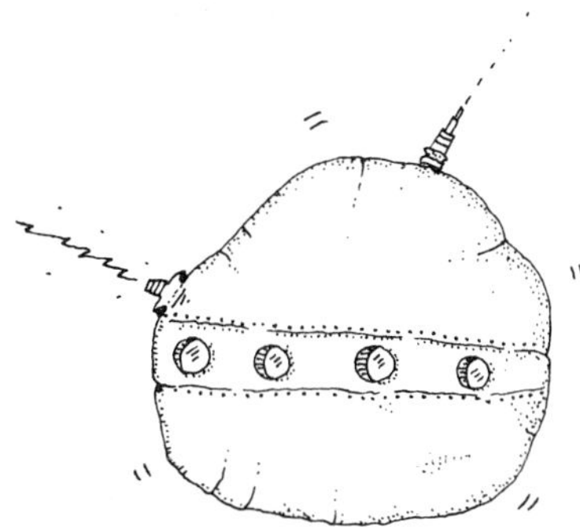

Solution

FIGURE 11.1

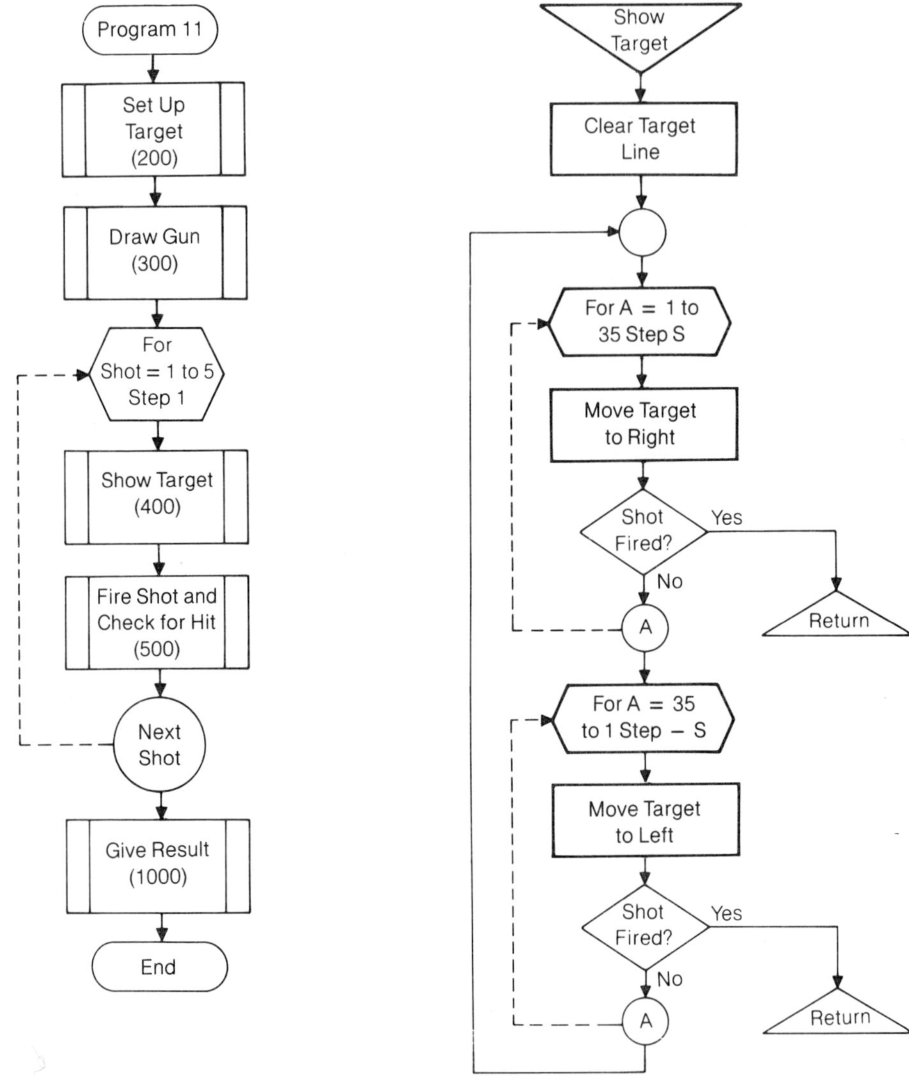

(Figure continued)

(Figure 11.1 continued)

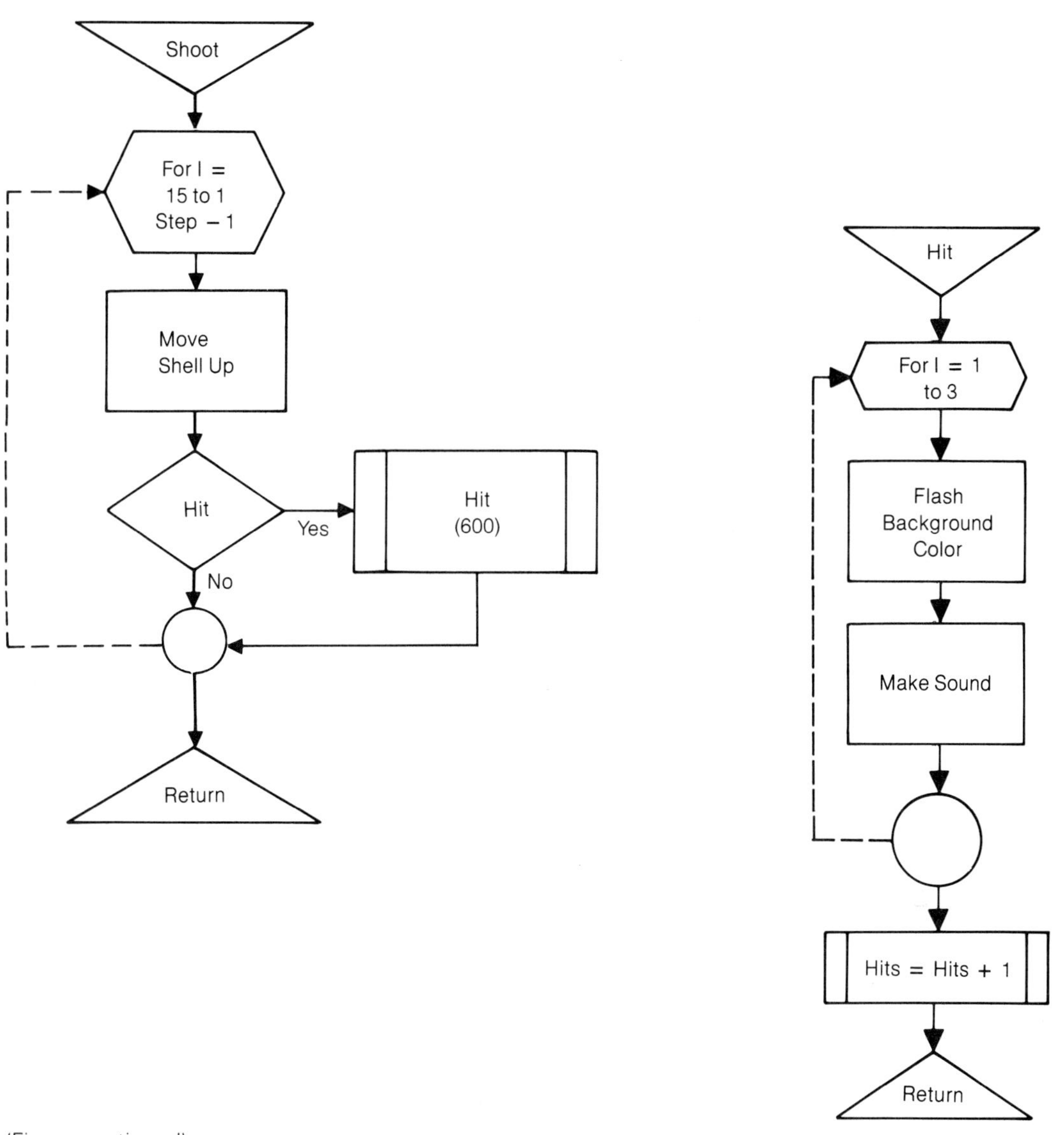

(Figure continued)

(Figure 11.1 continued)

P11A-COLOR VERSION

```
LIST
1     PN$ = "P11A-COL"
2     NA$ = "YOUR NAME"
3     DA$ = "00/00/00"
10    ' ===== VARIABLES =====
11    ' A = LEFT EDGE OF TARGET
12    ' SIDE$ = SIDES OF TARGET
13    ' I = LOOP COUNTER
14    ' J = LOOP COUNTER
15    ' MIDDLE$ = MIDDLE OF TARGET
16    ' S = SPEED OF TARGET
17    ' SHIP$ = SHAPE OF TARGET
18    ' SHOT = SHOT NUMBER
19    ' W = WIDTH OF TARGET
20    ' Z = DUMMY VARIABLE
100   ' ========== MAIN ==========
101   KEY OFF
102   SCREEN 1,0 :                          '  SET GRAPHICS MODE 1 IN COLOR
110   GOSUB 200 :                           '  SET UP TARGET
120   CLS
130   GOSUB 300:                            '  DRAW GUN
140   FOR SHOT = 1 TO 5
150      GOSUB 400:                         '  SHOW TARGET
160      GOSUB 500:                         '  FIRE SHOT & CHECK FOR HIT
170   NEXT SHOT
180   GOSUB 1000:                           '  GIVE RESULTS
190   END
200   ' =========== SET UP TARGET ==========
210   S = 2 :                               '  SET SPEED
220   W = 3 :                               '  WIDTH OF TARGET
230   SIDE$ = CHR$(21)
240   MIDDLE$ = STRING$(W-2,23)
250   SHIP$ = SIDE$ + MIDDLE$ + SIDE$ :'  DEFINE TARGET
260   RETURN
270   '
300   ' ========== DRAW GUN ==========
310   COLOR 1,1
320   LINE (97,165)-(202,175),1,B
330   LINE (142,130)-(153,170),1,BF
340   LOCATE 24, 8
350   PRINT "PRESS SPACE BAR TO FIRE";
360   RETURN
370   '
```

(Figure continued)

(Figure 11.1 continued)

```
400  ' ========== SHOW TARGET ==========
405  IF INKEY$ <> "" THEN GOTO 405 :  '  WAIT UNTIL BUFFER IS CLEAR
410  LOCATE 1,1
415  FOR I = 1 TO 39
420     PRINT " " ;:                  '  CLEAR FIRST LINE
425  NEXT I
430  '                                '  MOVE TARGET TO RIGHT
435  FOR A = 1 TO 35 STEP S
440     LOCATE 1,A : PRINT SHIP$ :    '    DRAW TARGET
445     IF INKEY$ = " " THEN RETURN : '    RETURN IF SHOT FIRED
450     LOCATE 1,A : PRINT SPACE$(W) :'    ERASE PREVIOUS TARGET
455  NEXT A
460  '                                '  MOVE TARGET TO LEFT
465  FOR A = 35 TO 1 STEP -S
470     LOCATE 1,A : PRINT SHIP$ :    '    DRAW TARGET
475     IF INKEY$ = " " THEN RETURN : '    RETURN IF SHOT FIRED
480     LOCATE 1,A : PRINT SPACE$(W) :'    ERASE PREVIOUS TARGET
485  NEXT A
490  GOTO 430
495  STOP :                           '  THIS SHOULDN'T HAPPEN
499  '
500  ' =========== SHOOT ===========
510  FOR I = 15 TO 1 STEP -1
520     LOCATE I,19: PRINT CHR$(24) : '  DRAW SHELL
530     LOCATE I,19: PRINT " " :      '  ERASE SHELL
540  NEXT I
550  IF A <= 19 AND A + W - 1 >= 19 THEN GOSUB 600 : '  HIT
560  RETURN
570  '
600  ' =========== HIT ===========
610  FOR I = 1 TO 3
620     COLOR 4,1 : COLOR 1,1
630     BEEP : SOUND 220,1
640  NEXT I
650  LET HITS = HITS + 1
660  RETURN
670  '
1000  ' ========== GIVE RESULTS ==========
1010  CLS : PRINT "HITS = "HITS
1020  RETURN
Ok
RUN
```

(Figure continued)

(Figure 11.1 continued)

P11A-MONOCHROME VERSION

```
LIST
1     PN$ = "P11A-MON"
2     NA$ = "YOUR NAME"
3     DA$ = "00/00/00"
10    ' ===== VARIABLES =====
11    ' A = POSITION OF LEFT EDGE OF TARGET
12    ' SIDE$ = SIDES OF TARGET
13    ' I = LOOP COUNTER
14    ' J = LOOP COUNTER
15    ' MIDDLE$ = MIDDLE OF TARGET
16    ' S = SPEED OF TARGET
17    ' SHIP$ = SHAPE OF TARGET
18    ' SHOT = SHOT NUMBER
19    ' W = WIDTH OF TARGET
20    ' Z = DUMMY VARIABLE
100   ' ========== MAIN ==========
105   KEY OFF
110   GOSUB 200 :                   '  SET UP TARGET
120   CLS
130   GOSUB 300:                    '  DRAW GUN
140   FOR SHOT = 1 TO 5
150      GOSUB 400:                 '  SHOW TARGET
160      GOSUB 500:                 '  FIRE SHOT & CHECK FOR HIT
170   NEXT SHOT
180   GOSUB 1000:                   '  GIVE RESULTS
190   END
195   '
200   ' =========== SET UP TARGET ==========
210   S = 2 :                       '  SET SPEED
220   W = 3 :                       '  WIDTH OF TARGET
230   SIDE$ = CHR$(21)
240   MIDDLE$ = STRING$(W-2,23)
250   SHIP$ = SIDE$ + MIDDLE$ + SIDE$ :'  DEFINE TARGET
260   RETURN
270   '
300   ' ========== DRAW GUN ==========
310   FOR I = 19 TO 21
320      LOCATE I,39 : PRINT "|" :  '  DRAW GUN
330   NEXT I
340   LOCATE 22,1
350   FOR I = 1 TO 79
360      PRINT "-";                 '  DRAW BASE
370   NEXT I
380   LOCATE 24,28 : PRINT "PRESS SPACE BAR TO FIRE";
390   RETURN
399   '
```

(Figure continued)

(Figure 11.1 continued)

```
400  ' ========== SHOW TARGET ==========
405  IF INKEY$ <> "" THEN GOTO 405 :  '  WAIT UNTIL BUFFER IS CLEAR
410  LOCATE 1,1
415  FOR I = 1 TO 79
420     PRINT " "; :                  '  CLEAR FIRST LINE
425  NEXT I
430  '                                '  MOVE TARGET TO RIGHT
435  FOR A = 1 TO 75 STEP S
440     LOCATE 1,A : PRINT SHIP$ :    '    DRAW TARGET
445     IF INKEY$ = " " THEN RETURN : '    RETURN IF SHOT FIRED
450     LOCATE 1,A : PRINT SPACE$(W) :'    ERASE PREVIOUS TARGET
455  NEXT A
460  '                                '  MOVE TARGET TO LEFT
465  FOR A = 75 TO 1 STEP -S
470     LOCATE 1,A : PRINT SHIP$ :    '    DRAW TARGET
475     IF INKEY$ = " " THEN RETURN : '    RETURN IF SHOT FIRED
480     LOCATE 1,A : PRINT SPACE$(W) :'    ERASE PREVIOUS TARGET
485  NEXT A
490  GOTO 430 :                       '  LOOP BACK
495  STOP :                           '  THIS SHOULDN"T HAPPEN
499  '
500  ' ============ SHOOT ============
510  FOR I = 15 TO 1 STEP -1
520     LOCATE I,39: PRINT CHR$(24) : '  DRAW SHELL
530     LOCATE I,39: PRINT " " :      '  ERASE SHELL
540  NEXT I
550  IF A <= 39 AND A + W - 1 >= 39 THEN GOSUB 600 : '  HIT
560  RETURN
570  '
600  ' =========== HIT ===========
610  FOR I = 1 TO 3
630     BEEP : SOUND 220,1
640  NEXT I
650  LET HITS = HITS
660  RETURN
670  '
1000  ' =========== GIVE RESULTS ===========
1010  CLS : PRINT "HITS = "HITS
1020  RETURN
Ok
```

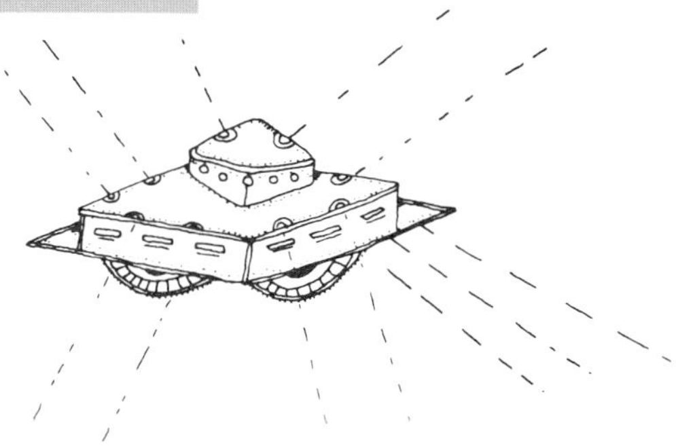

EXERCISES

Choose One of the Following

11.1 Use medium-resolution graphics to animate a simple figure (a square or line) that moves back and forth across the screen. The figure should appear to "bounce" back and forth between the edges of the screen. Have the speaker make a sound when the figure changes direction.

TIPS

1. **Use one subroutine to move the figure to the right and a separate subroutine to move it to the left.**
2. **Don't forget to erase the figure before drawing it in each new location.**
3. **Be sure to set the color of the figure so it will be visible.**

11.2 Write a program that will use medium-resolution graphics to draw a figure on the screen. Then move the figure back and forth by repeatedly drawing it, then erasing it and redrawing it in a new location. Have the program make a sound each time the figure moves.

TIPS

1. **Use a subroutine for drawing the figure in one location, a separate subroutine to draw it in the other location.**
2. **Erase the figure by setting the color to 0 and calling the same subroutine used to draw it.**
3. **Do not put a COLOR statement in the subroutines that draw the figure. Set the color before calling the subroutines.**

11.3 Write a program using sound and medium-resolution graphics to simulate program 11A, but with the following differences. Instead of a gun, draw a ship that sits at the top of the screen. Change the saucer to a submarine and have it move back and forth at the bottom of the screen. When the player presses the space bar, have the ship drop a depth charge that falls to the bottom of the screen.

In addition, add a subroutine to give the player a choice of several target widths and speeds, and print various messages at the end depending on the score (e.g., "Your score of 5 qualifies you as a master gunner"). Have the program make another sound when the player shoots and misses the target.

TIPS

1. **Type in the program as in program 11A and get it working before modifying it in any way.**
2. **Change the shape of the ship, sub, and shell and then move them to their new locations.**
3. **Add a new subroutine that asks the player to choose the values for speed and target size.**
4. **Remember that any operation you put inside an animation loop will slow down the animation.**

APPENDIX A

The Mini-Manual Table of Contents

THE MINI-MANUAL

1. KEYS AND COMMANDS

1.1 Keys

1.11 Cursor The cursor is a blinking underline character that marks the current location on the screen. When a key is pressed, the character appears on the screen where the cursor was and the cursor is moved one position to the right.

1.12 Arrow keys The right arrow key moves the cursor to the right and the left arrow key moves the cursor to the left. Both arrow keys can move the cursor over characters on the screen without changing them. The arrow keys are used to make changes in a program line. The arrows are to the right of the keyboard. The up and down arrows are also used in editing (described in chapter 0).

1.13 Ctrl-Break Ctrl-Break is accomplished by holding the Ctrl, or Control, key down and pressing the Break key at the upper right of the keyboard. On the PCjr, press ⟨Fn Break⟩. The effect of these keys is to stop a computer run or list. If a run has been stopped, you can sometimes resume the run by typing the letters CONT and pressing the Enter key. Ctrl-Break is also used to exit the AUTO line numbering mode.

1.14 Del and Ins keys The Del, or Delete, key is used in editing to delete the character at the cursor position. The Ins, or Insert, key is used to insert characters at the cursor position. See chapter 0 for more information about editing.

1.15 Enter key You press the Enter key at the end of each line in your program and after typing a command such as RUN or LIST. The Enter key initiates the computer's response to the line you just finished typing.

1.16 Space bar This is the long bar at the bottom of the keyboard. The space bar is used to produce blank spaces on the screen.

1.17 Ctrl-Num Lock Holding the Control key and the Num Lock key at the upper right of the keyboard at the same time will stop any output to the screen. Whatever is on the screen will be "frozen" there until output is restarted. Pressing any key will restart the output. On the PCjr this is accomplished with ⟨Fn-Pause⟩. Holding the Control key and alternately pressing the Num Lock key and the Home key is a convenient way to stop and start the listing of a long program.

1.18 Num Lock The Num Lock key switches the keys of the IBM PC's numeric keypad at the right of the keyboard between their two uses. These keys can be used to move the cursor on the screen. They can also be used as a numeric keypad like the one on an electronic calculator. Whichever mode these keys are in, the Num Lock key will switch them to the other mode. If you are trying to move the cursor and the computer is typing numbers on the screen, you need to press the Num Lock key. If you have accidentally typed some numbers, be careful not to type ⟨Enter⟩ or you may delete a line of your program (typing a line number by itself followed by ⟨Enter⟩ deletes a program line).

1.19 Function keys The function keys are located at the left side of the IBM PC keyboard and marked F1 through F10. They can be used as shortcuts to typing some of the more common commands in BASIC. They may also be reprogrammed for other uses (see the KEY ON OFF LIST, section 1.24, for more details). On the PCjr, which does not have separate function keys, type the Fn key followed by one of the number keys at the top of the keyboard. The current settings of the function keys are displayed at the bottom of the screen.

1.2 Screen Commands

1.21 CLS CLS may be used when no program is running or in a program line. The result is to clear the screen and move the cursor to the upper left of the screen.

Example:

```
10  CLS
```

When no program is running, typing ⟨Ctrl-Home⟩ will have the same effect. On the PCjr you must type ⟨Ctrl-Fn-Home⟩.

1.22 SCREEN A full description of the SCREEN command is beyond the scope of this book. In the form we will use it, the SCREEN command is used as follows:

`SCREEN` *mode*, *colorflag*

where *mode* is the video mode and *colorflag* is a numeric expression resulting in either 0 or 1. (IBM's name for the colorflag is "burst.") The effect of *colorflag* depends on the current video mode. Valid modes are 0–2 for the PC and 0–6 for the PCjr.

Video Modes

Mode	Effect
0	Text mode at current width.
1	Medium-resolution graphics mode (320x200 dots). 4 colors.
2	High-resolution graphics mode (640x200 dots). 2 colors.
3	Low-resolution graphics mode (160x200 dots). 16 colors. Available only with Cartridge BASIC.
4	Medium-resolution graphics mode (320x200 dots). 4 colors. Available only with Cartridge BASIC.
5	Medium-resolution graphics mode (320x200 dots). 16 colors. Available only with Cartridge BASIC. Requires 128K of memory.
6	High-resolution graphics mode (640x200 dots). 4 colors. Available only with Cartridge BASIC. Requires 128K of memory.

In text mode (mode 0), a *colorflag* of 1 enables (allows) color and a *colorflag* of 0 disables color. In color modes 1 and 4, this effect is reversed. A *colorflag* of 0 enables color and a *colorflag* of 1 disables color. In the other modes (2, 3, 5, and 6), the *colorflag* has no effect; in these modes, color is always on.

1.23 WIDTH The WIDTH statement may be used when no program is running or in a program line. On a computer with a color display adapter, the WIDTH statement sets the screen width. The only acceptable values are 40 and 80. On a computer with a monochrome display adapter, the WIDTH statement has no effect.

Examples:

```
10  WIDTH 40 : ' SETS THE SCREEN TO 40 COLUMNS
20  WIDTH 80 : ' SETS THE SCREEN TO 80 COLUMNS
```

The WIDTH statement may also be used to set the width of the printer or of a file but is seldom used in this way.

1.24 KEY ON OFF LIST The KEY command controls the key display at the bottom of the screen and also allows the programming of the function keys. See section 1.19 for a discussion of the function keys and how to use them.

`KEY ON` turns on the function key display
`KEY OFF` turns off the function key display
`KEY LIST` lists the current settings of the function keys
`KEY` *n*, "*string*" sets function key *n* so that when it is pressed, the string *string* is printed. The string must not be more than 15 characters long.

Example: If you type:

```
KEY 4,"SAVE PN$"
```

and press ⟨Enter⟩, function key F4 will be redefined for convenient saving of a program immediately after a successful run of the program. This assumes that line 1 assigns the program name to PN$ as illustrated below.

```
1   PN$ = "P11A-MON"
```

Following a run of the program, PN$ will contain the name of the program. You can save the program by simply pressing the redefined F4 key followed by the Enter key.

1.25 LOCATE Used prior to a PRINT or INPUT statement to set the position of the cursor on the screen. The general form is

`LOCATE` *row* **,** *column*

where *row* is the distance of the cursor from the top of the screen and *column* is the distance of the cursor from the left side of the screen. Legal values are 1–25 for *row* and 1–80 for *column*.

Example:

```
10  LOCATE 12,20
20  PRINT "X"
```

The above example will print an "X" 12 rows from the top of the screen and 20 columns from the left.

1.3 Disk Commands

1.31 BASIC and BASICA From the DOS prompt (usually A⟩), typing BASIC or BASICA will run the program that puts you in the BASIC language system. Both BASIC and BASICA are versions of disk BASIC. BASICA is called advanced BASIC and has several features that BASIC does not, including some graphics and sound commands. This book assumes you are using BASICA.

1.32 Filenames IBM BASIC has very strict rules concerning filenames. A filename consists of two parts, a name and an extension. The name can be up to eight characters long. The extension can be up to three characters long. The name and the extension are separated by a period (.):

```
NAME.EXT
```

Although certain other characters are legal in a filename, it is usually a good practice to use only the letters A–Z and the numerals 0–9. **Filenames should not contain spaces.** Putting spaces in a filename can cause you a great deal of trouble. In BASIC it is common to leave off the extension when specifying a filename. BASIC will add the default extension:

```
.BAS
```

This addition is automatic for the LOAD, RUN, and SAVE commands. For the KILL command the entire filename and extension must be specified.

1.33 FILES If there is a disk in the disk drive and you type FILES and press ⟨Enter⟩, a list of the programs stored on the disk will be displayed on the screen. FILES" *.BAS" will display only BASIC programs. If you have two disk drives

```
FILES"B:*.BAS"
```

will list all BASIC programs on drive B:.

1.34 KILL If you type KILL followed by the name of a program on the disk in the disk drive (in quotes) and press ⟨Enter⟩, the named program will be removed from the disk. You must give the full name including the extension.

Example:

```
KILL "PROGRAM1.BAS"
```

would remove PROGRAM1.BAS from the disk.

1.35 LOAD and MERGE If you type LOAD followed by the name of a program on the disk in the disk drive (in quotes), then press ⟨Enter⟩, the named program will be copied from the disk into the computer memory.

Example:

```
LOAD"PROGRAM1.BAS"
```

or

```
LOAD"PROGRAM1"
```

the extension need not be specified if it is "BAS". ⟨F3⟩ may be used as a shortcut instead of typing:

```
LOAD"
```

The MERGE command works like the LOAD command except that it merges the program on the disk with the one in memory. If there is any overlap in the line numbers, the ones in the merged program replace those in the program in memory. For this command to work, the file to be merged must have been saved in ASCII format with the ",A" option of the SAVE command (see SAVE).

1.36 SAVE If you type SAVE followed by a name for your program (in quotes) and press ⟨Enter⟩, the program in computer memory will be saved on your disk with the given name. If you give a name with no extension, the computer will add the extension "BAS". If the SAVE command is followed by ",A" as follows:

```
SAVE "PROGRAM1",A
```

the program will be saved to the disk in ASCII format. Normally BASIC programs are stored in an abbreviated code that is readable only by the BASIC language system. Using the ",A" option saves the program in a literal form, letter by letter. Saving a program in ASCII format is a little slower and is usually not necessary. An ASCII-formatted file can be merged with another program using the MERGE command and can also be edited using most word processors.

If line 1 of the program assigns the name of the program to PN$, e.g.:

```
1   PN$ = "P8A-TAB"
```

You can save the program immediately after a run by typing:

```
SAVE PN$  <Enter>
```

This method saves time and eliminates possible typing errors that result in a difference between the name on line 1 and the actual file name.

1.37 RUN If you type RUN followed by the name of a program on the disk in the disk drive (in quotes) and then press ⟨Enter⟩, the named program will be copied from the disk into computer memory and a run will be executed.

Example:

```
RUN "PROGRAM1"
```

will cause PROGRAM1 to be loaded and run. Any program in memory will be lost.

1.38 SYSTEM If you type SYSTEM, the computer will exit from the BASIC language program and return you to DOS.

1.39 NAME Files may be renamed by using the NAME command as follows:

```
NAME "OLDNAME.BAS" AS "NEWNAME.BAS"
```

The file to be renamed must exist, and both files must have legal filenames and include the extension.

1.4 Program Commands

1.41 CONT When a program run has been halted by a STOP, END, or Ctrl-Break, you can resume the run at the next instruction after the halt by typing CONT and pressing ⟨Enter⟩.

1.42 DELETE You can remove a section of a program by typing DELETE followed by the beginning and ending line numbers separated by a hyphen ("–"). As usual, press ⟨Enter⟩ to initiate the computer action. In some cases both line numbers must exist for this command to work properly.

Example:

Type `DELETE 60 - 120` and press ⟨Enter⟩ to remove all instructions from 60 to 120 inclusive.

1.43 LIST If you type LIST and then press ⟨Enter⟩, your entire program will be listed on the screen. Other possibilities are illustrated below (any numbers may be substituted for 60 and 120 in the examples below as long as the second number is larger than the first).

Example 1: `LIST 60` will list only line 60 of your program.

Example 2: `LIST 60-120` will list all lines in your program from line 60 to line 120 inclusive.

Example 3: `LIST 60-` will list all lines in your program from line 60 to the end of the program.

Example 4: `LIST -60` will list all lines in your program from the beginning to line 60 inclusive.

⟨F1⟩ can be used as a shortcut for the LIST command.

1.44 NEW If you type NEW and press ⟨Enter⟩, the program in your computer's memory will be removed. It cannot be recovered, so use this command carefully.

1.45 RUN If you type RUN and press ⟨Enter⟩, the computer will begin to carry out the program in memory (if any) at the lowest line number. ⟨F2⟩ may be used as a shortcut for this command.

Another possibility is: `RUN 60`
This will begin execution of the program at line 60

1.46 AUTO The AUTO command saves you the trouble of typing line numbers. The AUTO command used alone will start line numbering at 10 and use an increment of 10. You may also specify the starting line number and the increment between lines by putting the desired numbers after the AUTO command, separated by a comma.

Examples: `AUTO`

produces line numbers 10, 20, 30, ...

`AUTO 100,`

produces line numbers 100, 110, 120, ...

```
AUTO 15,5
```

produces line numbers 15, 20, 25, 30 ...

If the current line number is in use, AUTO flags it with an asterisk (*). If you press ⟨Enter⟩, the line will not be changed and AUTO will go to the next line number in the sequence. You may exit AUTO by typing ⟨Ctrl-C⟩ or ⟨Ctrl-Break⟩. ⟨Alt-A⟩ may be used as a shortcut for the AUTO command.

1.47 RENUM The RENUM command allows the renumbering of a BASIC program. Using RENUM alone renumbers the entire program. The new version of the program will start at line 10 and have a line increment of 10. Optionally, RENUM may be followed by up to three numbers that specify how the renumbering is to be done. The first number specifies the starting line number of the new version of the program. The second number specifies the line number in the old version where the renumbering operation is to start. Lines with numbers below this will not be changed. The third number specifies the increment to be used in the renumbering operation. If a program line contains a line number (as in `100   GOTO 500`), RENUM will change it if the line number referenced is changed by the renumbering operation.

Examples: `RENUM`

renumbers the entire program. The first new line number is 10. The line increment is also 10.

```
RENUM 500,100,5
```

renumbers all program lines starting with line 100. The new lines will start at line 500 and will have an increment of 5.

```
RENUM 100,,1
```

renumbers the entire program. The new program will begin at line 100 and have an increment of 1.

1.48 TRON/TROFF TRON stands for "Trace On." It causes the line number of the lines being executed to be displayed during the run of a program. This can be useful for debugging. TROFF turns this feature off.

1.5 Printer Commands

1.51 PrtSc The PrtSc key at the lower right of the keyboard allows you to "dump" what is on the screen to the printer. The shift key must be held down in order for this key to work. The function key display at the bottom of the screen will also be printed. If you don't want it in your printed output, use the KEY OFF command to turn the display off. The printer must be turned on and ready for this command to work. This command can be used even when a program is running.

1.52 Ctrl-PrtSc If you hold the Ctrl key down and press the PrtSc key, it turns on output to the printer. Everything that is printed from that point on will also appear on the printer. Typing the Ctrl-PrtSc key again turns this effect off. The printer must be turned on and ready for this command to work.

1.53 LLIST The LLIST command is used to list all or part of a program on the printer. Typing LLIST by itself will cause the entire program to be listed on the printer. Following LLIST with line numbers in the same form as the LIST command will cause part of the program to be listed. See section 1.43 on the LIST command for more details. The printer must be turned on and ready for this command to work.

1.54 LPRINT The LPRINT command can be used in a program to print messages on the printer.

Example: `10  LPRINT "HELLO THERE"`

will cause HELLO THERE to be printed on the printer. LPRINT can also be used in direct mode (at the BASIC prompt) to print a message on the printer. This can be useful for printing a heading at the top of a program listing.

Example: `LPRINT "PROGRAM ONE VERSION THREE"`

The printer must be turned on and ready for this command to work.

2. NUMBERS, VARIABLES, AND EXPRESSIONS

2.1 Number Format

In IBM BASIC, there are three kinds of numbers: integer, single-precision, and double-precision.

An integer can be any number from −32768 to 32767. Single- and double-precision numbers must be in the range from -1.7×10^{38} to 1.7×10^{38}. (An error message is printed when the absolute value of a number is greater than 1.7×10^{38}.)

Single-precision numbers are printed with up to seven digits, but only six digits will be accurate. Commas are not allowed to separate the digits into groups of three.

Examples: 27.345 is printed as 27.345
−1,000 is printed as −1000
1,263,457 is printed as 1263457

Numbers with absolute values less than 2.9×10^{-39} are converted to zero.

Examples: 1.63×10^{-50} is printed as 0
-4.7×10^{-40} is printed as 0

Single-precision numbers with absolute values greater than 9,999,999 or less than 0.0000001 are printed in scientific notation. In place of the normal superscript notation of the exponent, the letter E (or D) is used to indicate scientific notation. Single-precision numbers use E, double-precision numbers use D.

Examples: E or D means "times 10 to the power of"

1,000,000,000 is printed as 1E + 09
-24.632×10^{10} is printed as $-2.4632E+11$
0.0000000236 is printed as $-2.4362E+11$

Double-precision numbers are stored with 17 digits of precision and printed with up to 16 digits.

2.2 Variable Names

Variable names are used to identify memory cells that each contain a single number or a group of characters called a string. A variable name must begin with a letter of the alphabet and may be followed by additional letters of the alphabet or digits from 0 through 9. In some BASIC systems, only the first two characters of a variable name are significant (i.e., used to distinguish one variable name from another). However, in IBM BASIC, the first 40 characters are significant. Variable names may not be reserved words (i.e., words that have special meaning to BASIC—see appendix C).

A variable name determines whether a number or a string is stored in the named memory cell. For numbers, the variable name also determines the type and precision of the number. Numbers may be stored as integers, single-precision values (seven digits or less), or double-precision values (up to 17 digits). Single- and double-precision numbers generally include a decimal point and may be printed in an exponential form. For further information, see section 2.1, Number Format.

String variable names end with a $. Integer variable names end with a %. Single-precision variable names end with a !. Double-precision variable names end with a #. If no explicit identifier is used, the variable is single-precision (unless it is predefined as described below).

Variables with no explicit identifier may be predefined to have a given precision using the BASIC statements DEFINT, DEFSNG, DEFDBL, and DEFSTR—which define variables to be integer, single, double, and string, respectively. The statement

```
10  DEFINT I,J,K
```

tells the computer to treat variables beginning with the letters I, J, and K as integer variables. The following statement does the same thing:

```
10  DEFINT I-K
```

Examples of variable names:

```
A     C$     B%     C2!     BOX     SUM     PRODUCT
```

2.3 Names and Messages

Names and messages are enclosed between quotation marks to distinguish them from numbers. Any character except a quotation mark may be used in a message, including spaces. Names and messages are called strings because they consist of a string of characters.

Example: The following instruction will print the message. "MY NAME IS JOHN"

```
10  PRINT "MY NAME IS JOHN"
```

A message is printed exactly as it appears, including all spaces that are placed between the quotation marks. A single string may include as many as 255 characters or as few as 0 characters.

2.4 String Variable Names

When a memory cell is used to store a message, a dollar symbol ($) is appended to the variable name that identifies the memory cell. Such names are sometimes called string variable names to differentiate them from variable names that identify memory cells that store numbers. String variable names must begin with a letter of the alphabet and may be followed by one or more alphanumeric characters.

Examples of string variable names:

```
A$          B$          C1$          NAME$          ADDRESS$
```

2.5 Arithmetic Symbols

The following symbols are used in BASIC programs to form arithmetic expressions:

Symbol	Operation	Priority	Example
( )	do what is inside the parentheses first	1	$\frac{1}{A + B}$ is written 1/(A + B)
^	exponentiation	2	X^2 is written X ^ 2
–	negation	3	– 5 is written as – 5
/	division	4	2 ÷ A is written 2 / A
*	multiplication	4	2 x A is written 2 * A
\	integer division	5	X \ Y
MOD	modular arithmetic	6	X MOD Y (spaces are critical)
–	subtraction	7	B – A is written B – A
+	addition	7	A + 2 is written A + 2

Priority 3 is reserved for the minus sign when it is used to indicate the negative value of a quantity. This occurs only when there is no number or variable name to the immediate left of the minus sign. For example, the minus sign has priority 3 in the statement X = −2*2, which results in a value of −4 for the variable X. However, the minus sign has priority 5 in the statement Y = 4 − 2*2, which sets Y equal to 0. Also see section 2.8.

Integer division gives only the quotient of the division operation as we do it longhand. The remainder is discarded. For example, X = 5\2 results in a value of 2 for X.

Modulo arithmetic gives only the remainder of an integer division operation. The quotient is discarded. For example:

```
Y = 5 MOD 2
```

results in a value of 1 for Y. The MOD operator must have a space on each side of it. Y = 5MOD2 will give an erroneous result.

2.6 Arithmetic Expressions

A BASIC arithmetic expression consists of variable names and numbers separated by arithmetic operators. The computer evaluates arithmetic expressions from left to right in priority order—priority 1 is first and priority 5 is last (see section 2.5).

Examples:
```
4 * X ^ 2 + 6 * X - 7
(A + B) / (A - B)
```

When the value of an arithmetic expression is to be put in a memory cell, an equal sign is placed between the variable name on the left and the expression on the right.

Example:

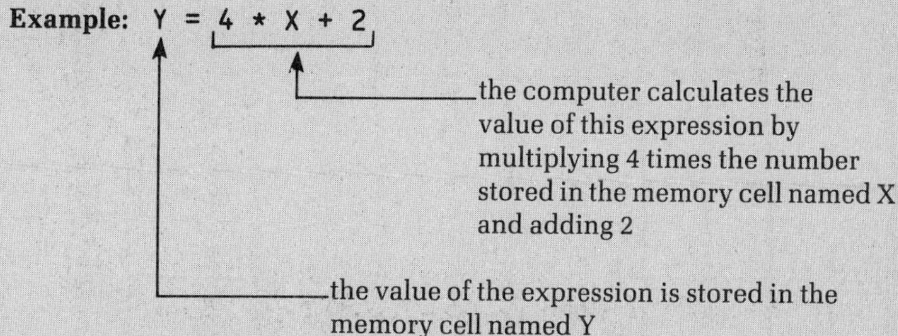

Y = 4 * X + 2
the computer calculates the value of this expression by multiplying 4 times the number stored in the memory cell named X and adding 2
the value of the expression is stored in the memory cell named Y

2.7 Relational Symbols and Conditionals

Conditionals are used in IF statements between the word IF and the word THEN or GOTO. A conditional has only two possible values: TRUE or FALSE. TRUE expressions have a value of −1; FALSE expressions have a value of 0.

A conditional consists of two expressions separated by one of the following relational symbols:

Relational Symbol	Meaning
=	equal to
>	greater than
<	less than
< > or > <	not equal to
< =	less than or equal to
> =	greater than or equal to

Examples of relational expressions :

```
A = B + C
X - Y < = 27
2 * X -2 > = 5 *  Y + 2
```

2.8 Logical Operators and Expressions

IBM BASIC allows the use of logical operators to form more complex conditionals in IF statements. The logical operators are: NOT, AND, OR, XOR, EQV, and IMP.

Logical operators are used to connect two or more conditionals (also called relations) and return a true or false value. A true value is assigned the number −1, and a false value is assigned the number 0.

If X and Y are two conditionals, then the following tables define the result of connecting X and Y with a logical operator.

NOT

X	NOT X
F	T
T	F

i.e., NOT X is the opposite of X

AND

X	Y	X AND Y
F	F	F
F	T	F
T	F	F
T	T	T

i.e., X AND Y is true only if both X and Y are true

OR

X	Y	X OR Y
F	F	F
F	T	T
T	F	T
T	T	T

i.e., X OR Y is true if either X or Y is true

XOR

X	Y	X XOR Y
F	F	F
F	T	T
T	F	T
T	F	F

i.e., X XOR Y is true if X and Y have opposite values

EQV

X	Y	X EQV Y
F	F	T
F	T	F
T	F	F
T	T	T

i.e., X EQV Y is true if X and Y have same values

IMP

X	Y	X IMP Y
F	F	T
F	T	T
T	F	F
T	T	T

i.e., X IMP Y is false if X is true and Y is false

A complex conditional may consist of any meaningful combination of numbers, variable names, arithmetic symbols, logical operators, and relational symbols. The combined operators and symbols are listed in priority order in the following table:

Symbol	Priority	Meaning
( )	1	do what is inside the parentheses first
^	2	exponentiation
-	3	indicates a negative quantity (only when there is nothing on the left of the minus sign)
*	4	multiplication
/	4	division
/	5	integer division
MOD	6	modulo arithmetic
+	7	addition
-	7	subtraction
=	8	equal to
>	8	greater than
<	8	less than
> = or = >	8	greater than or equal to
< = or = <	8	less than or equal to
< > or > <	8	not equal to
NOT	9	logic negation operator
AND	10	logic intersection operator
OR	11	logic summation operator
XOR	12	logic exclusive or operator
EQV	13	logic equivalence operator
IMP	14	logic implication operator

Symbols of the same priority are evaluated from left to right.

Examples of complex expressions:

1. `A < B AND C = D` Expression 1 is TRUE only if both A < B and C = D.

2. `X < = Y OR Z = 5` Expression 2 is TRUE if either X < = Y or Z = 5.

2.9 Subscripted Variables

The subscripted variable makes it more convenient for us to use a group of memory cells to store a list or table of names or numbers. By using a subscripted variable, we give the same name to every memory cell in the group and use the subscript value to distinguish between the memory cells in the group. This is a distinct advantage, because it is much easier to change the subscript value in a program than it is to change a variable name. A list of subscripted variables is called an array.

A subscripted variable name consists of a variable name followed by a subscript enclosed in parentheses. The subscript may be a number, a variable name, or an arithmetic expression.

Examples:

```
A(1)
B$(2)
C2(I)
SUM(J + 2 * I)
F3$(3 * I)
```

See chapter 9 for a further discussion of subscripts. Also see section 3.51 for a discussion of the DIM statement.

3. PROGRAM STATEMENTS

3.1 Statements That Put Names or Numbers into Memory Cells

3.11 LET The LET statement is used to assign a name to a memory cell and put a number or message into the named memory cell. The general form of the LET statement is:

line number `LET` *variable name* = *number or arithmetic expression whose value will be placed in memory*

or

line number `LET` *string variable* = *"message"*

The equal sign in the LET statement has a different meaning than it does in a mathematical equation. The LET statement instructs the computer to replace the contents of the memory cell named on the left side of the equal sign by the value of the expression on the right side. For this reason the equal sign in the LET statement is sometimes referred to as the "replaced by" symbol. Computer scientists would have preferred to use a left arrow rather than an equal sign to express this operation, but it wasn't available on the keyboard.

The statement LET X = X + 1 means replace the contents of the memory cell named X with the old contents of X plus 1. If the memory cell named X contains the number 3, the statement LET X = X + 1 will replace that 3 with a 4.

Examples of LET statements:

```
10  LET A = 2
20  LET X = 2 * A + 4.324
30  LET B$ = "JOHN JOHNSON"
```

The use of the word LET is optional; the following statements are equivalent:

```
10  LET A = 2
10  A = 2
```

3.12 INPUT The INPUT statement is used to assign names to memory cells. When the program runs and the INPUT statement is executed, the computer waits for the user to type the data to be put in the memory cell named in the INPUT statement. The most common form of the INPUT statement is:

line number INPUT "*prompt*"; *variable name*

or

line number INPUT "*prompt*", *variable name*

The prompt is optional. If a semicolon (;) is used before the variable name, a question mark will be printed. If a comma is used, no question mark will appear.

Examples of INPUT statements:

```
10 INPUT X
20 INPUT A$
30 INPUT "HOW MANY TRIPS? ",T1
40 INPUT "TYPE YOUR NAME"; NAME$
```

3.13 INPUT# The INPUT# statement is used to get input from a file rather than from the keyboard. The # stands for the number under which the file was opened. See the OPEN statement for more information.

Example:

```
10  OPEN "DATAFILE" FOR INPUT AS #1
20  INPUT #1, A$
```

The above example will read a string item from the file DATAFILE and put it in the string variable A$. Leading spaces, carriage returns, and line feeds are ignored. If a string item begins with a quotation mark, the string will include everything up to the second quotation mark, excluding the quotes (however, strings are limited to 256 characters). If a string item does not begin with a quotation mark, the string includes everything up to the first comma, carriage return, or line feed.

3.14 LINE INPUT The LINE INPUT statement allows keyboard entry of a string that has commas or other delimiters in it. The INPUT command cannot accept a string with a comma in it.

3.15 LINE INPUT# The LINE INPUT# statement is used just like the INPUT# statement except that it allows the program to read from a file a line that has commas in it.

Example:
```
10  OPEN "DATAFILE" FOR INPUT AS #1
20  LINE INPUT #1, A$
```

3.16 READ, DATA, and RESTORE The READ and DATA statements are used together to assign names and put numbers or messages in memory cells. The READ statement gives the names for the memory cells. The DATA statement gives the numbers or messages that go into the named memory cells. The names and numbers or messages must be in exactly the same order in the READ and the DATA statements. All the DATA statements in a program are considered to be part of one overall DATA statement with the same order of occurrence of the numbers and messages. When the program run begins, the computer sets a DATA pointer above the first quantity in the overall DATA list. Each time the computer encounters a variable name in a READ statement, it puts that name on a memory cell, copies the quantity under the DATA pointer into the named memory cell, and moves the DATA pointer over the next quantity in the overall DATA list.

The computer prints the message OUT OF DATA when it encounters a name in a READ statement and the DATA pointer has moved past the last quantity in the overall DATA list.

The RESTORE statement moves the DATA pointer back to the first quantity in the overall DATA list. If the RESTORE statement is followed by a line number (e.g., RESTORE 100), the DATA pointer will be moved to point at the first DATA value on the specified line.

The general form of the READ and DATA statements are:

line number `READ` *any combination of variable names and string variable names separated by commas*

and

line number `DATA` *a corresponding combination of numbers and messages separated by commas*

NOTE: A message that includes a comma or colon must be enclosed in quotation marks.

Examples:

```
10 READ X
20 DATA 7.642

50 READ X,Y,Z
60 DATA 7.642, 3.25, -1.43

120 READ A$
200 DATA PETER

220 READ N$,M$
230 DATA "JONES, PETER", "MACKEY, ORVILLE"

500 READ N$, S1, S2, S3
510 DATA "JONES,PETER"
511 DATA 364, 34, 7652
```

**3.17 INKEY$** The INKEY$ variable is used to get a single keypress from the keyboard. It is like the INPUT statement except that it can get only a single keypress and the user does not press ⟨Enter⟩.

Example:

```
10  K$ = INKEY$
```

The above example sets K$ to the value of the key pressed by the user. If no key has been pressed, the program continues and the value of K$ is "" (nothing). The following statement waits for a keypress and sets K$ to the key pressed:

```
10  K$ = INKEY$ : IF K$ = "" GOTO 10
```

3.18 SWAP The SWAP statement exchanges the values of two variables.

```
10  SWAP v1,v2
```

swaps the values of the two variables *v1* and *v2*. The two variables can be either string or numeric variables.

3.2 Statements That Display Names or Numbers

3.21 PRINT The PRINT statement is used to display the contents of memory cells or the value of an expression. The general form of the PRINT statement is:

> *line number* `PRINT` *any combination of variable names, string variable names, and arithmetic expressions separated by commas or semicolons*

When the comma is used as the delimiter separating the items in the PRINT statement, the monitor screen is divided into print zones of 14 spaces each. The commas cause each succeeding variable to be printed in the next zone.

Semicolons may be used as the delimiter separating the items in a PRINT statement. When a semicolon is used at the end of a PRINT statement, the usual carriage return is suppressed.

The PRINT statement prints a blank space in front of positive numbers so that if X = 1, the statement

```
10  PRINT "THE NUMBER IS";X
```

will result in the printed output:

```
THE NUMBER IS 1
```

If X = −1 the result will be

```
THE NUMBER IS-1
```

While you are programming, the question mark (?) may be used as a shorthand for the word PRINT at any time.

Examples of PRINT statements:

Statement	Result
`70  PRINT`	leaves a blank line on the screen or paper
`80  PRINT X`	displays the value of X in zone 1, beginning in position 1 (left adjusted)
`90  PRINT A,B,C`	displays the value of A in zone 1, B in zone 2, and C in zone 3
`100 PRINT "X = "; X`	displays the message, followed immediately by the value of X

`200 PRINT A,`
`201 PRINT B,`
`202 PRINT C`
	result is identical to 90 PRINT A,B,C as shown above

`300 PRINT A`
`301 PRINT B`
`302 PRINT C`
	displays the value of A in zone 1 of the first line, the value of B in zone 1 of the next line, and the value of C in zone 1 of the third line

3.22 PRINT USING The PRINT USING statement allows the programmer a great deal of control over the format of printed output. A complete explanation of the PRINT USING statement is beyond the scope of this book. The following are some common forms and their effects. The # sign is used to represent numbers in the PRINT USING statement. The symbols in the PRINT USING statement give the computer a kind of "picture" of what you want the output to look like. A decimal point may be placed in the format string to tell the computer where the decimal point goes in the printed output. If the number to be printed does not fill the whole field, a zero will be added in front of the decimal point. If the number to be printed extends beyond the right of the format string, it will be rounded off. If the number to be printed is larger than the specified format string, a percent sign (%) is printed in front of the number. A dollar sign ($) in front of the format string causes the number to be printed with a leading dollar sign. Two dollar signs ($$) in front of the format string cause the dollar sign to be placed right next to the first digit of the number. Several numbers or variables may be placed at the end of the PRINT USING statement separated by commas. They will be formatted according to the PRINT USING format string.

Examples:

```
STATEMENT                                 RESULT

PRINT USING "##.##";.99                    Ø.99
PRINT USING "###.##";123.456              123.46
PRINT USING "##.##";999.11                %999.11
PRINT USING "$####.##";25                 $  25.ØØ
PRINT USING "$$####.##";25                   $25.ØØ
PRINT USING "   ##";1,2,3                      1    2    3
```

3.23 LPRINT USING This statement is just like the PRINT USING statement except that it prints its output to the printer rather than the screen.

3.24 TAB The TAB command is used in a PRINT statement to cause the display to begin in a particular column. The next item will be printed in the named column (counting from the left side of the display). TAB must be used in a PRINT statement and, unlike LOCATE, can cause movement only to the right of the current position.

The general form of TAB is:

line number `PRINT TAB(`*number or expression*`);` *Variable Name*

The value of the number or expression following the word TAB is the position on the line where the next character will be placed.

String variable names, expressions, numbers, and messages may be used where the variable name appears in the general form above.

Examples of the TAB command:

```
10 READ A,B,C,D,E$,F$
20 DATA 1,2,-3,JOE,SUE
30 PRINT TAB(12);A;TAB(24);B;TAB(36);C;
40 PRINT TAB(48);D;TAB(60);E;TAB(72);F
```

The above instructions will produce the following printed output.

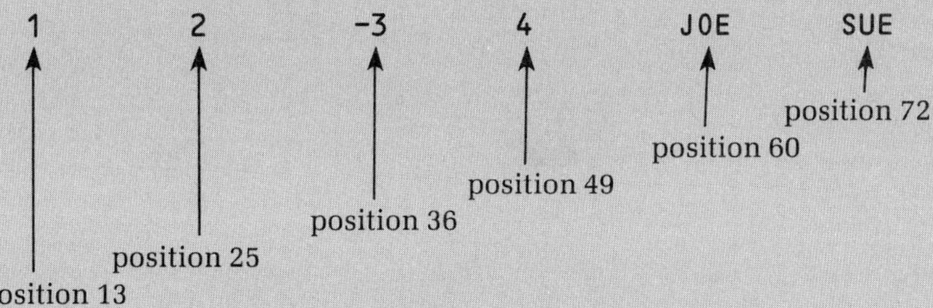

3.3 Statements That Terminate a Program

3.31 END The END statement halts the run of a program and no message is printed.

Example: `200 END`

3.32 STOP The STOP statement halts the run of a program and prints this message:

```
Break in 70
```

line number of the statement that caused the halt.

Example: `70 STOP`

3.4 Statement to Put Remarks in a Program

3.41 REM The REM statement allows us to insert any message we wish in a program. REM statements are ignored by the program.

Example:

```
5 REM     THIS IS AN EXAMPLE OF A REMARK.
6 REM     ALL CHARACTERS ON THE KEYBOARD
7 REM     CAN BE INCLUDED IN A REMARK.
8 REM     THE COMPUTER IGNORES ALL REM
9 REM     STATEMENTS WHEN IT RUNS A PROGRAM.
10 '      REMARK STATEMENTS MAY ALSO BEGIN
11 '      WITH AN APOSTROPHE (')
```

3.5 Statement That Reserves Memory Cells for Lists or Tables

3.51 DIM The DIM statement reserves memory cells for subscripted variables used to store lists or tables. If a DIM statement is not used, BASIC assigns a maximum value of 10 for each subscript in subscripted variables used in the program. If you see the message "Bad subscript error" it means that you have more subscripts than your DIM statement allows for. If you see the "Duplicate definition" error message, it means that you have used a subscripted variable before it was defined by a DEF statement or you used two DEF statements to define the same subscripted variable.

Examples of DIM statements:

`10 DIM A(20)`	assigns a maximum value of 20 for the subscript of A(I).
`20 DIM B(30,40)`	assigns a maximum value of 30 for the first subscript and 40 for the second subscript of B(I,J).
`10 DIM A(20),B(30,40)`	assigns a maximum value of 20 for the subscript of A(I), 30 for the first subscript of B(I,J), and 40 for the second subscript of B(I,J).
`5 DIM C$(15)`	assigns a maximum value of 15 for the subscript of C$(I).

3.6 Statements That Alter Program Flow

3.61 GOTO The GOTO statement causes an unconditional jump to the line number written after the word GOTO.

Example: `120 GOTO 80`

3.62 IF/GOTO This is the simpler form of the IF statement. The general form is:

line number `IF` *conditional* `GOTO` *line number #2*

If the conditional following the IF statement is TRUE, then the computer will jump to line number #2. If the conditional is FALSE, then the computer will go to the line immediately following the IF statement.

Refer to section 2.7 for details of the conditional.

Example:

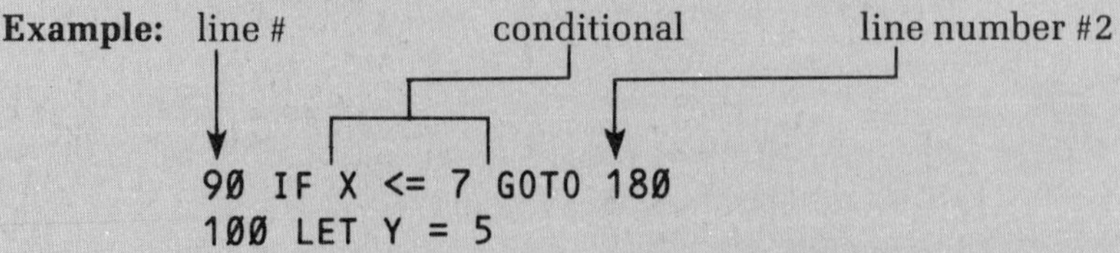

If X is less than or equal to 7 (i.e., conditional is TRUE), then the instruction at line 180 will be executed next. If X is greater than 7 (i.e., the conditional is FALSE), then the instruction at line 100 will be executed next.

3.63 IF/THEN ELSE A more complex form of the IF statement. The general form is:

line number `IF` *conditional* `THEN` *one or more instructions separated by colons,:* `ELSE` *more statements*

If the conditional is TRUE (greater than 0), then all the instructions between the word THEN and the word ELSE will be executed in order from left to right. If the conditional is FALSE (0 or less), then *all* the instructions between the word THEN and the word ELSE will be ignored and the instructions following the word ELSE will be executed next. The ELSE and the statements following it are optional. If they are omitted and the conditional is false, the program goes on to the next line, ignoring the statements following the word THEN. Refer to section 2.7 for details of the conditional.

Examples:

```
1Ø INPUT X
2Ø IF X < Ø THEN PRINT "X IS NEGATIVE" ELSE PRINT X

1Ø INPUT H : INPUT W
2Ø IF H < = 4Ø THEN P = H * W
3Ø IF H  4Ø THEN P = 4Ø * W + (H - 4Ø) + 1.5 * W
4Ø PRINT H, W, P
5Ø END
```

3.64 FOR/TO/STEP/NEXT The FOR and NEXT statements are used together (always) to form a loop to carry out a sequence of instructions more than once.

The general form of a FOR/NEXT loop is:

line number `FOR` *variable name* `=` *a* `TO` *b* `STEP` *c*

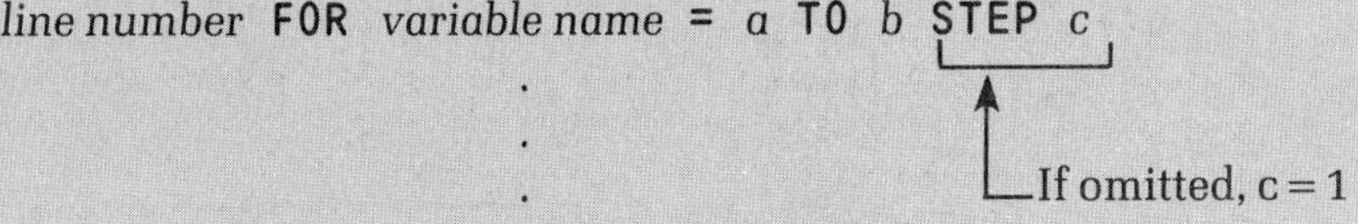

sequence of instructions to be repeated

line number `NEXT` *variable name—same as in FOR statement*

Notes:

1. The letters *a*, *b*, and *c* in the FOR statement represent numbers or arithmetic expressions.
2. The variable name in the FOR and NEXT statements is called the control variable. The same control variable must be used in the FOR and the NEXT statements that form a loop.
3. The sequence of instructions located between the FOR and NEXT statements is called the body of the loop.
4. Each time the computer carries out the instructions in the body of the loop, the control variable takes on a different value. These values of the control variable are determined by the numbers represented by *a*, *b*, and *c* in the FOR statement.
   - The value of *a* is the initial value of the control variable.
   - The value of *b* is the final value of the control variable. The looping stops after the control variable passes the final value.
   - The value of *c* is the amount by which the value of the control variable increases between passes through the loop.
5. If the value of *b* is less than the value of *a*, the body of the loop is passed over and the statement following NEXT is executed.

Example:

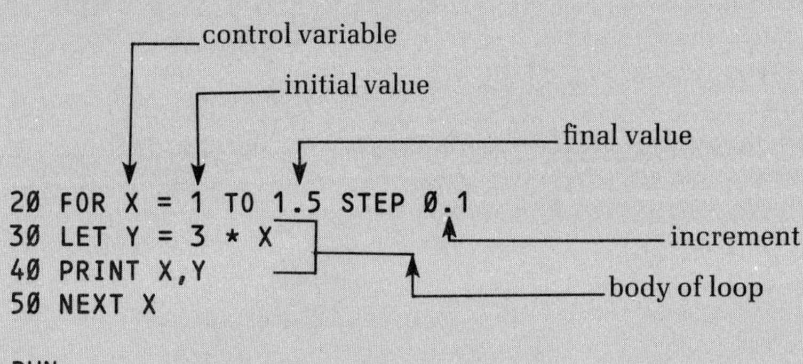


```
RUN

1.0            3.0
1.1            3.3
1.2            3.6
1.3            3.9
1.4            4.2
1.5            4.5
Ok
```

3.65 GOSUB and RETURN Sometimes you will find it necessary to use the same sequence of instructions in several places in your program. The GOSUB and RETURN statements allow you to write this sequence of instructions once as a subroutine. You use a GOSUB statement each time you need the subroutine, and a RETURN statement in the subroutine transfers control back to the next statement in your main program.

Example:

```
10 FOR J = 1 TO 4
20 GOSUB 500
30 PRINT "*";
40 GOSUB 500
50 PRINT "*"
60 NEXT J
70 GOSUB 500
80 PRINT "*"
90 STOP
100 DATA 15,7,16,5,17,3,18,1,19
```

```
500 REM SUBROUTINE TO PRINT SPACES
510 READ S
520 FOR I = 1 TO S
530 PRINT " ";
540 NEXT I
550 RETURN
```

In the above example, the GOSUB at line 20 transfers control to the subroutine at line 500, and the RETURN at line 550 transfers control back to line 30. The GOSUB at line 40 transfers control to the subroutine at line 500, and the RETURN at line 550 transfers control back to line 50. The GOSUB at line 70 transfers control to the subroutine, and the RETURN transfers control back to line 80. The result is the same as it would be if the three GOSUB statements were each replaced by lines 510, 520, 530, and 540.

```
RUN

               *       *
                *     *
                 *   *
                  * *
                   *
Ok
```

3.66 ON/GOTO The seldom-used ON/GOTO statement is used to form a multiple branch in a program.

Example:

```
10 INPUT X
20 ON X GOTO 100,200,300,400
30 GOTO 10
```

The above instructions will transfer control to

```
line 100 if X = 1
line 200 if X = 2
line 300 if X = 3
line 400 if X = 4
line 30 if X < > 1, 2, 3, or 4
```

The general form of the ON/GOTO is:

> *line number* `ON` *arithmetic expression* `GOTO` *a sequence of line numbers separated by commas*

3.67 ON/GOSUB The ON/GOSUB statement is the preferred statement to form multiple branches in a program.

Example:

```
10 INPUT "ENTER AN INTEGER FROM 1 TO 6 ";C
20 ON C GOSUB 1100, 1200, 1300, 1400, 1500, 300
30 . . .
```

The above instructions will call the subroutine at

```
1100 if C = 1
1200 if C = 2
1300 if C = 3
1400 if C = 4
1500 if C = 5
300  if C =  6
30   if C < > 1, 2, 3, 4, 5, or 6
```

The general form of the ON/GOSUB is as follows:

> *line number* `ON` *arithmetic expression* `GOSUB` *sequence of line numbers separated by commas*

3.68 WHILE/WEND The WHILE/WEND loop is seldom used since it is so much slower than the FOR/NEXT loop. The general form is

line number `WHILE` *conditional*

.

.

sequence of instructions to be repeated

.

.

line number `WEND`

The sequence of instructions will be repeated until the conditional is false. When the conditional is false, the program will skip to the line following the WEND. If the conditional is false to begin with, the sequence of instructions will not be executed at all.

4. FUNCTIONS

4.1 Statement for Defining a Function

4.11 DEF FN The DEF statement allows you to define a function, give the function a name, and then use the name of the function each time you wish to use the function in your program.

Example:

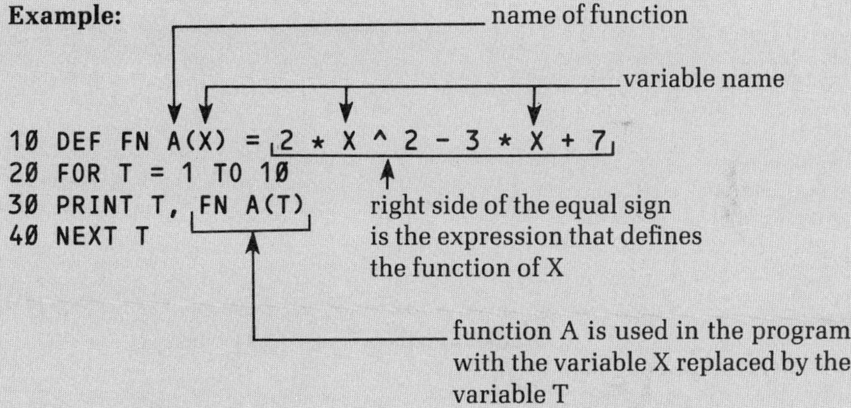
name of function
variable name
10 DEF FN A(X) = 2 * X ^ 2 - 3 * X + 7
20 FOR T = 1 TO 10
30 PRINT T, FN A(T)
40 NEXT T
right side of the equal sign is the expression that defines the function of X
function A is used in the program with the variable X replaced by the variable T

The value of function A is `2 * T ^ 2 - 3 * T + 7`

4.2 Numeric Functions

4.21 ABS(*arithmetic expression*) The ABS function gives the absolute value of the expression in parentheses.

Example:
```
10 LET Y = ABS(X)
```

4.22 INT(*arithmetic expression*) The INT function gives the largest integer less than or equal to the value of the expression in parentheses.

Example:
```
20 LET Y = INT(7.2)    '  PUTS  7 IN Y
30 LET X = INT(-7.2)   '  PUTS -8 IN X
```

4.23 RND and RANDOMIZE The RND function gives a random number that is greater than or equal to 0 and less than 1.

Example:
```
10  LET X = RND
```

To get a random number between 1 and a certain number *n*, use:

```
10  LET X = INT(RND * n + 1)
```

RND can be followed by a number in parentheses (e.g., RND(1)), but this is seldom done since RND is almost always used to get a new random number between 0 and 1 and this is the result when RND is used with no number.

The RANDOMIZE statement is used to reseed the random number generator. Without this, the program will produce the same sequence of random numbers each time it is run. If the RANDOMIZE statement is used without a number following it, the program will stop and ask the user for a number to use to reseed the generator. The following example shows how to reseed the random number generator using the current value of hundredths of a second on the system clock. This will reseed the generator without bothering the user and will produce a new sequence of random numbers each time the program is run:

```
102  RANDOMIZE VAL(RIGHT$(TIME$,2))
```

This line is explained more fully in chapter 8.

4.24 SGN(*arithmetic expression*) The SGN function gives the following:

−1 if the arithmetic expression has a negative value
0 if the value of the arithmetic expression is 0
1 if the arithmetic expression has a positive value.

4.25 SQR(*arithmetic expression*) The SQR function gives the positive square root of the arithmetic expression.

4.26 FIX(*arithmetic expression*) The FIX statement gives the integer part of a positive or negative number. The FIX statement is just like the INT statement except that it does not return the next lower number when *arithmetic expression* is negative.

Example:
```
20  LET Y = FIX(7.8)    '   PUTS 7 IN Y
30  LET X = FIX(-7.8)   '   PUTS -7 IN X
```

4.27 CDBL, CINT, and CSNG These three functions are used to convert numbers from one numeric precision to another. CDBL converts numbers to double-precision, CSNG converts numbers to single-precision, and CINT converts numbers to integers. Numbers changed from greater to lesser precision are rounded. The CINT function is like the INT function except that it rounds the number being converted instead of truncating it.

4.3 Trigonometric Functions

4.31 ATN(*arithmetic expression*) The ATN function gives the arc tangent in radians of the arithmetic expression.

4.32 COS(*arithmetic expression*) The COS function gives the cosine of the angle in radians equal to the value of the arithmetic expression.

4.33 SIN(*arithmetic expression*) The SIN function gives the sine of the angle in radians equal to the value of the arithmetic expression.

4.34 TAN(*arithmetic expression*) The TAN function gives the tangent of the angle in radians equal to the value of the arithmetic expression.

4.4 Logarithmic and Exponential Expressions

4.41 EXP(*arithmetic expression*) The EXP function gives the value of e = 2.718289... raised to a power equal to the value of the arithmetic expression.

4.42 LOG(*arithmetic expression*) The LOG function gives the natural log of the arithmetic expression.

Examples:

```
V = 5 * EXP(5 * T)    '   SETS V = 5 * e^5 * T
X = LOG(3 * A)        '   SETS X = LOG(3 * A)
```

4.5 String Functions

4.51 LEFT$ RIGHT$, and MID$ These functions allow the programmer to alter, manipulate, and create strings from parts of other strings.

The string function LEFT$ has the general form:

LEFT$(*string variable name, n*)

This expression refers to the leftmost *n* characters of the variable named.

Example:
```
10 LET C$ = "PETER PAN"
20 LET L$ = LEFT$ (C$, 7)
```

sets L$ to "PETER P"

The RIGHT$ function is exactly like the LEFT$ function, except that it refers to the rightmost *n* characters of the variable named.

Example:
```
10 LET C$ = "PETER PAN"
20 LET R$ = RIGHT$ (C$, 7)
```

sets R$ to "TER PAN"

The MID$ function is similar to the LEFT$ and RIGHT$ functions, but has three arguments in the parentheses: the first is the name of the string variable referred to, the second is the starting position of the substring, and the third is the number of characters in the substring.

Example:
```
10 LET C$ = "PETER PAN"
20 LET M$ = MID$ (C$, 5, 3)
```

sets M$ to "R P"

MID$ may also be used on the left side of the equal sign to change the value of part of a string. In this case the first variable following MID$ is the name of the string variable to be changed and the second is the position of the character in that string where the changing is to start. The following example shows how MID$ can be used to change the value of part of a string:

```
10  C$ = "MY FEET ARE HURTING ME"
20  MID$(C$,13) = "KILL"
30  PRINT C$

RUN

MY FEET ARE KILLING ME
Ok
```

4.52 STR$ and VAL These functions complement each other. They are used to turn a number into a string or a string into a number.

The STR$ function is used to convert a numeric variable to a string.

Example:
```
10 LET C = 93421
20 LET S$ = STR$ (C)
```

S$ is now the string "93421." It may not be used in an arithmetic expression. In fact, no mathematical operations can be performed on it at all. Since it is a string, however, you may use other string functions like LEFT$, RIGHT$, and MID$ to modify it.

The VAL function is the opposite of the STR$ function. It is used to convert a string version of a number into a numeric value.

Example:
```
10 LET S$ = "93421"
20 LET N = VAL(S$)
```

If S$ starts with a letter, N will be set to zero.

4.53 ASC and CHR$ Every keyboard character has a number associated with it. The set of numbers is called the American Standard Code for Information Interchange (ASCII).

The ASC function is used to convert a string made up of a single character to its ASCII value.

Example:
```
10  LET C$ = "A"
20  LET N = ASC(C$)
```

N is set to 65, which is the ASCII value of an uppercase A.

The CHR$ function is used to refer to a character by its ASCII value.

Examples:

```
10 LET N = 65
20 PRINT CHR$ (N)
```

will cause an uppercase A to be printed.

```
30 LET S$ = CHR$ (65)
```

or

```
30 LET S$ = CHR$ (N)
```

is equivalent to

```
30 LET S$ = "A"
```

4.54 LEN The string function LEN has the general form:

LEN (*string variable name*)

This function gives the number of characters in the string variable named.

Example:
```
10 LET C$ = "PETER PAN"
20 LET N = LEN(C$)
```

The above instruction sets N to 9.

4.55 Concatenation Sometimes it is necessary to join two or more strings together to form a single string. This is called concatenation and is accomplished by using the " + " symbol.

Example:

```
10 S1$ = "HOLD"
20 S2$ = "THE"
30 S3$ = "ONIONS"
40 LET S$ = "S1$ + " " + S2$ + " " + S3$
```

is equivalent to

```
40 LET S$ = "HOLD THE ONIONS"
```

4.56 SPACE$(*n*) and SPC(*n*) SPACE$ can be used to create a string variable made up of nothing but spaces. A number (*n*) is placed inside the parentheses to specify the length of the string. SPACE(10) would create a string made up of ten spaces.

Example:
```
10  LET C$ = SPACE$(20)
```

The SPC(*n*) function is used to print a certain number of spaces. It cannot be used to create a variable. It can be used only with PRINT, LPRINT, and PRINT#.

Example:
```
10  PRINT  "LEFT" SPC(14) "RIGHT"

RUN

LEFT              RIGHT
Ok
```

4.57 *STRING$(n,c)* This function creates a string of *n* characters, all of which are the same. The character used is specified by *c*, which may be a number representing the ASCII value of the desired character, a string variable, or the character itself in quotes.

Examples:

FORM	RESULT
`PRINT STRING$(5,45)`	`-----`
`C$ = "$"`	
`PRINT STRING$(3,C$)`	`$$$`
`PRINT STRING$(11,"&")`	`&&&&&&&&&&&`

4.58 *INSTR(n,x$,y$)* The INSTR function is used to search for the occurrence of one string in another string. String *x$* is searched to see if it contains string *y$*. The optional number *n* specifies the point in string *x$* where the search is to begin. INSTR returns the position of string *y$* in string *x$* or 0 if the search string is not found.

Example:

```
10  X$ = "THIS IS THE STRING TO BE SEARCHED"
20  Y$ = "STRING" : ' STRING TO BE SEARCHED FOR
30  P = INSTR(X$,Y$)
30  PRINT P

RUN

 13
Ok
```

4.59 *HEX$(n)* and *OCT$(n)* These functions can be used to get a string that represents the hexadecimal or octal value of a number *n*.

Example:

```
10  X = 255
20  H$ = HEX$(X)
30  PRINT H$

RUN

FF
Ok
```

4.6 Miscellaneous Functions

4.61 FRE(0) In BASIC, strings can have variable lengths and the length of a given string can change during the course of a program. To speed up the process of allocating space, BASIC creates a new string every time a string is reassigned or changes its length. This is very wasteful of space and causes the string space to become fragmented. If a BASIC program ever fills the string space, a long delay results while memory is reorganized. This process is called "garbage collection." The FRE(0) function forces garbage collection and, in programs that do enough string manipulation to cause garbage collection, it is sometimes a good idea to use the FRE(0) function periodically to cause garbage collection before there is so much garbage that it would take a long time. Actually the 0 in FRE(0) is a dummy variable and could be replaced by any number or variable.

Example: `10  X = FRE(0)`

4.62 CSRLIN The CSRLIN variable tells the current line (row) that the cursor is on. If the cursor is on line 10 (from the top of the screen), then

```
LET R = CSRLIN
```

will result in R being set to 10.

4.63 POS(0) The POS(0) function tells the current horizontal (column) position of the cursor. As with the FRE(0) command, the number in the parentheses is a dummy argument and can have any value. If the cursor is at column 8, then LET C = POS(0) will result in C being set to 8.

4.64 SCREEN(*row,column*) This should not be confused with the SCREEN statement in section 6. This function (the simple form of the function is given here) tells the ASCII value of the character on the screen at the location specified by *row* and *column*.

5. DATA FILES

5.1 General Information on Files

5.11 Naming Files A file is a storage area on your floppy disk. All files are identified by a name that must be unique (i.e., no two files can have the same name). See section 1.32 for more information about filenames.

5.12 Disk Commands Used on Data Files You may use the KILL" command to remove a data file from your disk. Just type the command KILL", followed by the name (in quotes) of the file to be deleted. The command is executed when you press the Enter key. The SAVE", LOAD", and RUN" commands are not used with data files because they are not programs. See section 5.3 for details on creating and reading sequential data files.

5.13 Field A field is a single item of data such as a name, an ID number, a score, a wage rate, etc.

5.14 Record A record is a group of fields that are related in some way. For example, a student's name, ID number, and exam scores could be a record. There would be a similar record for each student in the class. From a different viewpoint, the names of all the students in the class could be a record, and there would be a similar record for each class in the school.

5.15 File A file is a group of related records. For example, a class file could consist of the records of all the students in the class. Also, the school file could consist of all class records in the school.

5.16 Sequential Access File (Sequential File) In a sequential file, the records are stored in sequential order in much the same manner as names and numbers are stored in DATA statements in a program. Sequential files are created and read in sequential order. The entries in a sequential file may all be of different lengths, and any combination of strings and numbers is permitted.

5.17 Random Access File (Direct File) In a random access file, all records must be the same length. Thus each record must be as long as the longest record, with the extra space unused. The advantage of a random access file is that a single record can be read directly, regardless of its location in the file; it is not necessary to read all of the preceding records in order to get to the one you want.

5.2 BASIC File Commands

5.21 OPEN The OPEN command tells the computer that we want to read from or print to a disk file. When opening a file, we must specify whether we plan to use the file for input, output, or appending. The most common form of the OPEN statement is:

line number `OPEN` *filename* `FOR` *mode* `AS` *#filenum*

where *mode* is INPUT, OUTPUT, or APPEND and *filenum* is the number we intend to refer to the file by.

The following opens the file "DATAFILE" for input:

```
10  OPEN "DATAFILE" FOR INPUT AS #1
```

The number 1 is the file number and can be any number from 1 to the maximum number of allowable open files (usually 3 or 4). The file number is used in other BASIC commands that read from or print to the file.

5.22 INPUT# and LINE INPUT# These commands work just like the INPUT and LINE INPUT commands except that they get their input from a file rather than from the keyboard. See section 3.1 for more information about these commands.

Examples:

```
10  OPEN "DATAFILE" FOR INPUT AS #1
20  INPUT#1, A$
30  LINE INPUT#1, B$
```

5.23 PRINT# and PRINT# USING These are the same as the PRINT and PRINT USING statements except that they print the information to a file rather than to the screen. See section 3.22 for more information.

Example:
```
10  OPEN "DATAFILE" FOR OUTPUT AS #1
20  PRINT#1, "HELLO"
30  PRINT#1, USING "##.##"; A
```

Line 20, above, prints the word HELLO and the value of A in the DATAFILE disk file.

5.24 CLOSE Information to be written to a file is not always written to the file right away. It is stored in a buffer and is often written to the file only when the buffer is full. The CLOSE command makes sure everything is written properly to the file and also releases the file number for use by another file. Files should always be closed when you are through with them.

Example:
```
10 CLOSE#1
```

Using CLOSE with no file number causes all open files to be closed.

5.3 Using Sequential Files

5.31 Creating a Sequential File The following program will create a sequential file (also called a text file) containing N numbers as data entries. The first entry in the file is the value of N, so the file actually contains N + 1 entries. A file of names could be created in the same way, using a string variable such as N$(I) in place of A(I) in lines 17, 26, and 55.

```
10 PRINT "ENTER THE FILE NAME"
11 INPUT F$
15 PRINT "HOW MANY NUMBERS";
16 INPUT N
17 DIM A(N)
20 FOR I = 1 TO N
25 PRINT I; TAB(5);
26 INPUT A(I)
30 NEXT I
35 OPEN F$ FOR OUTPUT AS #1
40 PRINT#1, N
50 FOR I = 1 TO N
55 PRINT#1, A(I)
60 NEXT I
90 CLOSE#1
```

5.32 Reading a Sequential File The following program will copy and print the entries in a sequential file created by the program in section 5.31. Line 70 copies numbers from the file into A(I), and line 75 prints the value of A(I) on the screen. A file of names could be read in the same way, using N$(I) in place of A(I) in lines 50, 70, and 75.

```
10 PRINT "ENTER THE FILE NAME"
12 INPUT F$
20 OPEN F$ FOR INPUT AS #1
40 INPUT#1, N
50 DIM A(N)
60 FOR I = 1 TO N
70 INPUT#1, A(I)
75 PRINT A(I)
80 NEXT I
90 CLOSE#1
```

6. MEDIUM-RESOLUTION GRAPHICS

6.1 Graphics Commands

Graphics statements for the IBM are difficult and sometimes confusing. We have not attempted to cover all possible graphics statements, but have confined our discussion to a subset of the graphics statements available in medium-resolution graphics mode 1.

6.11 Rows and Columns Points on the graphics screen are described in terms of rows and columns. Rows are horizontal, and columns, like the columns that hold up buildings, are vertical.

Example:

```
ROW 0          C        C          *
ROW 1          O        O          ↑
ROW 2          L        L          |
ROW 3          U        U          |________35,0
ROW 4          M        M
ROW 5          N        N
ROW 6          15       25
```

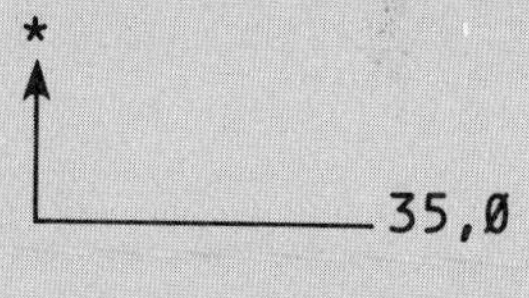

When plotting a point on the screen, the column is specified first and the row second. The asterisk (*) on the screen is at column 35 and row 0.

The medium-resolution graphics screen is 320 squares wide and 200 squares high. Some of the graphics commands require information about points on this grid. Although the grid is 320 × 200, the columns are numbered from 0 to 319 and the rows from 0 to 199.

6.12 SCREEN The SCREEN statement is used to set the attributes of the screen. Many of the graphics statements require that the screen attributes be set properly before they will work. The most common form of the SCREEN statement is:

line number `SCREEN` *mode, colorflag*

where *mode* is the desired video mode and *colorflag* determines whether color will be enabled (allowed).

Valid modes for the IBM PC are:

0 Text mode at the current width (40 or 80)
1 Medium-resolution graphics mode (320 x 200)
2 High-resolution graphics mode (640 x 200)

The value of *colorflag* must be either 0 or 1. Its effect depends on the mode selected. In mode 0 (text), a *colorflag* value of 1 enables color and a value of 0 disables color. In mode 1 (medium-resolution graphics), this is reversed; a *colorflag* value of 0 enables color, and a value of 1 disables color. In mode 2 the value of *colorflag* has no effect.

The PCjr has additional graphics modes 3 through 6, which are variations of the first three modes.

6.13 COLOR In the text mode, the COLOR statement sets the colors of the foreground, background, and border. In the medium-resolution graphics mode, the COLOR statement sets the color of the background and selects one of two *palette* choices. A *palette* is a set of three colors as defined in table 6.13B. The high-resolution graphics mode does not use the COLOR statement.

In the text mode, the COLOR statement has the following form:

`COLOR` *foreground, background, border*

where *foreground* can be any number from 0 to 31, *background* can be any number from 0 to 7, and *border* can be any number from 0 to 15.

If you have an IBM PC with a color monitor, the numbers from 0 to 15 set the color as defined in table 6.13A. The *foreground* values from 16 to 31 make blinking characters with the color of the character set by the *foreground* number minus 16. For example, a *foreground* number of 23 will result in blinking white characters (color number 23 − 16 = 7).

If you have an IBM PC with a monochrome monitor, *background* values 0–6 give a black background and 7 gives a white background. The following *foreground* values can be used:

0,8,16,24	Black (must be used with white background)
1	Underlined, white characters
9	Underlined, bold, white characters
17	Underlined, blinking, white characters
25	Underlined, blinking, bold, white characters
2–7	White characters
10–15	Bold, white characters
18–23	Blinking, white characters
26–31	Blinking, bold, white characters

In the medium-resolution graphics mode, the COLOR statement has the following form:

`COLOR` *background,palette*

where *background* is a number from 1 to 15 chosen from table 6.13A and *palette* is either 1 or 0. The *palette* value determines which of the two palettes will be used by the following graphic statements: CIRCLE, DRAW, LINE, PAINT, PRESET, and PSET. Each palette gives a choice of three palette colors as defined in table 6.13B. A parameter in the graphic statements chooses the palette color that will be used to draw the shape on the screen.

TABLE 6.13A COLOR CODES

Code	Color	Code	Color
0	BLACK	8	ORANGE
1	BLUE	9	LIGHT BLUE
2	GREEN	10	LIGHT GREEN
3	CYAN	11	LIGHT CYAN
4	RED	12	LIGHT RED
5	MAGENTA	13	LIGHT MAGENTA
6	BROWN	14	YELLOW
7	WHITE	15	HIGH-INTENSITY WHITE

Table 6.13A shows the two color palettes we can choose from in graphics mode 1.

```
10  COLOR  4,1
```

tells the computer to use color 4 from table 6.13A as the background color (red) and to select palette number 1. The palette selected determines what color will be used in certain graphics statements (PSET, PRESET, LINE, and CIRCLE). We have found that palette 1 usually gives the best results when text and graphics are mixed.

TABLE 6.13B PALETTES

COLOR	PALETTE 0	PALETTE 1
1	GREEN	CYAN
2	RED	MAGENTA
3	BROWN	WHITE

Example:

```
5   CLS
10  SCREEN 1,0
20  COLOR 2,1
30  LINE (20,20) - (90,90),2,BF
40  CIRCLE (250,150),25,2
50  PAINT (250,150),2
60  FOR I = 20 TO 30
70  PSET (300,I),2
80  NEXT I
```

Line 5 clears the screen. Line 10 selects medium-resolution graphics (mode 1) and enables the use of color. Line 20 selects background color 2 (green) and palette 1 (cyan, magenta, white). Line 30 draws a filled box in palette color 2 (magenta). Line 40 draws a circle with a radius of 25 and a center located at column 250 and row 150. At this point the circle is just a magenta line. Line 50 fills in the circle with the color magenta. Lines 60 to 80 plot a series of points that form a line in column 300 from row 20 to row 30.

6.14 LINE The LINE statement is used to draw lines and boxes on the graphics screen. The general form of the LINE statement is:

line number `LINE (`*x1*`,`*y1*`) - (`*x2*`,`*y2*`),` *color*`, BF`

Each pair of numbers in parentheses specifies a single point on the screen (x,y), where x is the column or horizontal position on the screen and *y* is the row or vertical position on the screen. The simplest form of the LINE statement is:

line number `LINE -(`*x*`,`*y*`)`

This draws a line from the last point referenced to the point specified by (x,*y*). The form used above:

line number `LINE (`*x1*`,`*y1*`) - (`*x2*`,`*y2*`)`

draws a line between the two points specified by (*x1*, *y1*) and (*x2*, *y2*). The LINE statement may also be followed by a comma and a palette color number that will cause the line to be drawn in color.

```
10  LINE  (20,20) - (30-30),2
```

will draw a line at the upper left of the screen in palette color 2.

If the palette color number is followed by a comma and B or BF, a colored box will be drawn instead of a line, using the two points specified as the corners of the box. B causes an empty box to be drawn, and BF causes the box to be filled. If the palette color number is left out, the box will be drawn in the current foreground color:

```
10  LINE  (20,20) - (30-30),,BF
```

Both commas must be present.

```
10  LINE  (0,0) - (319,199)
```

will draw a diagonal line from the upper left corner to the lower right corner of the screen in the current color.

```
10  LINE  (319,0) - (0,199)
```

will draw a line from the upper right corner to the lower left corner.

6.15 CIRCLE The most common form of the circle statement is:

line number `CIRCLE (x,y),` *radius, color*

Where x, and y, specify a point of the screen, r gives the *radius* (size) of the circle, and *color* is a color selected from table 1.63B. If *color* is omitted, the current foreground color is used.

6.16 PSET and PRESET The PSET statement causes a dot to be plotted at the point specified in the statement. The general form of the PSET statement is:

line number `PSET (x,y),` *color*

The coordinates x and *y* specify a dot on the screen as described earlier; *color* is a number specifying a color from table 6.13B. If *color* is omitted, the current foreground color is used.

Example: `110  PSET (5,5), 2`

The program line above will draw a dot near the upper left corner of the screen in color 2. The PRESET statement is nearly identical to the PSET statement and has the same form. The only difference is that if *color* is omitted, PRESET uses the current *background* color. It is often used to erase points. If *color* is specified, PRESET and PSET are identical.

6.17 PALETTE (PCjr only) On the PCjr the number of available colors can be extended with the use of the PALETTE statement. The PALETTE statement does not set the current palette, although it seems that it should. Instead, it allows the LINE, COLOR, PSET, and PRESET statements (and other graphics commands) to use all 15 of the colors from table 6.13A. It does this by allowing the substitution of one color for another.

```
PALETTE c1,c2
```

substitutes color *c2* from the list of 15 in table 6.13A for *c1*, which is a number from 1 to 3.

Example:

```
10  SCREEN 1,0
20  COLOR 2,1
25  PALETTE 2,4
30  LINE (20,20) - (90,90),2,BF
```

Without the PALETTE statement, line 30 would draw a filled box in green. Now, however, the PALETTE statement tells the computer to substitute color 4 (red) from table 6.13A whenever it sees a 2 in a graphics statement, so the box is drawn in red. The PALETTE statement can also be used to change the background color. If the first number in the PALETTE statement is a 0, the second number will set the background color.

```
PALETTE  0,5
```

will set the background color to magenta (color 5 from table 6.13A). Used this way, the PALETTE statement works a little different from the COLOR statement, which can also be used to set the background. The COLOR statement sets both the screen background and the screen border to the same color. The PALETTE statement sets only the screen background without changing the border. If you add the following line 26 to the example above:

```
26  PALETTE 0,5
```

you will get a red box on a magenta background with the screen border in green. The PALETTE statement by itself will set the screen back to white letters on a black background. It is especially handy to know this when you have accidentally set the foreground and the background to the same color. This makes all text invisible. If this happens or if the characters on the screen become hard to read, just type:

```
PALETTE
```

and things will get back to normal. Notice the spelling of PALETTE; it is easy to misspell.

6.18 PAINT The PAINT statement fills in a shape on the screen with the selected color. The format of the PAINT statement is:

PAINT (*column*, *row*), *fillcolor*, *bordercolor*

where *column* is the column number and *row* is the row number of any point inside the shape to be filled. The painting will begin at the point specified by (*column*,*row*) and will continue until the entire shape is filled in. The value of *fillcolor* chooses the palette color used to fill in the shape, and *bordercolor* is the color of the edges of the shape.

7. SOUND

7.1 The Bell

The bell is a built-in sound effect in the IBM. There are several ways to ring it, but all have the same effect. If you type ⟨Ctrl-G⟩ at the keyboard, you will hear the bell.

In a program, any of the following may be used:

```
10  PRINT CHR$ (7) : REM  RING BELL
20  PRINT "" : REM  CTRL G INSIDE QUOTES DOESN'T PRINT ON SCREEN
30  BEEP : REM  THE BEEP COMMAND IS THE SIMPLEST WAY TO RING THE BELL
40  LET BELL$ = CHR$ (7) : REM  SET UP VARIABLE
50  PRINT BELL$ : REM RING BELL
```

7.2 The SOUND Statement

A more sophisticated way of creating sounds is to use the SOUND statement. The simple form of the SOUND statement is:

SOUND *f*, *d*

where *f* is the frequency of the sound (in hertz) and *d* is the duration. Legal values for frequency are from 37 to 32767. Duration is measured in clock ticks. Clock ticks occur 18.2 times per second, so a duration of 18 means the sound lasts about a second. Legal values for duration range from .0015 to 65535. If you use a large value for duration, you may have to listen to the sound for quite a while.

APPENDIX B

Error Messages

The following are error message generated by the computer when there is an error in a BASIC program. The messages are in alphabetical order.

Advanced Feature (73)

This results from trying to use an advanced BASIC feature without running BASICA (advanced BASIC).

Bad File Mode (54)

Usually caused by an improper OPEN statement. The only proper modes for a sequential file are INPUT, OUTPUT, and APPEND. This error can also result from trying to merge a file that is not in ASCII format and from using GET or PUT with a sequential file.

Bad file name (64)

This is caused by using an invalid file name with KILL, NAME, or FILES.

Bad file number (52)

This error has several possible causes. The most likely is referring to a file by its file number when the file is not open. Other possibilities are that the file number is outside the normal range, the device name in the file specification is too long or invalid, or the filename is too long or invalid.

Bad record number (63)

Usually caused by referring to a record number of 0.

Can't continue (17)

If you try to start up a program that has halted by typing CONT, you will get this error if the program stopped due to a fatal error or if you made any changes in the program before attempting to restart it. This message will also occur if you type CONT when there is no program in memory.

Cartridge Required

This results when you try to run BASIC from a diskette on the PCjr without the BASIC cartridge installed.

Communications buffer overflow (69)

You have sent more information to the communications port than it can handle.

Device Fault (25)

This usually indicates a problem with the printer.

Device I/O error (57)

This is most often caused by trying to perform a disk operation (FILES, KILL, NAME, OPEN, etc.) using a diskette that has not been formatted. It can also be associated with problems at the COM: port.

Device Timeout (24)

This can mean a problem in reading from cassette, writing to the printer, or the failure of an OPEN command to open the COM: port. It means that the computer did not get a reply from the device within a predetermined amount of time.

Device Unavailable (68)

You have tried to open a file to a device that doesn't exist.

Direct statement in file (66)

A direct statement (one with no line number) was encountered in a file you tried to LOAD or MERGE. This may also occur when a file contains a line feed or was created by a word processor.

Disk full (61)

You have tried to store more on a disk than it will hold. Whatever you have tried to save or write has not been successfully stored on the disk.

Disk Media Error (72)

This usually means that your diskette is bad. Before giving up on it, you should try the diskette in several different drives. If you find one that can read it, copy all the files to a good diskette and reformat the bad one. If the format operation fails, throw the disk away.

Disk not Ready (71)

This is most often caused by leaving the drive door open or (on the PCjr internal drives or other half-height drives) by not closing the drive latch. Not having a diskette in the drive or having the diskette in sideways, backward, or upside down can also cause this problem.

Disk Write Protect (70)

Trying to perform a disk operation that writes information to the disk (e.g., SAVE", NAME", KILL", or PRINT#) on a disk that is write-protected will generate this error message. IBM disks are write-protected by putting tape over the write-protect notch (more correctly called the "write-enable notch"). Some disks are produced with no notch at all, and cannot be written to unless notched.

Division by zero (11)

This is an easy message to get. All you need to do is try PRINT X/0 , or X/N where N is any expression that evaluates to zero. Dividing something by zero gives infinity as an answer, and the concept of infinity is too much for the poor computer. This error does not stop execution of a program.

Duplicate Definition (10)

The program has come to a DIM statement for an array that has already been dimensioned. This usually happens in one of two ways. Either a line containing a DIM statement is executed twice, or, more often, an array is dimensioned that was previously dimensioned before, as in the following:

```
10 A(1)=256
20 DIM A(19)
```

In this example, the variable A is dimensioned in line 10, since subscripted variables that have not been dimensioned previously are automatically dimensioned to 10. When A is dimensioned again in line 20, the program balks. A good way to avoid this is to dimension all subscripted variables at the beginning of a program.

FIELD overflow (50)

If a FIELD statement tries to allocate more bytes than the record length in a random file in the OPEN statement, this error message will result. This can also result from running into the end of the FIELD buffer when doing sequential operations on a random file.

File already exists (58)

This happens when the filename specified in the NAME command matches the name of an existing file on the diskette.

File already open (55)

This means that you have tried to OPEN a file that is already open or KILL an open file.

File not found (53)

A LOAD, KILL, NAME, or FILES command has referenced a file that does not exist on the disk. Usually this means that you have misspelled the filename. Remember that filenames must be spelled *exactly* as they were when you saved the file. Be sure to explore this possibility fully before trying the following suggestion. If you saved the file using a name with a space in it, or using too long a name, it may be hard (or impossible) to get the computer to recognize its name. Use the FILES command to see what happened. If you can see the filename but can't get the computer to recognize that name, sometimes you can use wildcards and the NAME command to rename the file to something the computer will recognize. This can be dangerous, however, so try everything else first.

FOR without NEXT (26)

Usually this means that the end of the file is reached during the execution of a FOR loop.

Illegal direct (12)

Some messages—such as INPUT, DEF FN, and GET—must be in a line of the program to be legal. If you type them without a line number, this message will result.

Illegal function call (5)

This is a general message that appears when you try to do some operation the computer doesn't understand or can't perform.

The following is a list of the more common causes of this error:

a negative or very large subscript

an improper argument to a function or statement (e.g., a syntax error in a LINE or COLOR statement)

trying to delete a nonexistent line

Incorrect DOS version

You have entered a command that requires a different version of DOS than the one you are running.

Input past end (62)

This message means you have tried to read from a text file or part of a text file that doesn't exist. The most common causes of this are reading beyond the end of a file, misspelling the name of a file, and trying to read from a file that has not been written properly (e.g., written to without being opened first). Other common causes are trying to read from a file that has been opened for output or append.

Internal error (51)

This is a very rare error. It means that something has gone wrong with the BASIC interpreter. It is usually caused by having a bad copy of BASIC on the disk. It can also mean a hardware problem with your computer or a defective BASIC cartridge.

Line buffer overflow (23)

This message results when you try to enter a program line containing too many characters.

Missing operand (22)

A logical, mathematical, or relational operator is missing something to operate on.

Example: `10 LET X = 2 *`

NEXT without FOR (1)

Every NEXT statement in a program must be preceded by a FOR statement. As the program encounters FOR statements and NEXT statements, it counts them. If the number of NEXT statements counted ever gets to be greater than the number of FOR statements counted, you will see this message.

Example:
```
10 FOR I = 1 TO 5
20 FOR J = 1 TO 7
30 NEXT J
40 NEXT I
50 NEXT I
```

Indenting your FOR/NEXT loops will help prevent this problem. With indentation, the error above is easier to spot.

```
10 FOR I = 1 TO 5
20      FOR J = 1 TO 7
30      NEXT J
40 NEXT I
50 NEXT I
```

No RESUME (19)

This results when the program branches to an error-trapping routine as a result of an ONERR statement or ERROR statement and the error-trapping routine has no RESUME statement.

Out of DATA (4)

When you use READ and DATA statements to set the values of variables, every execution of a READ must have a DATA value to go with it. Every time a piece of DATA is "read," a pointer in memory is moved to the next position in the DATA list. If the pointer is at the end of the list and another "read" is called for, an "Out of data" message is printed and the program stops. One common cause of this is leaving one or two DATA items out of the DATA statement when you type it. Another common cause is to try to read the same set of DATA statements twice without using RESTORE to return the pointer to the beginning of the list after reading it the first time.

Out of memory (7)

This one is pretty obvious. It may mean your program is too large or that a DIM statement has set aside more memory than is available (e.g., 10 DIM A$(65000). It may also be caused by having too many variables, FOR loops, or GOSUBS or by using expressions that are too complex.

Out of paper (27)

The printer has run out of paper or is not turned on and switched to on line.

Out of string space (14)

This means the strings of your program have filled up all the available memory.

Overflow (6)

You have entered or had the program calculate a positive or negative number that is too big for the computer to handle.

Path/file access error (75)

A disk operation has failed. Most often this is caused by trying to open a read only file for writing, trying to remove the current directory, or trying to open a directory instead of a file.

Path not found (76)

The pathname specified in a filename, MKDIR, CHDIR, or RMDIR operation is not valid.

Rename across disks (74)

This is caused by trying to rename a file but specifying the wrong disk.

Example: `NAME "A:DUMMY.BAS" AS "B:FILE1"`

RESUME without error (20)

The RESUME statement must be in an error-trapping routine. The program must have encountered an ERROR statement or an actual error before reaching the RESUME statement or this message will result.

RETURN without Gosub (3)

This works very much like the NEXT without FOR error. It means that more RETURN statements than GOSUB statements have been executed. The most common cause of this is forgetting to put an END statement in a program where the main program is followed by subroutines. At the end of the main section, the program "falls through" to the following subroutine instead of ending.

Example:

```
100 REM MAIN PROGRAM
110 PRINT "HELLO"
120 GOSUB 200
190 REM END SHOULD GO HERE
200 PRINT "GOODBYE"
210 RETURN
```

In this example, the section at line 100 should have an END statement at line 190. At line 120 the program is sent to the subroutine at line 200. When the program returns from this subroutine, it should encounter the END statement at line 190; instead the program "falls through" to line 200 again, and when it hits the RETURN in line 210, the error message is generated.

String formula too complex (16)

This means that a string expression is too long or too complex.

String too long (15)

This message occurs when you try by concatenation to create a string that would be longer than 255 characters (e.g., C$ = A$ + B$, where the total length of A$ plus B$ is greater than 255).

Subscript out of range (9)

This message implies an error involving a subscripted variable such as A(1) or A$(1). If a subscript greater than 10 is to be used, you must use a DIM statement to save space in memory for the variables [e.g., DIM A$(25)]. The most common form of this error is an attempt to print a variable like A(11) or A(N), where N is 11, without first dimensioning the variable. Another possibility is that an array has been specified with one dimension, as in DIM A(25), and later in the program it is referred to with two or more dimensions, as in PRINT A(22,1).

A very common (and very confusing) cause of this error is to use a TAB statement with a space following the TAB:

```
10 PRINT TAB (20); "HELLO"
```

Fix the error by deleting the space following the word "TAB."

Syntax error (2)

The form of a statement is not correct. This may be the result of a spelling, punctuation, or sequence error. The most common causes are missing parentheses and quotes, misplaced punctuation marks, and reserved words used as variable names. One good troubleshooting technique is to make sure that you have an even number of quotation marks and an equal number of left and right parentheses. One confusing cause of this message is that the type of variable in a READ statement does not match the item being read from the DATA statement (i.e., one is a string and one is a number).

When this error message is printed, BASIC automatically displays the offending line with the cursor positioned at the beginning of the line so it can be easily corrected.

Too many files (67)

This usually means that there are too many files on the diskette and its directory is full. It can also result when trying to save or open a file with an invalid file specification.

Type mismatch (13)

The most common cause of this error is forgotten quotation marks. It results when you match a string with a numeric expression or variable, as in the following examples.

```
10 LET NAME$ = PETER RAYGOR
20 LET N = "43"
30 LET L$ = 255
40 LET G = "A"
```

Another common cause of this problem is an incorrect match of variable names and data when reading from DATA statements or from a file. This error can also result from trying to swap numeric variables of different precision.

Undefined line number (8)

You or your program have referred to a line that does not exist. During execution of a program, this usually means that the most recently executed GOTO or GOSUB statement has sent the program to a line that does not exist. One common cause of this for beginners is accidentally deleting a line while editing, or mistyping the number in a GOSUB or GOTO statement.

Undefined user function (18)

You have referred to a user-defined function that has not been defined yet.

Unprintable error

This is usually caused by an ERROR statement with a nonexistent error code.

Example: `10 ERROR 245`

WEND without WHILE (30)

This is just like the "RETURN without Gosub" error. For every WEND statement a program encounters, it must first have passed a WHILE statement; otherwise this error occurs.

WHILE without WEND (29)

The program has come to an end inside a WHILE loop. All WHILE loops must be closed with a WEND statement, and that statement must be passed before the program ends.

APPENDIX C

Basic Reserved Words

The following words may not be used as variable names in IBM BASIC. The line

```
10 LET TO  = 100
```

would be illegal since it uses the reserved word "TO" as a variable name. When a program encounters a line with an improperly used reserved word, the program halts and a Syntax Error message is displayed.

RESERVED WORDS

ABS
AND
ASC
ATN
AUTO
BEEP
BLOAD
BSAVE
CALL
CDBL
CHAIN
CHR$
CINT
CIRCLE
CLEAR
CLOSE
CLS
COLOR
COM
COMMON
CONT
COS
CSNG
CSRLIN
CVD
CVI
CVS
DATA
DATE$
DEF
DEFDBL
DEFINT
DEFSNG
DEFSTR
DELETE
DIM
DRAW
EDIT
ELSE
END
EOF
EQV
ERASE
ERL
ERR
ERROR
EXP
FIELD
FILES
FIX
FN
FOR
FRE
GET
GOSUB
GOTO
HEX$
IF
IMP
INKEY$
INP
INPUT
INPUT#
INPUT$
INSTR
INT
KEY
KILL
LEFT$
LEN
LET
LINE
LIST
LLIST
LOAD
LOC
LOCATE
LOF
LOG
LPOS
LPRINT
LSET
MERGE
MID$
MKD$
MKI$
MKS$
MOD
MOTOR
NAME
NEW
NEXT
NOT
OCT$
OFF
ON
OPEN
OPTION
OR
OUT
PAINT
PEEK
PEN
PLAY
POINT
POKE
POS
PRESET
PRINT
PRINT#
PSET
PUT
RANDOMIZE
READ
REM

RENUM	SAVE	STICK	THEN	VARPTR$
RESET	SCREEN	STOP	TIME$	WAIT
RESTORE	SGN	STR$	TO	WEND
RESUME	SIN	STRIG	TROFF	WHILE
RETURN	SOUND	STRING$	TRON	WIDTH
RIGHT$	SPACE$	SWAP	USING	WRITE
RND	SPC(	SYSTEM	USR	WRITE#
RSET	SQR	TAB(	VAL	XOR
RUN	STEP	TAN	VARPTR	

APPENDIX D

Formatting a Diskette

To format a blank diskette, you must also have a diskette that has a copy of the DOS FORMAT.COM program on it. Usually a copy of the DOS master diskette is used.

WARNING: The formatting process will destroy any data on the disk to be formatted, so be **very sure** there is nothing valuable on the disk you intend to format.

If the diskette containing the copy of the DOS format program has a write-protect notch on one side (see figure 1), cover it with a write-protect tab (these should be provided with every box of new diskettes). This will prevent you from accidentally destroying data on this diskette.

FIGURE 1

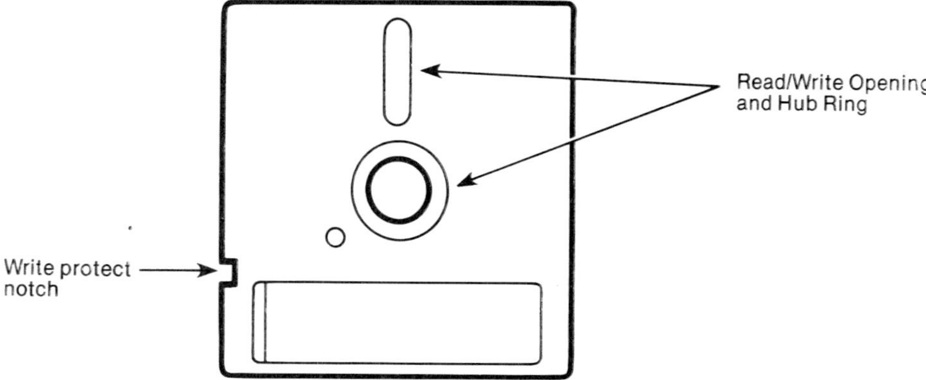

Be careful not to touch the magnetic surface of the diskette where it is exposed at the Read/Write opening and the Hub Ring.

Place the DOS master (or other diskette containing the FORMAT program) in the drive with the machine turned off. Close or latch the drive door and turn on the power. If the light stays on indefinitely, try again or use another diskette. When the light goes out, you should be asked to enter the date and time. You may enter the date and time or you may simply press ⟨Enter⟩ at each prompt. You should then see the DOS prompt (A⟩) followed by the cursor (the little blinking underline). If not, make sure the monitor (TV screen) is turned on. Try again if necessary. When you see the prompt and cursor, format your new diskette according to one of the following procedures.

ONE-DRIVE FORMATTING PROCEDURE

If you have only one drive, with the master diskette (the one with the copy of the DOS format program on it) in the drive, type:

```
FORMAT A:/S
```

followed by ⟨Enter⟩ (the carriage return key)
You should see the message:

```
Insert new diskette for drive A:
and strike any key when ready
```

At this point, place the new diskette to be formatted in your drive and hit the space bar once. Formatting takes a while, so be patient. Depending on how much memory you have in your machine, you may be prompted to replace the original (or source) diskette in the drive and strike a key, then prompted again to put the new diskette back in. This may happen more than once.

TWO-DRIVE FORMATTING PROCEDURE

Place the diskette with the copy of the DOS format program in drive A: (the left-hand drive or, if your drives are one above the other, the upper drive). Then place the new diskette to be formatted in drive B: (the other drive). Type

```
FORMAT B:/S ⟨Enter⟩
```

Be patient, formatting takes a while.

FOR BOTH METHODS

Eventually you should see the message:

```
Formatting...Format complete
System transferred

      362496 bytes total disk space
      40960  bytes used by system
      321536 bytes available on disk

Format another (Y/N) ?
```

The numbers may not match those above. Also, there may be a fourth number giving the number of bytes of bad sectors. This means that some parts of the diskette are unusable. DOS automatically marks them as bad sectors that are not to be used, so this is no problem unless the number is very large (over 30,000 or 40,000), in which case the diskette is not a very good one and should probably not be used for anything important.

If you would like to format another diskette at this time, press the "Y" key and repeat the formatting procedure. If not, press the "N" key.

Your newly formatted diskette should have a copy of the BASIC language program called BASICA.COM. You can use the following procedure to copy BASICA.COM from the DOS master diskette (or any other disk that has the BASICA.COM program).

Begin the copy procedure with the A> DOS prompt displayed on the screen. Insert the diskette with the BASICA.COM file on it into drive A:. If you have two disk drives, insert your newly formatted diskette into drive B:. If you have only one disk drive, DOS will tell you when to insert your newly formatted disk. Type:

```
COPY BASICA.COM B:
```

and press the Enter key.

If you have only one drive, the following message will appear:

```
insert diskette for drive B: and strike
any key when ready
```

Remove the source diskette from the drive and insert your newly formatted diskette into drive A:. Press any key to continue with the copy procedure.

When the copy procedure is completed, the following message will appear on the screen.

```
1 File(s) copied
```

NOTE: Diskettes, formatted or not, should be treated very carefully. They should not be bent, folded, or mutilated. They should not be exposed to extremes of heat or cold. Putting a diskette near a magnet will not hurt the diskette, but it will destroy the data on the diskette. The paper cover on a diskette is designed to protect the sensitive magnetic surface inside from dirt and fingerprints. Care should be taken not to get your fingers in contact with the magnetic medium where it shows through the holes in the sleeve.

APPENDIX E

Flowcharts and Programming Techniques

YOU CAN'T GET THERE FROM HERE

A person learning to program a computer is faced with an almost insurmountable problem. The problem is that you must use a programming language you have not yet learned, apply programming concepts you have not yet mastered, and run the program on a computer you are just learning to operate. This triple whammy can make the first programming experience a difficult and frustrating experience. In this section we have attempted to prevent some of this frustration with an explanation of some simple programming techniques.

A computer program is similar to a recipe for baking a cake. The recipe is a sequence of steps the baker follows to produce a cake. A computer program is a sequence of steps the computer follows to produce a desired result. We use the term *algorithm* to name the step-by-step procedure followed by the computer, just as the term recipe names the procedure used by the baker. Computer programming can be divided into two major tasks: (1) developing the algorithm that will produce the desired result, and (2) translating the algorithm into a computer program. This section is concerned with the first task: developing the algorithm.

In the past 15 or 20 years, we have experienced an amazing increase in computer hardware capabilities and an equally amazing decrease in the cost of computer hardware. We have reached the point where software (i.e., the computer programs or the labor necessary to produce them) is the most expensive part of a computer system. In the past, memory hardware was extremely expensive and it was cheaper to pay programmers to write obscure, poorly structured programs that made very efficient use of memory than to buy more memory. With the tremendous decrease in cost of memory and computing power, the current trend is to write programs in a way that reduces the software cost. This means writing programs that are easy to understand and easy to modify when the inevitable need for change arises.

Some techniques used in this text that make a program easier to understand include the following: placing the program name on line 1; including a list of variables at the beginning of the program; using remarks to explain parts of the program; and breaking a large program into small, manageable units. These techniques sometimes use up extra memory and slow down the execution speed of the programs, but are more than worth it because of the added clarity they provide.

STEPS IN WRITING A PROGRAM

Many people, when confronted with their first programming assignments, are unsure of the steps that are necessary, or even where to begin the task. The following ten steps outline a procedure for writing, debugging, and documenting a computer program. A sample problem will be used as an example.

Sample Programming Problem

STEP 1: Study the problem, determine the variables that will be required, and pick names for the variables.

Example:

a. Problem statement: Write a program that computes the cost of gasoline for a single trip in a car.
b. Three variables are required: the gallons of gasoline used, the price of a gallon of gasoline, and the cost of the trip.
c. We will use G for the gallons used, P for the price of a gallon of gas, and C for the cost of the trip.

STEP 2: Develop a method for solving the problem.

Example: A four-step algorithm is all that is required for this simple problem.

a. Enter values of G and P
b. Calculate C (C = G * P)
c. Round C to the nearest cent
d. Print C

STEP 3: Calculate one or more answers by hand for testing the program.

Example:

1.
```
G = 10, P = 1.249
C = 10 * 1.249 = 12.49
```

2.
```
G = 15, P = 1.249
C = 15 * 1.249 = 18.745
```

STEP 4: Write the BASIC program.

Example:

```
110  INPUT "GALLONS USED? ", G
120  INPUT "PRICE OF A GALLON? ", P
130  LET C = G * P
140  PRINT "COST OF THE TRIP IS $";C
150  END
```

STEP 5: Enter the program into the computer.

STEP 6: List and run the program.

STEP 7: Correct syntax errors.
A syntax error is anything in your program that the computer cannot interpret as it attempts to run the program. The error message will include the line number of the problem line. List the line and look for errors such as a missing symbol, a comma, semicolon, or quotation mark, or a spelling error.

STEP 8: Check for logic errors.
If the answers you calculated in step 3 do not agree with the answers produced by the computer, then your program has a logic error—i.e., the program runs but the answers are incorrect.

STEP 9: Correct the logic errors.
A logic error is any error in a program that runs but produces the wrong result. List the program and look for an incorrect formula. Step through the program and look for an incorrect sequence of operations.

STEP 10: Save the final version of your program and produce a list and run for the final documentation of the program.

The first two steps in the programming process are the most difficult for students to master. The remainder of this section explains in more detail techniques for accomplishing steps 1 and 2.

Problem Definition

The first step in the programming process is to study and define the problem to be solved. Start by describing the output that is to be produced by the program. Use a piece of graph paper to make a layout of the output as it will appear on the monitor screen or printed page. Four or five lines per inch is a convenient size for this purpose.

With the output firmly established, determine what input data are required to generate the output. In other words, what information will the computer need from the user to do the job (input data) and what information will the computer give to the user (output data)? Prepare a list of the variables required for input and output and select a name for each variable.

Examine the input and output. Write down any equations that are required and determine the steps required to produce the output. For simple programs, a list of the required steps is sufficient. A flow diagram is a useful tool for describing complex problems with decision points and multiple branches. Large problems are often divided into smaller, more manageable modules. A structure chart is used to show the interconnections of the modules.

FLOWCHARTS

A flowchart is a useful tool for describing the sequence of steps in complex programs with multiple branches. Not all programs require a flowchart. Large, modular programs are often best described by a structure chart. The "big one" in this text, program 10A, is an example of such a program.

Flowcharts use standard symbols to represent various programming functions. In this text, line 1 in every program assigns the name of the program to the string variable PN$. An oval-shaped symbol is used to represent the beginning of the program (line 1) and the end of the program.

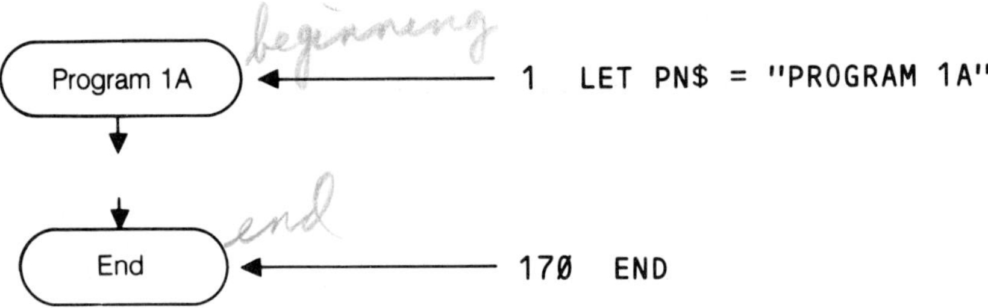

The parallelogram-shaped symbol is used for INPUT or READ statements.

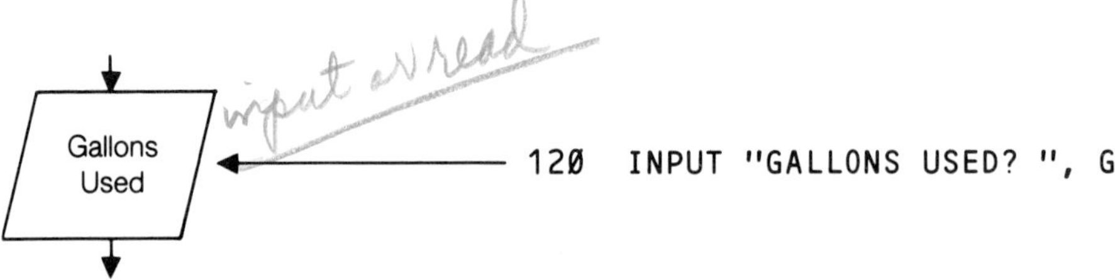

The rectangular-shaped symbol is used for assignment statements (i.e statements).

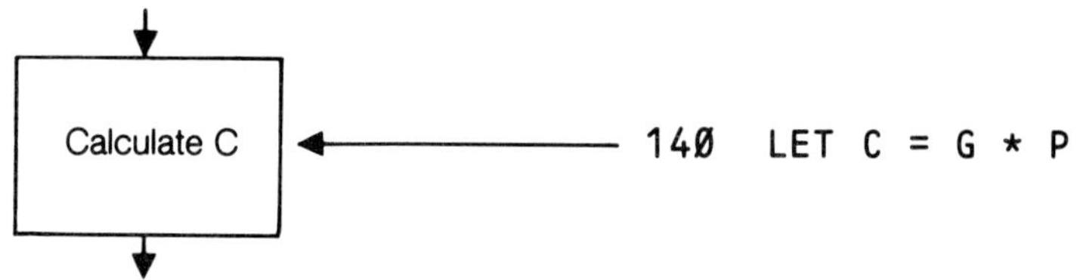

The torn-sheet symbol is used for PRINT statements.

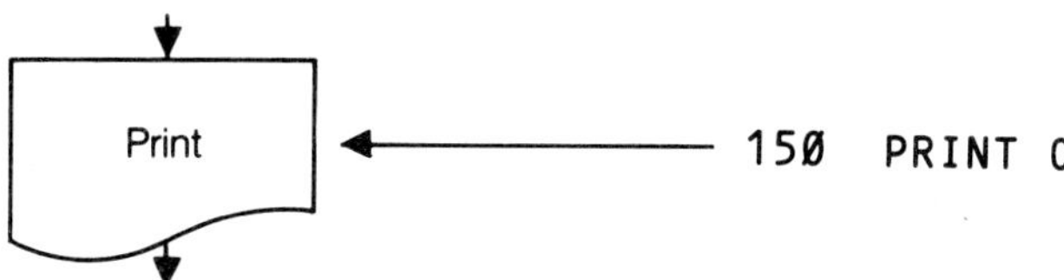

The diamond-shaped symbol is used for IF statements.

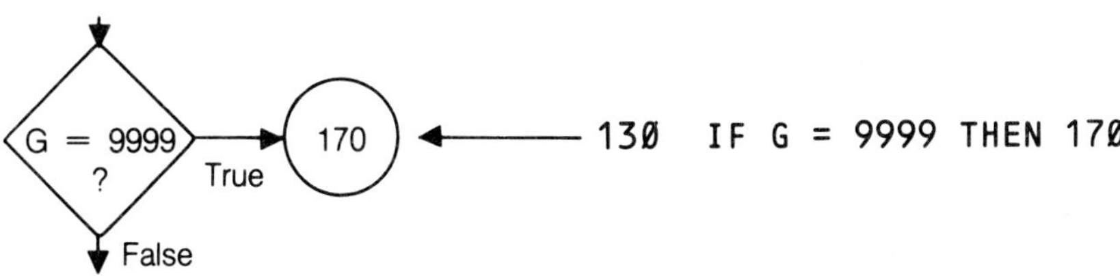

his text, the hexagonal-shaped symbol is used for the FOR statement, and a cle is used for the NEXT statement. A dotted line indicates the return path at forms the loop.

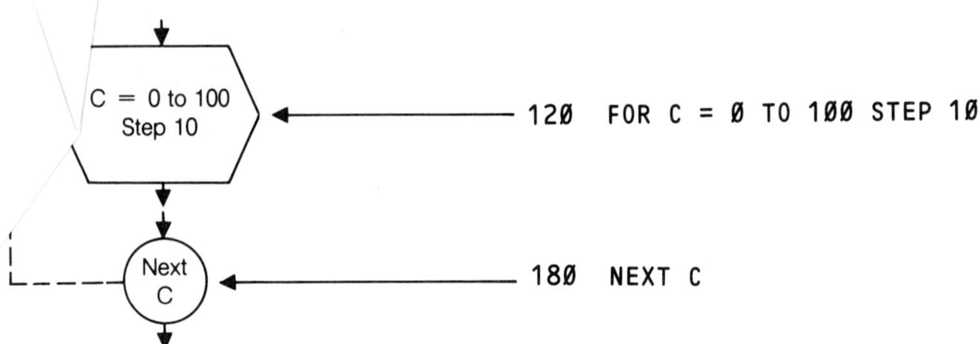

Finally, the circle is used as a connector between two parts of the flowchart where it would be too confusing or take up too much space to draw the connections.

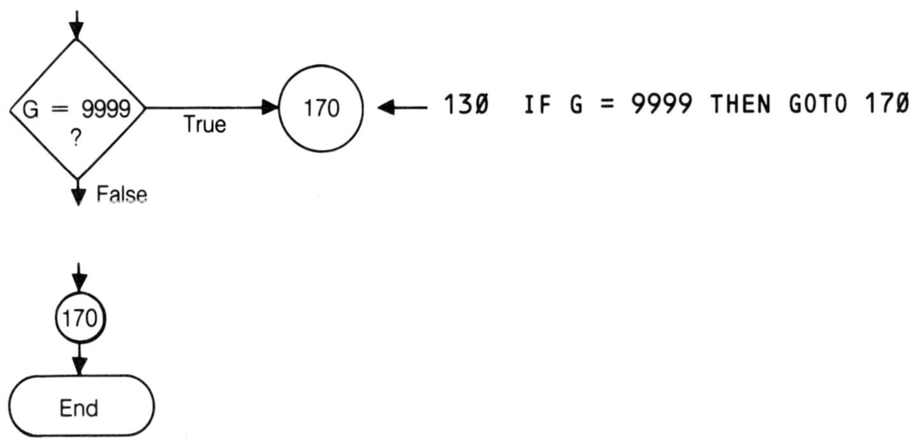

The following examples show typical flowcharts and the programs they represent.

EXAMPLE 1: The Cost of a Trip

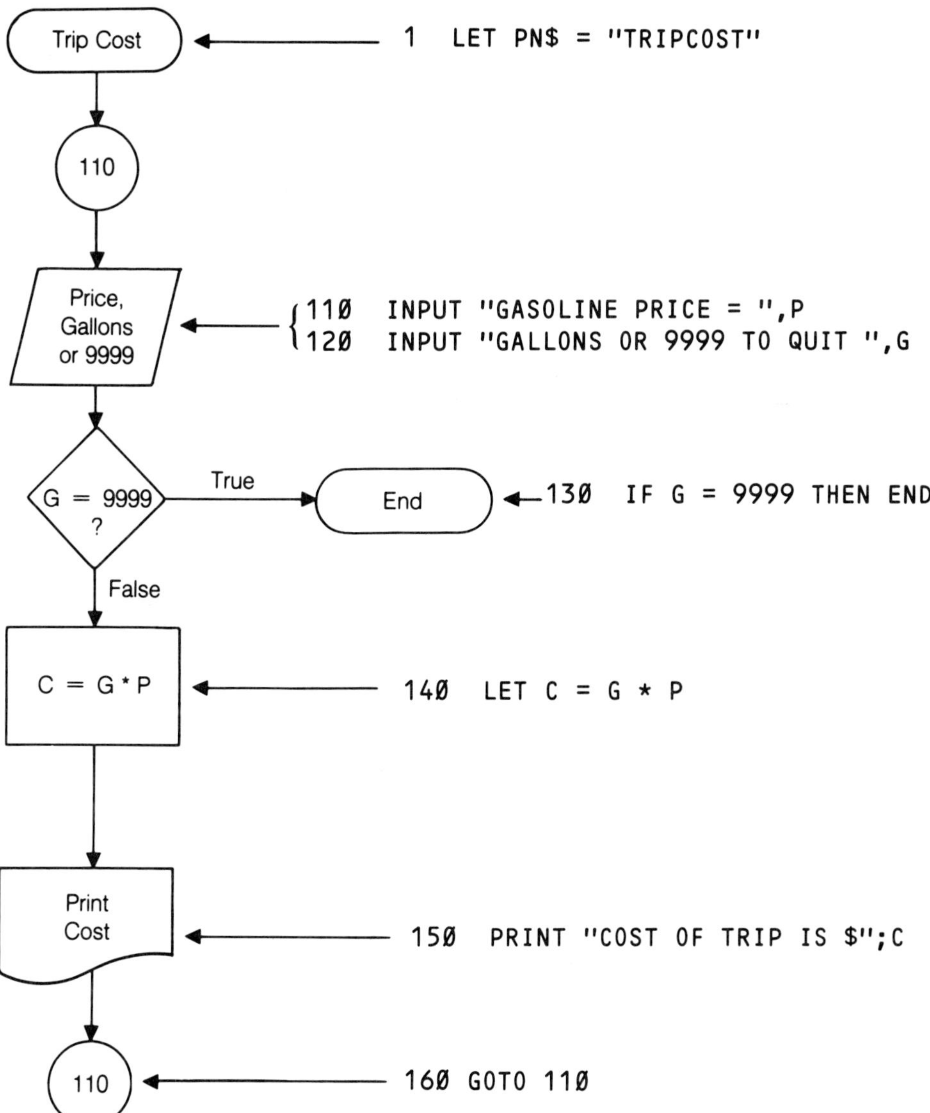
Trip Cost
1 LET PN$ = "TRIPCOST"
110
Price,
Gallons
or 9999
110 INPUT "GASOLINE PRICE = ",P
120 INPUT "GALLONS OR 9999 TO QUIT ",G
G = 9999
?
True
End
130 IF G = 9999 THEN END
False
C = G * P
140 LET C = G * P
Print
Cost
150 PRINT "COST OF TRIP IS $";C
110
160 GOTO 110

EXAMPLE 2: Weekly Wages

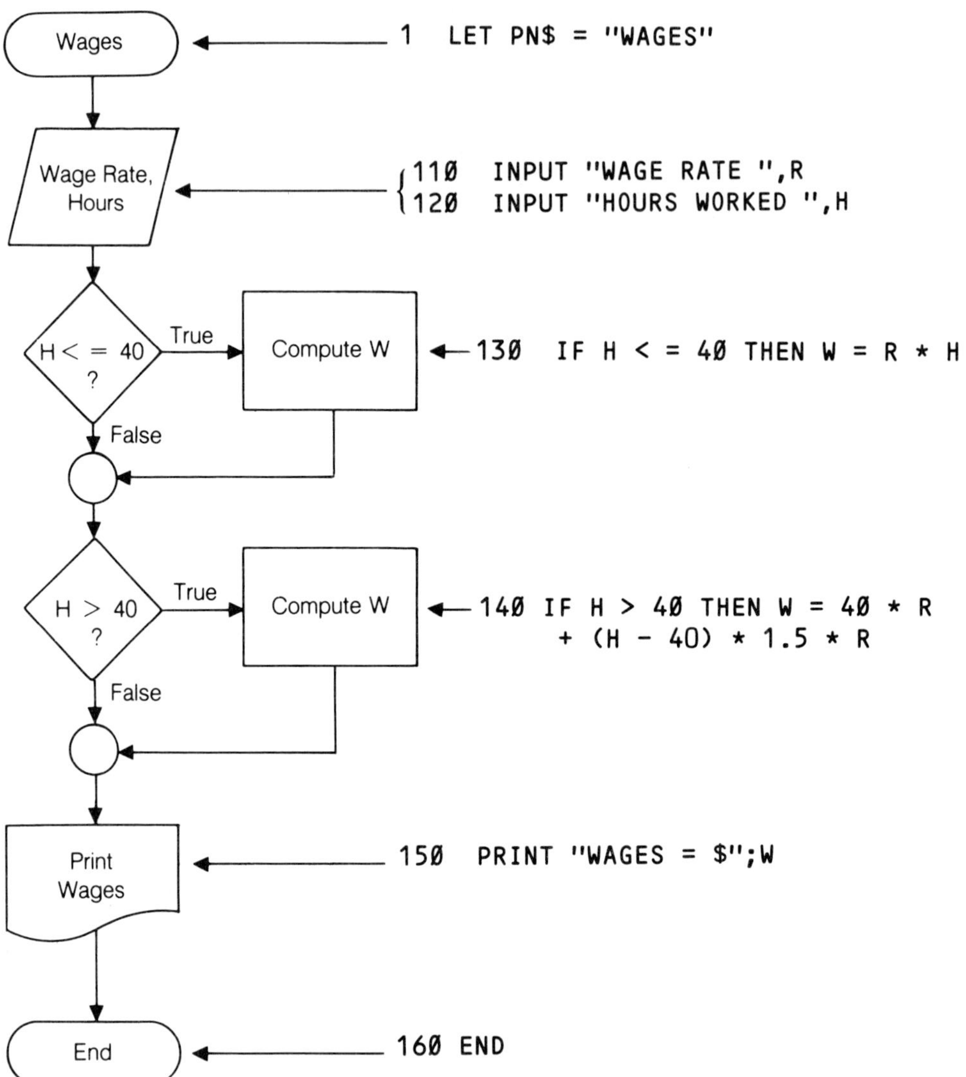
Wages
Wage Rate, Hours
H < = 40 ?
True
False
Compute W
H > 40 ?
True
False
Compute W
Print Wages
End
1 LET PN$ = "WAGES"
110 INPUT "WAGE RATE ",R
120 INPUT "HOURS WORKED ",H
130 IF H < = 40 THEN W = R * H
140 IF H > 40 THEN W = 40 * R + (H - 40) * 1.5 * R
150 PRINT "WAGES = $";W
160 END

EXAMPLE 3: Conversion of Feet to Meters

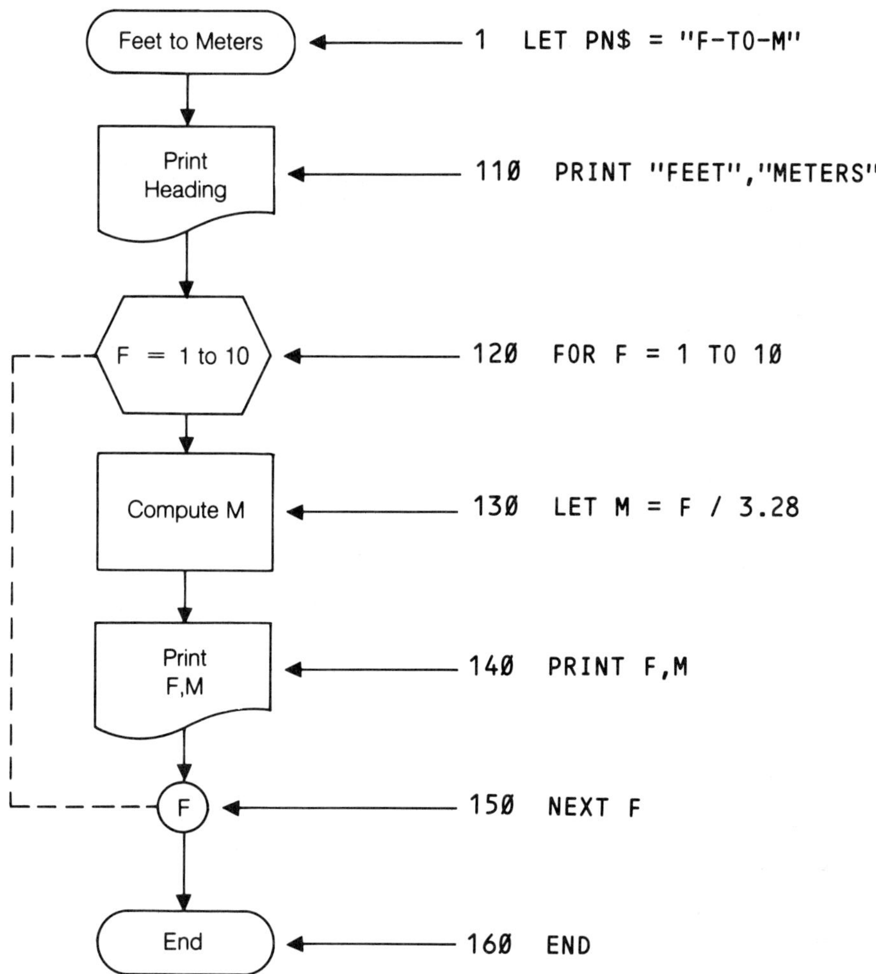

Modular Programming and Structure Charts

Large programs such as program 10A can be made more manageable by a technique known as top-down program design. The entire program is divided into several segments, which are in turn divided into small modules that each perform a single function. A good rule on the size of a module is that the entire module should be shown in a single view on the screen. Modules should be small and should do only a single job. For example, if you need to sort and print a list of names, you should use two separate modules: one to sort the list, and another to print it. A point to keep in mind is that a proper module can be a programming tool that can be used in many different programs. If your module to sort a list is written properly, it can sort *any* list and can be used in many programs.

The relationship between the modules of a program is shown in a diagram called a structure chart. In programs with a menu, the menu is often the basis for the structure chart. The structure chart for program 10A is shown below.

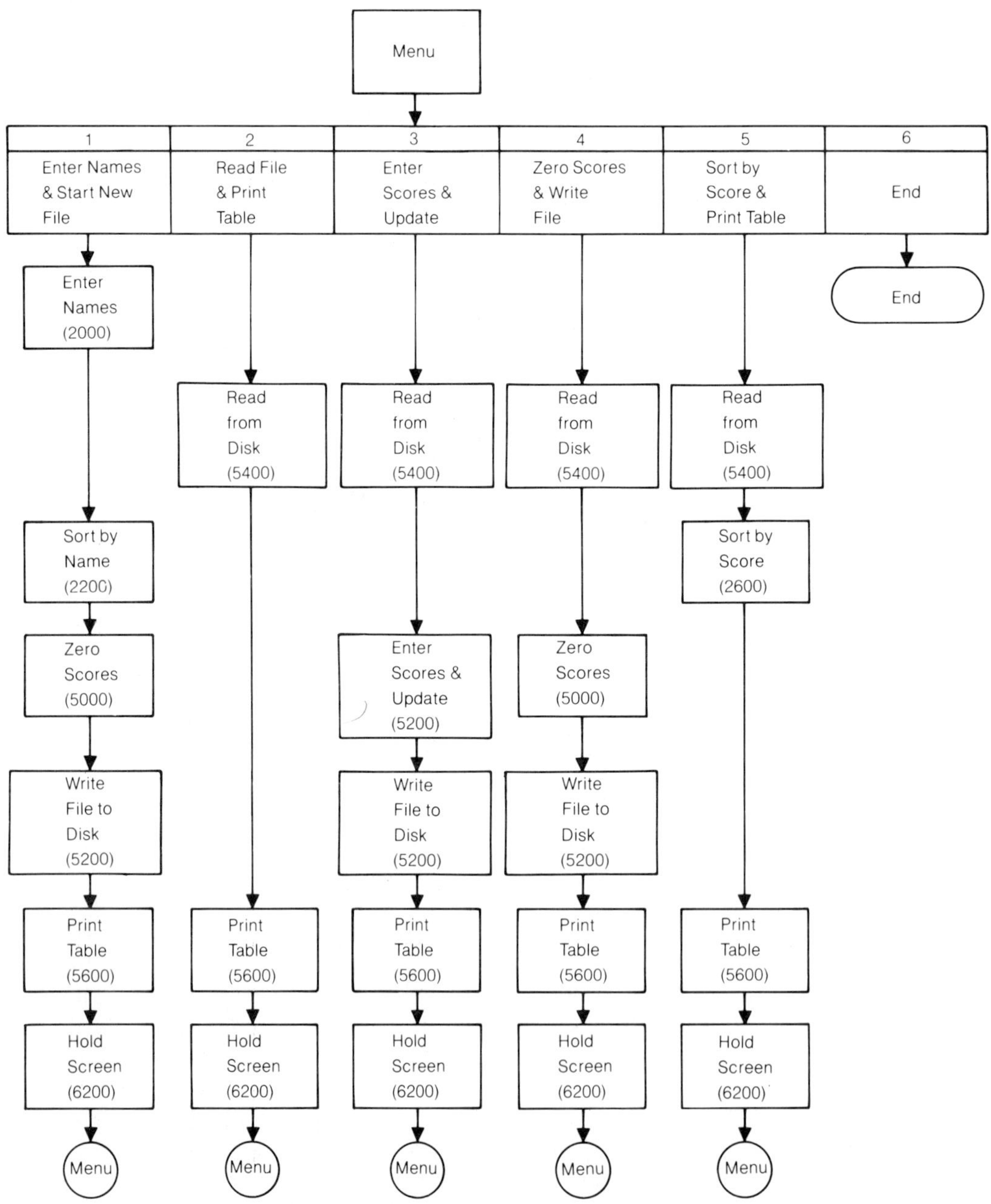

STRUCTURE CHART FOR PROGRAM 10A

APPENDIX F

ASCII Character Codes

TABLE OF ASCII CHARACTER CODES

ASCII value	Character	ASCII value	Character	ASCII value	Character
000	(null)	032	(space)	064	@
001	☺	033	!	065	A
002	☻	034	"	066	B
003	♥	035	#	067	C
004	♦	036	$	068	D
005	♣	037	%	069	E
006	♠	038	&	070	F
007	(beep)	039	'	071	G
008	◘	040	(	072	H
009	(tab)	041	)	073	I
010	(line feed)	042	*	074	J
011	(home)	043	+	075	K
012	(form feed)	044	,	076	L
013	(carriage return)	045	-	077	M
014	♫	046	.	078	N
015	☼	047	/	079	O
016	►	048	0	080	P
017	◄	049	1	081	Q
018	↕	050	2	082	R
019	‼	051	3	083	S
020	¶	052	4	084	T
021	§	053	5	085	U
022	▬	054	6	086	V
023	↨	055	7	087	W
024	↑	056	8	088	X
025	↓	057	9	089	Y
026	→	058	:	090	Z
027	←	059	;	091	[
028	(cursor right)	060	<	092	\
029	(cursor left)	061	=	093	]
030	(cursor up)	062	>	094	^
031	(cursor down)	063	?	095	_

ASCII value	Character	ASCII value	Character	ASCII value	Character
096	`	128	Ç	160	á
097	a	129	ü	161	í
098	b	130	é	162	ó
099	c	131	â	163	ú
100	d	132	ä	164	ñ
101	e	133	à	165	Ñ
102	f	134	å	166	ª
103	g	135	ç	167	º
104	h	136	ê	168	¿
105	i	137	ë	169	⌐
106	j	138	è	170	¬
107	k	139	ï	171	½
108	l	140	î	172	¼
109	m	141	ì	173	¡
110	n	142	Ä	174	«
111	o	143	Å	175	»
112	p	144	É	176	░
113	q	145	æ	177	▒
114	r	146	Æ	178	▓
115	s	147	ô	179	│
116	t	148	ö	180	┤
117	u	149	ò	181	╡
118	v	150	û	182	╢
119	w	151	ù	183	╖
120	x	152	ÿ	184	╕
121	y	153	Ö	185	╣
122	z	154	Ü	186	║
123	{	155	¢	187	╗
124	¦	156	£	188	╝
125	}	157	¥	189	╜
126	~	158	Pt	190	╛
127	⌂	159	ƒ	191	┐

ASCII value	Character	ASCII value	Character
192	└	224	α
193	┴	225	β
194	┬	226	Γ
195	├	227	π
196	─	228	Σ
197	┼	229	σ
198	╞	230	μ
199	╟	231	τ
200	╚	232	Φ
201	╔	233	θ
202	╩	234	Ω
203	╦	235	δ
204	╠	236	∞
205	═	237	$\emptyset$
206	╬	238	ϵ
207	╧	239	$\cap$
208	╨	240	$\equiv$
209	╤	241	$\pm$
210	╥	242	$\geq$
211	╙	243	$\leq$
212	╘	244	⌠
213	╒	245	⌡
214	╓	246	$\div$
215	╫	247	$\approx$
216	╪	248	°
217	┘	249	•
218	┌	250	·
219	█	251	$\sqrt{}$
220	▄	252	^{n}
221	▌	253	^{2}
222	▐	254	■
223	▀	255	(blank 'FF')

APPENDIX G

Answers to the Self-Testing Questions

CHAPTER 1

1.1	J	1.5	G	1.9	A	1.13	B
1.2	F	1.6	K	1.10	E	1.14	I
1.3	L	1.7	M	1.11	C	1.15	N
1.4	H	1.8	P	1.12	O	1.16	D

CHAPTER 2

2.1 25 MILES PER GALLON
2.2 7 MILES PER GALLON
2.3 6.7 MILES PER GALLON
2.4 6.67 MILES PER GALLON
2.5 6.667 MILES PER GALLON

CHAPTER 3

3.1 28 MILES PER GALLON
3.2 3Ø.6 MILES PER GALLON
3.3 (a) 36.6 MILES PER GALLON
(b) 36.2 MILES PER GALLON
3.4 THE LAST NUMBER IS 7

CHAPTER 4

4.1
```
 7
 8
OUT OF DATA IN 12Ø
```

4.2
```
HOW MANY TRIPS? 3

HOW MANY MILES? 412
HOW MANY GALLONS? 11.8
 34.9 MILES PER GALLON

HOW MANY MILES? 360
HOW MANY GALLONS? 21.2
 17.0 MILES PER GALLON

HOW MANY MILES? 385
HOW MANY GALLONS? 14.5
 26.6 MILES PER GALLON
```

4.3
```
ENTER A DISTANCE OR 9999
TO TERMINATE THE PROGRAM

HOW MANY MILES? 250
HOW MANY GALLONS? 12
 20.8 MILES PER GALLON

HOW MANY MILES? 225
HOW MANY GALLONS? 11
 20.5 MILES PER GALLON

HOW MANY MILES? 9999
```

4.4
```
ENTER A DISTANCE OR 9999
TO TERMINATE THE PROGRAM

HOW MANY MILES? 250
HOW MANY GALLONS? 12
 20.8 MILES PER GALLON

HOW MANY MILES? 225
HOW MANY GALLONS? 11
 20.5 MILES PER GALLON

HOW MANY MILES? 9999

PROGRAM TERMINATED AFTER
 2 TRIPS.  GOODBYE.
```

CHAPTER 5

5.1
```
YARDS          FEET
 1              3
 2              6
 3              9
 4              12
 5              15
```

5.2
```
YARDS          FEET
 1              3
YARDS          FEET
 2              6
YARDS          FEET
 3              9
YARDS          FEET
 4              12
YARDS          FEET
 5              15
```

5.3
```
ENTER NUMBERS TO BE ADDED
OR ENTER 9999 TO QUIT

? 7
? 18
? 5
? 9
? 6
? 9999
 5 NUMBERS WERE ADDED
THE TOTAL IS 45
```

5.4 `1  2  3  4  5`

5.5 `1  3  5  7`

5.6 `1  4  7  1  Ø  1  3`

5.7 `8  7  9  4`

5.8 `3  3  3`

5.9 `5  9  4  7  8  8`

5.10 `1  5  3  4  5  3  7  2  9  1`

CHAPTER 6

6.1
```
B IS GREATER
A IS GREATER
EQUAL
A IS GREATER
```

6.2 EEEEE

6.3 BB

6.4 AAAA

6.5 KKKK

6.6 1 1 1 2 2 2 3 3 3

6.7 1 2 3 1 2 3 1 2 3

6.8 1 1 1 2 2 1 2 2 3 1 3 2

6.9 1 2 3 1 2 3 1 2 3

6.10 3 2 1 3 2 1 3 2 1

6.11 3 3 3 2 2 2 1 1 1

6.12
```
1 2 3
1 2 3
1 2 3
```

6.13 1 2 1 2 1 2 1 2

6.14
```
1 2
1 2
1 2
1 2
```

6.15
```
1 2
1 2

1 2
1 2
```

6.16
```
YEAR = 1
QUARTER = 1 : MONTHS = 1, 2, 3
QUARTER = 2 : MONTHS = 4, 5, 6
QUARTER = 3 : MONTHS = 7, 8, 9
QUARTER = 4 : MONTHS = 10, 11, 12

YEAR = 2
QUARTER = 1 : MONTHS= 1, 2, 3
QUARTER = 2 : MONTHS= 4, 5, 6
QUARTER = 3 : MONTHS= 7, 8, 9
QUARTER = 4 : MONTHS= 10, 11, 12

YEAR = 3
QUARTER = 1 : MONTHS= 1, 2, 3
QUARTER = 2 : MONTHS= 4, 5, 6
QUARTER = 3 : MONTHS= 7, 8, 9
QUARTER = 4 : MONTHS= 10, 11, 12
```

CHAPTER 7

7.1
```
*****
```

7.2
```
*
*
*
*
*
```

7.3
```
 ***
  *
 ***
*****
*****
```

7.4
```
****
*
***
*
****
```

7.5
```
******
******
  **
  **
  **
```

7.6
```
*****
    *
    *
    *
   **
```

CHAPTER 8

8.1 (a) `Ø,1,2,3` (b) `1,2,3,4`

(c) `11,12,13,14` (d) `1,2,3,4,5,6,7,8,9,1Ø,11,12,13`

(e) `1,2,3,4,5,6`

8.2
```
*
*
*
*
*
*
```

8.3
```
******
```

8.4
```
*
 *
  *
   *
    *
     *
```

8.5
```
*  *  *  *  *  *
```

8.6
```
     *
    *
   *
  *
 *
*
```

8.7
```
STRING MANIPULATION
```

CHAPTER 9

9.1
```
8 7 5 4 3
```

9.2
```
3 8 4 2 7
```

9.3 (a)
```
JANE        80
DAVE        82
CAROL       90
FRANK       88
```

(b)
```
JANE          DAVE          CAROL         FRANK
 80            82            90            88
```

9.4 (a)
```
8 14 15
21 3 7
19 2 9
```

(b)
```
8 21 19
14 3 2
15 7 9
```

(c)
```
8 3 9
```

(d)
```
8 21 19
14 3 2
15 7 9
```

(e)
```
9 2 19
7 3 21
15 14 8
```

9.5 (a)
```
TERRY   82   78   90
CARL    88   80   85
JUNE    86   90   84
```

(b)
```
TERRY   CARL   JUNE
 82      88     86
 78      80     90
 90      85     84
```

(c)
```
TERRY    90
CARL     85
JUNE     84
```

(d)
```
TERRY    250
CARL     253
JUNE     260
```

(e)
```
TERRY    83
CARL     84
JUNE     87
```

9.6 (a)
```
CARL     78
JUNE     64
TERRY    76
```

(b)
```
TERRY    64
CARL     76
JUNE     78
```

(c) Add the following three lines.

```
205  LET T = S(I)
215  LET S(I) = S(J)
225  LET S(J) = T
```

(d) Add the following three lines.

```
205  LET T$ = N$(I)
215  LET N$(I) = N$(J)
225  LET N$(J) = T$
```

CHAPTER 10

10.1 (a)
```
8 63 4
```
(b)
```
63 4 71
```
(c)
```
12 47 18
8 63 4
71 21 7
```

10.2 (a)
```
 3
 4
TERRY
 92
CARL
 88
JUNE
 84
```
(b)
```
 3
 4
TERRY
 92
 4
CARL
 88
 4
JUNE
 84
```
(c)
```
 3
TERRY
 92
CARL
 88
JUNE
 84
 4
```

INDEX*

*Boldface page numbers given in this index refer to pages in the Mini-Manual (Appendix A).